Navigating New Media Networks

Acknowledgments

This is a book about communication networks and the ability to form relationships and gather resources in this network. This is also a book that has only come to fruition due to the support of a wide-ranging network. In addition, this is a first book and thus represents the long effort of a network over time to produce and support an individual to be put into the privileged position of having the time, the means, and the ability to write a book and thus these acknowledgements span that network.

First, to my strongest ties—my family. To Colin who is the heart of our family, the calm spot in a sometimes hectic life. To Branwen, Oriana, and Cael who have been more patient while mama is working. I received the book contract a few weeks before Cael was born, so his mother has been "writing a book" his whole life. To my parents—all of them. To my dad who is the most likely source of the nautical terms that appear here and there in the text. To my mom who told me to go to Michigan State for undergrad despite having more scholarships for other places.

Second, to those who have given their time and energy to educate me over the years. To Jackie Ruppel who taught us how to write and whose lessons perpetuate as I try to impart her systems to my own students. To Gail Dawson who taught us how to find our voices. To the faculty from Michigan State whose work was and continues to be inspirational, particularly Tim Levine, Steve McCornack, Kelly Morrison, and Sandi Smith. To the Arizona State faculty who pushed me to think both deeper and wider and provided a broad skill set to find and answer new questions. To Laura Guerrero, who gently pushes and strongly supports. To Dan Canary, Paul Mongeau, Kory Floyd, Linda Lederman, and Susan Messman's carefully constructed communication courses. To Angela Trethewey and Sarah Tracy who I never actually took a class from but whose work on identity strongly influences my own thoughts on online identity production. To all of the fantastic ASU co-alums who I had the opportunity to study alongside and in particular a group of very smart, very funny, very confident women—Miriam Sobre-Denton, Alice Veksler, and Jen Eden.

I also want to acknowledge the network of scholars who have accepted me into the world of communication technology scholarship. Each of these scholars whether they realize it or not has influenced some part of this book, provided some inspiration, some support, and are my go-to's when I think of solid scholars in communication technology. These are the scholars who are working hard to identify real effects rather than urban myths, develop and apply theoretical perspectives and just do good work in an area overrun with popular misconceptions. These include Art Ramirez, Nick Bowman, David Westerman, Nick Brody, Erin (Bryant) Sumner, Jesse Fox, Katy Pearce, Caleb Carr, Becky Hayes, Jimmy Manning, Brandon Van Der Heide, Stephanie Tom Tong, and Jamie Banks. In particular, I want to acknowledge Andrew Ledbetter who has been a constant supporter and promoter of my work.

Also important has been the support at Western Illinois University. Roger Runquist's CITR faculty symposium program provided the motivation to write the first versions of chapters of this book. My GA, Monica Lombardo helped extensively with the formatting, learning more about Chicago-style than she ever wanted to. My department has been incredibly supportive in this endeavor.

I'd also like to acknowledge two individuals who have cheered me on in this project since the beginning: Chris Carpenter and Tessa Pfafman. In regard to the former, in a small department, having a colleague who is one of the top statistical minds in the field is fantastic; one that also laughs at your terrible jokes is priceless. The latter is the best example of a networked individual that I know. Her empathy, caring, and love for people shows in the wide-ranging and diverse network ties she creates.

Chapter One

Navigating Networks

Every day seems to bring a new alarm warning about how communication technologies are about to change social life for the worse. The average reader perusing the papers would read op-eds arguing the dangers of too much technology (Pinker 2015), that technology strips us of our ability to hold conversations (Bindley 2011; Turkle 2012; Ossola 2015), that technology will create echo chambers for negative behavior (Bine; Nagourney, 2005), and reduce our memory capacity (Carr, 2008, 2012). At the same time, opinion writers and scholars alike have expressed concerns that people are becoming more isolated and less tied to our social groups (McPherson et al. 2006, Putnam 2000, Turkle 2011).

These fears are unsurprising given that new advances in communication technology can often usher in a new age of anxiety (McLuhan 1964), where our social organizing is in upheaval and people are learning new norms regarding appropriate uses of technologies. Make no mistake, the channels that humans have for communication have changed dramatically in recent years. A forty-year-old in the United States has experienced the widespread adoption of personal computers, GPS, cellular phones, dvds, email, the internet, websites, web browsers, Windows, message boards, text messaging, instant message services, online shopping, social network sites (SNS), wi-fi, and most recently smart phones with applications that allow games, socializing, editing and sharing photos and more on the go. Compare that upheaval to the experience of a forty-year-old in 1974 that experienced relatively less upheaval in communication technology; a few advances in radio, the invention of the television, and the eventual upgrade to color television.

Coinciding with these technological changes, prominent sociologists have been making the argument that Western society is moving away from groups (Putnam 2000) and toward social organization through interconnected net-

1

works (Rainie and Wellman 2012). This change is also a potential cause for concern as humans require social connections not only for survival but also to thrive. People depend on their social connections including kin relationships, friendships, and acquaintances for resources ranging from instrumental (having someone who could take you to the doctor, or loan money, or babysit), to companionship, to personal (having someone to disclose to, to share emotions with) (McEwan and Guerrero 2012). Changes to how a society organizes itself could lead to changes, for better or worse, in how individuals in that society are able to access these necessary resources.

Furthermore, these social changes and the proliferation of communication technology are connected. The ability to communicate through mediated channels hastens the shift to networked individualism as these technologies allow communicators to reach out directly to networked connections. These social upheavals mean that the modern individual is faced with new challenges. The shift to networked individualism puts greater pressure on the individual to communicate competently in order to have access to the types of social resources that previously may have been available through belonging to social groups. The introduction of new communication technologies means that these individuals must navigate both how to physically use these technologies as well as stay abreast of changing social norms regarding the appropriate use of various mediated communication channels. In order to improve relationships within social networks and understand how people engage with each other in the age of communication technology it may be necessary to begin to understand communication patterns from a technologically networked perspective. This book seeks to strike a middle path between technology alarmists and the enthusiasm of early adopters by exploring both the opportunities and hazards that communication technologies offer for forming and maintaining resource-rich social networks.

THE SHIFT FROM GROUPS TO NETWORKS

At the turn of the millennium, scholars began to sound alarms regarding the decline of group membership in the Western world. Putnam (2000) argued that people were spending less time self-disclosing with their neighbors and fellow community members. An investigation of the General Social Survey found that between 1985 and 2007 Americans' core discussion networks have shrunk by as much as a third (McPherson et al. 2006).

An actual decline in sociability would be worrying given that human beings are by their very nature social beings. Our ability to communicate and form social structures is important both for the functioning of our society and our personal well-being. Access to network connections provides social capital (Putnam 2000). Putnam has argued that collective trust engendered by social capital helps society members resolve collective problems, become more tolerant of others, diffuse information, and even help us cope with trauma and fight off disease. Thus, declines in the sociability of our species would be a very concerning trend.

However, while membership in formal social organizations such as churches, civic organizations (e.g. Elks, Masons, Kiwanis, Rotary), and bowling leagues have been declining, different forms of social organizing and communicating have been on the rise. People have signed up in droves for social network sites such as Facebook, Twitter, Instagram, LinkedIn, and others. Eighty-seven percent of American adults use the internet and 73% of those internet users use social network sites (Pew 2013b, 2014b). "Social" has been the buzzword of multiple years at technology conferences (Griggs and Gross 2013). Gamers now play games that involve interacting with millions of others (Nardi and Harris 2006; Pew 2012; Williams, Ducheneaut, Xiong, Zhang, Yee, and Nickell 2006). Today's communicator has the ability to reach larger social networks and has access to millions of potential new acquaintances through various types of online communities (Baym 2010; Tufekci 2012). Rather than living in a world where people are becoming *less* social, technological advances mean people have the ability to remain hyper-connected to our social networks at all times.

Networked Individualism

The social world we live in appears to be moving from collections of groups and densely intertwined societies to social worlds based on *networked individualism* (Putnam 2000; Rainie and Wellman 2012). According to Rainie and Wellman (2012), "The hallmark of networked individualism is that people function more as connected individuals and less as embedded group members" (p. 11). Whereas in the past social networks were smaller and tightly bounded systems based around local groups, individuals today may be operating in looser, linked social networks (Rainie and Wellman 2012). Previously, kinship systems, locality, and perhaps work groups drove human connection. Today, communication technologies help facilitate the ability to communicate with network members of our choosing. Global citizens are no longer limited to choosing their friends and acquaintances from those who share a close proximity or are connected through kinship systems. Communication technologies provide exciting new possibilities in how we choose and maintain network connections as well as who those connections might be. Thus, people find themselves amidst this social shift from rigid and bounded groups to fluid and flexible personal networks.

In the past people were generally limited to their immediate communities for both their choice of social connections as well as their potential access to social resources such as support, information, and camaraderie. Although

Putnam argued that group membership may make people more tolerant, a long-standing finding on groups and communities is that they tend to privilege group harmony and create pressures toward uniformity (Asch 1956; Festinger 1950; Tuckman 1965). Societies that are more focused on the collective good may be even more likely to exhibit conformity effects (Bond and Smith 1996). These conformity effects can make it difficult for people who might be stigmatized by their community based on difference in opinions, attitudes, beliefs, or other personal characteristics. People who are viewed as different may be driven either to hide their differences or leave smaller communities. One example of this is migrations of LGBTQ youth from rural communities to more urban centers with existing gay communities (Weston 1995). Although this type of migration is not descriptive of the experience of every queer youth (Lewis 2012), the narrative of feeling the need to either hide one's identity or move to a more accepting place has occurred often enough to make it reasonable to question whether social organization in groups and small communities is always beneficial for society members.

Networked societies allow people to seek out connections with friends and acquaintances that share similar tastes and interests (Feld 1981; Lewis, Kaufman, Gonzalez, Wimmer, and Christakis 2008). Societies structured around networks rather than formal groups allow the members of such societies more autonomy to seek out the social relationships that the individual perceives to be most advantageous. Networked individuals may be able to push beyond the binds of legal or physical communities such as kin or neighborhoods and concentrate more specifically on social or personal interests that lead them to create new interpersonal connections (Lewis et al., 2008)

The Structure of Networks

Not every social connection is the same. Interpersonal connections within networks are called network ties and may be of varying levels of strength. Granovetter (1973) identified four dimensions of tie strength: intensity, intimacy, duration, and reciprocity. *Intensity* refers to the intensity of emotions network members connect to the tie. For example, an argument with a close friend would likely produce a greater emotional response than would be involved in a disagreement with an acquaintance. A meeting with a friend from out-of-town may produce more happiness than a pleasant encounter with a co-worker. *Intimacy* is the amount of self-disclosure shared between two network members. In most cases, an increase in the amount of self-disclosure between two network members leads those members to view the relationships as increasingly close (Altman and Taylor 1973). Duration is the amount of time spent with a particular network member. *Reciprocity* refers to services the support network members share with each other. Network members might provide each other with a variety of resources such as providing a sounding board, helping each other with tasks, sharing a meal, and countless other day-to-day exchanges in the course of interaction. We can say that two network ties experience reciprocity when the resources flow back-and-forth fairly equally between the two network members.

Other scholars have proposed additional dimensions that might influence the strength of network ties. In particular, the structure of the social network may influence tie strength (Burt 1995). Network members with whom we share a greater number of other network ties are likely to be stronger ties than individuals with whom we share few network connections. Other factors influencing social distances such as differences in socioeconomic status, education level, and political affiliation may also influence tie strength (Lin, Ensel, and Vaughn 1981).

Strong Ties

Strong ties are those individuals with whom people spend considerable amounts of time communicating. Network members self-disclose more to strong ties and are emotionally closer to stronger ties. People expect some level of reciprocity in their relational investments with strong ties, share additional network connections and experience a limited amount of social distance (Burt 1995; Granovetter 1973, 1983; Lin et al. 1981; Putnam 2000). These relationships are considered strong, personal relationships and people strive to keep in contact with their strong ties (Roberts et al. 2009). These core network members have the most influence over our attitudes, behavior, and well-being (McCallister and Fischer 1978). Of course, people are also likely to be similar to their strong ties in terms of values and status (DiPrete, Gelman, McCormack, Teitler, and Zheng 2011).

Weak Ties

Social networks also consist of weak ties (Granovetter 1983). Weak ties can be thought of as more casual friends and acquaintances. Examples of weak ties might include a friend of a friend, a former colleague that you see around town, a child's schoolmate's parent, or a former high school classmate. Weak ties do not communicate with each other on a regular basis but they form an important component of the overall communication network. Weak ties are often more diverse than strong ties in terms of values (DiPrete et al. 2011), attitudes, (McCallister and Fischer 1978) and available sources of social information (Granovetter 1983).

Latent Ties

Individuals may also have network connections that Haythornthwaite (2002) called latent ties. Latent ties are ties that essentially lay fallow until they need to be activated. They may be friends of friends of friends, a connection to a weak tie, and so on. These are individuals whom one would not typically count in their circle of acquaintances but in the right circumstances would be available to provide resources and information (Haythornthwaite 2002; Ellison, Steinfield, and Lampe 2011). Roberts et al. (2009) considered these types of ties to constitute one's global network: individuals that you would feel appropriate greeting but do not generally make a special effort to maintain the relationship.

RESOURCES WITHIN NETWORKS

Network connections can provide individuals with social capital. Social capital is the perceived potential resources that are available to an individual through the maintenance of social relationships (Bourdieu 1986). Social capital and network resources are an important component for allowing people to both survive and thrive in society. Different types of network ties may provide different types of social capital. Thus, it is important for individuals to manage not just close relationships or more distant connections but rather a wide variety of network ties.

Strong ties typically provide resources such as emotional support as well as other types of personal resources (McEwan and Guerrero 2012). However, these relationships can also be more cognitively demanding to maintain and may require greater levels of interpersonal investment (Roberts et al. 2009). Strong ties typically provide bonding social capital (Putnam 2000). Bonding social capital provides access to social resources through the reciprocal connections shared by strong ties. Strong tie relationships tend to be communal relationships (Clark and Mills 1979) where people share resources because network members know each other well enough to trust that they will eventually recoup their shared resources (O'Connell 1984).

Weak ties can provide access to a more diverse range of resources and information (DiPrete et al. 2011). Information and other resources can be more readily diffused across networks through weak tie connections. People maintaining greater numbers of weak tie relationships may be more likely to receive a greater diversity of ideas and information from their social network (Granovetter 1983). Weak ties provide connections to other individuals and groups that might not have otherwise been accessible. For this reason, weak ties have also been called bridging ties as they provide connections between denser network connections (Gittell and Vidal 1998; Putnam 2000; Rainie and Wellman 2012). Weak ties provide access to bridging social capital

(Putnam 2000). Bridging social capital refers to diversity in the social network that allows communication and resources to flow between different segments of the social network (Putnam 2000). Weak ties can also provide linkages to latent ties, which might provide network members with even greater amounts of diversity of thought, norms, and social knowledge.

THE ROLE OF COMMUNICATION TECHNOLOGY IN MANAGING AND MAINTAINING NETWORKS

The shift from groups to networks changes how society members approach the organization and management of their social life. On one hand, the possibility of increased diversity and size of our communication networks is likely to our social advantage. The autonomy and flexibility of networks allow individuals to find resources that might not be available within bounded systems. However, the ability to connect with various networks is restricted by limitations in communication abilities and capacities (Wellman and Guilia 1999). Networked relationships exist through communication. It takes cognitive and social time and effort to form and maintain social relationships (Roberts et al. 2009). In networked societies, either active communication or the structure of the network is required to maintain social relationships. It is necessary to continually reproduce networked relationships through interactions between network members (Corman and Scott 1994). These relationships *require* interaction between network members to remain in existence. Thus, the ability of the individual to communicate competently to form, maintain, and manage network connections takes on greater importance in a society based on network individualism. Whereas in a group-based society, the social group as a whole takes on some of the communication work needed to sustain the social relationships and resource flow to individuals within the group, in a network-based society that pressure falls more greatly on each individual network member. Communication technologies can assist networked individuals to manage their networks by making it possible to send messages faster, more conveniently, over greater distances, and to larger audiences. At the same time communication technologies introduce unique challenges for social communication.

TECHNOLOGY TURNS SOCIAL

Communication technologies are an important component of leading a networked life. Communication technology, including social media, can facilitate companionship, social support, an overall sense of belonging, and the diffusion of social capital (Ellison et al. 2011; Wellman and Guilia 1999). Our communication with network members is woven through emails, texts, instant messages, phone calls, tweets, posted photos, and status updates. As members of a networked society become less able to rely on group and kin structures to maintain their connections, technology provides the requisite tools to maintain a diverse set of network connections.

Despite concerns that the use of communication technology may lead to decreased social skills and increased isolation (Nie 2011; Pierce 2009; Turkle 2011), research has generally shown that using technology for communication leads to increased sociability. Those who have rich and involved social lives offline tend to be the heaviest users of the internet for social purposes (Dutton, Helsper, and Gerber 2009; Zhao 2006). Furthermore, the internet has been shown to facilitate increased social ties (Wang and Wellman 2010). A recent report by the *Pew and American Life Project* found that heavy internet users tend to have more offline friends than non-internet users (Hampton, Sessions, Her, and Rainie 2009). Similarly, researchers at the *Oxford Internet Institute* found that ex-users and non-users of the internet reported up to two times as much loneliness as internet users (Dutton, Helsper, and Gerber 2009).

Social technologies allow people to reach out beyond group structures to the connections that they choose to maintain. For example, communication technology can help communicators ameliorate the effects of distance on a network tie. Traditionally, decreases in proximity have a negative impact on social relationships with stronger ties experiencing larger negative impacts than weak ties when a proximally close relationship transitions to long-distance (Roberts and Dunbar 2011). However, communication technologies provide strong ties the ability to keep in touch across the miles (Rainie and Wellman 2012). In addition, mobile technologies can increase our ability to stay connected exponentially. Smart phones allow us to be connected to email, social media, messaging applications, and voice calls through a single device. Mobile allows communicators to move not only beyond being tied to groups, but also beyond being tied to specific places. Rather, mobile users can connect directly person to person (Campbell and Park 2008; Rainie and Wellman 2012).

Communication Technologies

For the purposes of this text, communication technologies refers to any form of technology that is intended for the purpose of facilitating communication, i.e. technology that allows individuals to send messages back and forth (Thurlow, Lengel, and Tomic 2001). Computer-mediated communication (CMC) typically refers to communication that is mediated through the internet. In this way, CMC is a slight misnomer in that often scholars using the term CMC are referring to communication mediated through the internet (or at the very least an intranet when considering internal organizational instant messaging systems) rather than just computers. For example, internet-based applications such as email, instant messaging, blogging, message boards, social network sites (SNS), and other forms of social media are all often considered to fall under the term CMC whereas short message services (SMS), more commonly called text messaging or texting are typically not thought of as CMC even though a phone that can handle sending text messages most certainly qualifies as a computing device. Text messaging, however, sends messages from device to device and does not use the internet. Telephone calls are also not typically considered CMC as they also involve messages sent directly from one device (phone) to another and usually bypass the internet. Of course newer mobile options such as smartphones, tablets, and the hybrid "phablets" allow people to make choices to communicate using internet-based applications (for example the mobile version of Facebook or a video call service such as Skype or FaceTime) or device-to-device systems such as phone calls or text messages.

Within the category of CMC or internet-mediated communication there are further distinctions. Social media are a particular type of CMC. A simple definition of social media is "user-generated content" (boyd 2009). The focus on user-generated content means that unlike other types of websites where content is provided by governmental, corporate, or journalistic sources, social media content is developed and posted directly by the users of that medium. Social media can refer to blogs where bloggers create stories for their audiences, micro-blogs such as Twitter or Tumblr, video services designed for user-postings such as YouTube or Vine, message board services like reddit or GitHub or social network sites together such as Facebook, Google+, and LinkedIn. Social network sites (SNS) are further defined as internet-based sites that allow people to construct a profile, create a list of network connections, and view communications from their connections (boyd and Ellison 2007).

Social media have particular properties that differentiate them from other forms of communication: *persistence, replicability, searchability, scalability, and (de)locatability* (boyd 2009). The first three characteristics are related to the need for messages to be recorded in some way for asynchronous accessibility by receivers. Persistence means that once something is posted it is generally retained by the website. Persistent information is replicable. Users can save the information posted to one site and re-post it somewhere else or reproduce the information in another context. Even if users attempt to delete messages, there is always the possibility that the information is still stored by the website or that it has been recorded and published by another entity. For example, the website, Politwoops (politwoops.sunlightfoundation.com) records politician's tweets that they (or their campaign) have later deleted. For this reason, many different types of communication technologies are persistent and replicable. Emails can be printed. Screenshots of text messages can be saved for later use. Persistent information is also searchable. People can use various search functions to find persistent posts. For example, one's Twitter account may show up in Google search. This issue recently came to light with Facebook's new graph search function (Goldman 2013; Tate 2013). Although the information that feeds the graph search has always been there, the graph made it easier than ever for users from different network segments to search for particulars.

Social media is also *scalable.* Users can broadcast messages or interpersonal messages can be reproduced and posted for much larger audiences than originally intended. Photos, videos, and memes can "go viral" and suddenly a video intended for a small audience of friends and family may now be viewed by millions of people across the globe. Finally, boyd (2009) also attributed the property of *(de)locatability* to social media. She argued that although media becomes dislocated from any single place in space, the proliferation of location-based technologies, such as foursquare, or using the GPS in your phone to note your location on Facebook can make location an even more salient feature of messages.

The proliferation of various communication technologies, including device-to-device, CMC, and social media allow people new options for maintaining a wide variety of network ties. As communicators' use of particular media channels has begun to stabilize, different rules and norms for different channels begin to emerge (Bryant and Marmo 2012; Grelhesl and Punya-nunt-Carter 2012; McEwan, 2013a; McLaughlin and Vitak 2012; Park et al. 2009; Raacke and Bonds-Raacke 2008). Different types of media may facilitate different types of ties or be viewed as more appropriate for particular types of network ties.

Media and Strong Ties

For strong or close ties, different forms of media provide additional channels which we can use to connect with our close friends and family on an everyday basis. Although strong ties typically engage in face-to-face communication more than weak ties, strong ties also use mediated channels more than they see each other face-to-face (van den Berg, Arentze, and Timmermans 2012). Strong ties typically use a greater number or *multiplex* of channels to communicate with each other than weak ties (Haythornthwaite 2005). Haythornthwaite and Wellman (1998) found that people who communicated frequently were more likely to communicate frequently in every medium. In 1998, this meant that people who talked face-to-face were also likely to call each other on the phone and email each other. Today media multiplexity may mean that while an individual may see their close friend face-to-face quite a bit, they also text each other through the day, comment on each other's'

Facebook status, and give a call when needed (Ellison et al. 2011; Ledbetter 2009b, 2010a; Miczo, Mariani, and Donahue 2011).

Media and Weak Ties

Although communication technologies are used frequently for strong tie communication, these media might be particularly useful for sustaining weak and latent ties (Ellison, Steinfield, and Lampe 2007; Ellison et al. 2011; Gilbert and Karahalios 2009; Haythornthwaite 2002). Whereas close ties tend to use social media channels as supplementary routes of communication, weak ties may rely more exclusively on channels such as SNS (Ellison et al. 2011; Haythornthwaite 2002). Internet use has been associated with having more non-kin members in one's core discussion network (Hampton et al. 2009). SNSs in particular help to make weaker social network connections continuously visible (Rainie and Wellman 2012). This visibility can substantially increase the number of weak ties people are able to maintain in their social network (Donath and boyd 2004, McPherson et al. 2006; Rainie and Wellman 2012). Dunbar's (1992, 1998) social brain hypotheses suggest there is a ceiling on the number of social connections our brain has the capacity to process. SNSs provide a way for people to work around this ceiling. By keeping track of social connections online, the maintenance of larger networks may be possible while simultaneously freeing up brain capacity. Indeed, people report that they enjoy SNSs due to the convenience of being connected to a large number of people (Debatin, Lovejoy, Horn, and Hughes 2009).

Media and New Ties

Although generally people use communication technology to maintain contact with people they have also met in person, communication technology, particularly the internet, offers the ability to meet a diverse range of individuals. Online message board communities can allow for the opportunity to establish new connections based on similarity in tastes and interests (Li 2004; McEwan and Zanolla 2013). Wang and Wellman (2010) reported that approximately a fifth of their sample reported having friends who are online only. The diversity of connections that social media and other forms of online communication afford may enhance our overall access to social support and social capital (Ellison et al. 2007; Rainie and Wellman 2012).

Managing Networks

Not only can we maintain individual ties, social media allows us to interact with our networks as networks. O'Sullivan (2005) noted that technology creates media where individuals can send interpersonal messages through mass channels or engage in mass and interpersonal communication simultaneously. O'Sullivan termed this convergence of mass and interpersonal mediums *masspersonal* communication. Masspersonal communication can occur on social media such as SNS, or micro-blogging sites such as Twitter allow individuals to communicate with a networked audience (Carr and Hayes 2015; Marwick and boyd 2011). A networked audience consists of real and potential viewers who are connected both to the user and each other. In a sense, communication technologies that allow communication to and within a networked audience allow for a type of many-to-many communication (Marwick and boyd 2011; Shirky 2009). These *masspersonal* and many-to-many communications have the advantage of not only communicating specific messages but also highlighting the relationships between various network members.

COMMUNICATION CHALLENGES IN NAVIGATING NETWORKS

Although communication technologies help to facilitate communication between network members, the ability to maintain resourceful networks depends upon communicators' abilities to competently communicate via technology. Understanding not only how different technologies work but also shifting norms regarding the use of communication technologies can be an arduous task. The introduction of communication technologies in combination with a shifting societal structure to networked individualism means that individuals may need new strategies to manage their social connections and access social resources. As Wellman and Rainie (2012) argued, "those who want to thrive in the network operating system need to take insight into its realities and need to practice how to function effectively in this changed world" (p. 255).

However, using social media to create and maintain network connections is unlikely to be a straightforward prospect. Individuals will likely need to learn new communication competencies in order to manage their mediated communication. Networked individualism may introduce new challenges for interpersonal processes such as forming and maintaining network connections. Identity performances may be altered due to the characteristics and affordances of mediated platforms. Trade-offs between privacy and disclosure have changed drastically. Communication technologies offer new opportunities for engaging in intercultural communication but to be beneficial that engagement must be mindful and empathic. Taking advantage of these new opportunities and navigating new communication challenges requires new communication competencies.

COMMUNICATION COMPETENCE IN A NETWORKED SOCIETY

Many scholars have discussed the various literacies needed to successfully navigate the internet. Internet users must be able to learn how to use computers or other devices that allow them to get online (Litt 2013a). Internet users must also be able to decipher content that they receive through online channels (Van Dijk 2005). While these literacies are important foundations for mediated communication (and will be discussed in greater detail in chapter 2), the focus of this book is not on literacy but competency. Communication competence refers to the ability to effectively and appropriately send and receive messages to achieve relational goals (Spitzberg and Cupach 1984). The in-depth understanding of various communicative activities provided by this text is intended to help readers understand not only the specific affordances and characteristics of online channels but also the social norms regarding technology use for interpersonal purposes. Of course, norms regarding the appropriateness of technology do shift over time; this text attempts to identify some areas of stabilization in how people perceive and use various technologies as well as indicate arenas that are still in formative stages.

CONCLUSION

A networked society offers new potential to the individual in terms of creating connections of choice and opening up wells of social resources that were hitherto difficult to access. Communication technology has accelerated the shift from a society based on group structure to one based on networks by allowing individuals to maintain connections with diverse social ties across barriers of time and space. These technologies also bring new complications and risks for individuals and relationships. A better understanding of the characteristics of various technology and the norms associated with particular technology uses can help an individual be a more informed and higher functioning networked citizen.

Chapter Two

Communication Competence

Although communication technologies offer fascinating new opportunities for social communication, people are only able to take advantage of these new opportunities if they are able to use these technologies competently (Litt 2013). Communication scholars generally define competence as messages that are delivered effectively and appropriately (Spitzberg and Cupach 1989). A communicator's ability to be effective refers to whether or not that communicator can successfully achieve their goals within a communicative interaction. Appropriateness, on the other hand, refers to how receivers and audiences judge the communicator and the communication. The judgments are based on how well the communicator adheres to social norms and meets certain interaction goals such as being tactful, warm, or sociable. A communicators' ability to craft competent messages relies on their motivation to do so, their knowledge of concepts related to their communicative task, and communication skills related to successfully sending and receiving messages (Spitzberg and Cupach, 1989). This framework for understanding communication competence has also been applied to CMC (Spitzberg 2006).

MOTIVATION

The first step in becoming a competent communicator via any medium is having a *desire* to be seen as a competent communicator. People are motivated to adopt technologies for both extrinsic and intrinsic reasons (Davis, Bagozzi, and Warshaw 1992). Extrinsic motivations are external rewards that communicators perceive that they will gain by using a technology. For example, someone might develop a LinkedIn profile because they perceive it will help them get a job or they might adopt a smart phone because they think the ability to get business emails during the day will help them make more money. Intrinsic motivations are the internal satisfaction individuals get from adopting a new technology (Davis et al. 1992). For some, the joy of being the first to have a new "toy" is enough reason to adopt the latest gadget or join the newest platform (Davis 1993) Other researchers have noted that enjoying the ability to interact with friends, family, and other network members is an intrinsic motivation for using communication technologies (Lin and Lu 2011). However, internal and external motivations are tightly intertwined. A person may in fact adopt a communication technology for enjoyment or entertainment. However, using the technology to persist within a communication network allows that person to increase their perception of the quantity and quality of network resources that are available to them.

Whether influenced by extrinsic or intrinsic motivations, primarily, people do use communication technology to build and persist within interpersonal networks (Davis 1993; Ellison et al. 2007; Lin and Lu 2011; Flanagin 2005; Stafford, Kline, and Dimmick 1999). Adoption of various communication technologies is likely driven by the realization that these technologies may facilitate more efficient means of communicating with network members. If individuals do not perceive there are benefits to using a new technology, they may be unmotivated to use or pursue competence using that technology (Melenhorst, Rogers, and Bowhuis 2006). For example, a grandmother may have avoided learning about computers until she realized she could view pictures of her grandchildren through a social network site. Some people might create a profile on a micro-blogging site such as Twitter in hopes of reaching new professional contacts. Others might develop private profiles on the same site in order to share secrets and gossip with a select few members of their inner circle. Regardless, the desire to connect to others provides motivation to learn how to use communication technologies to pursue communication goals in an appropriate manner.

When Competence Does Not Motivate

When people are motivated to communicate competently, they likely seek the knowledge and skills necessary to use communication technology to foster interpersonal connections. However, in spaces where online communicators are able to be anonymous (or at least less visible to their primary social network) people may be motivated by other goals such as expression, entertainment, or disruption. Anonymous spaces may lead to the online disinhibition effect (Suler 2004; Suler 2005). The online disinhibition effect occurs when people communicate online in ways that they would refrain from doing in offline venues (Suler 2004). Online disinhibition can take on both benign and toxic forms (Suler 2004). Benign disinhibition occurs when anonymity allows people to feel more comfortable expressing emotions and personal disclosures or perhaps even engaging in acts of kindness or generosity they might not otherwise. Toxic inhibition, on the other hand, may be when people interpret their freedom from other network influences as a license to be rude, critical, and threatening. Thus, people are not always motivated to be competent communicators. Indeed, online and anonymous environments may encourage behaviors that are deemed socially inappropriate like online trolling and flaming.

Trolling

The terms "trolls" and "trolling" can have different meaning in different online contexts (Bishop 2014) but generally refer to online communicators who take advantage of anonymous environments (or create fake profiles to operate anonymously in non-anonymous environments) in order to disrupt social communication of other online communicators (Buckels, Trapnell, and Paulhus 2014; Phillips 2011b; Shachaf and Hara 2010). Trolls are often looking to provoke a reaction from other internet users through a variety of deceptive and destructive practices (Buckels, Trapnell, and Paulhus 2014). Trolling behavior might include posting racist, sexist, or homophobic messages and imagery (Phillips 2011). Trolls might make posts that are designed to "bait" other users into a conflict and/or distort the communication of other community members (Donath 1999; Phillips 2011b). People who troll may have different personality traits than the average internet users. Buckels et al. (2014) found that trolls are much more likely to be sadists and extroverts. Essentially, trolls are people who like engaging in communication with others but also enjoy causing hurt and pain in those others.

Other users are likely to find trolls incompetent (Bishop 2014). Trolls may appear to have "no apparent instrumental purpose" (Buckels et al. 2014, 97). However, trolls provide a case where the motivations of the user are different than the motivations of other more typical online communicators. The goal of a troll is to disrupt online community processes. While non-troll users often see trolls as independent users motivated by boredom and a desire for malicious entertainment (Shachaf and Hara 2010), trolls themselves may belong to troll communities and see themselves as avengers of social norms and regulators of online spaces.

Trolls can meet up with other trolls online, coordinate attacks, discuss methods, and so on. (Phillips 2011b). They may use spaces within 4chan or Reddit dedicated to trolling or find each other through social network sites (Phillips 2011b). Trolls and troll communities often set themselves up as the sheriffs of appropriate online behavior. In trolling Facebook memorial pages, a practice known as RIP trolling, trolls argue Facebook is an inappropriate place to share news and emotions regarding death and that their role in trolling these pages is to have people keep real-life tragedy off of the internet (Phillips 2011a). In particular, trolls can set themselves up as the police of "grief tourists"—creating unofficial pages for real tragedies, allowing people (generally those who are not family and friends of the deceased) to join those pages and then ambushing them with offensive content. One troll argued that family and friends should be grieving together in private like normal people and those visiting memorial pages are "grief tourists" or "people who substitute online emotions and declarations of solidarity for real emotional relationships and friendships" (75).

Thus, many trolls are harmful to online communities (Shachaf and Hara 2010) *because* they are motivated to be harmful to online communities. Trolls may see online targets as fair game because they feel that either people should not be sharing those particular emotions online or forming social connections online. Those practices, trolls say, are more appropriate for off line spaces. Thus, the goals of trolls are in direct opposition to a society moving toward networked individualism. By disrupting online community spaces, trolls disrupt our ability to reach out to others, share, and trust.

Yet, however twisted troll goals may seem, trolls are motivated to be effective in subverting the purposes of others' online messages in ways deemed appropriate by online trolling communities. Trolls often know how to play the "game" of online communication. To gain access to groups trolls often pretend to be interested in the group but their real "intention(s) are to cause disruption and/or trigger or exacerbate conflict for their own amusement" (Hardaker 2010, 238). Trolls are not unaware of the protocols of socially acceptable behavior on the internet. Indeed, trolls create anonymous profiles (often multiple anonymous profiles) in order to hide their behavior (Phillips 2011a). On one hand they are hiding their identity from site administrators; on the other hand they are hiding their behavior from the rest of their social network who would likely disapprove of their online behavior.

The case of trolls provides an example of where an individual can have the knowledge and skill to be effective at certain communication goals. However, without the motivation to use this knowledge and skill in a prosocial manner, the average troll comes across as highly incompetent and disruptive (Bishop 2014).

Flaming

Even people who are not attempting to troll may not always be motivated to use socially appropriate communication online. Online spaces that allow for anonymity may seem more permissive in regard to engaging in negative communication behaviors (Dubrovsky et al. 1991; Kiesler et al. 1984; Lea and Spears 1992). Thus, anonymous online spaces may engender instances of flaming. Flaming is hostile communication via text-based CMC that violates the community and/or interpersonal norms of that particular online space (O'Sullivan and Flanagin 2003). Flaming might include aggression, hostility, or profanity. People may feel more comfortable flaming in online environments due to greater anonymity and reduced social cues. Anonymous spaces could invite more aggressive and less inhibited messages (Kiesler, Siegel, and McGuire 1984).

There are times that messages that include characteristics of flaming may in fact be perfectly acceptable in terms of the social norms of the online space (O'Sullivan and Flanagin 2003). Just as people may engage in profanity or harsh language in a joking or sarcastic manner in order to signal in-group status (McCormick and McCormick 1992), people may also be motivated to use certain forms of harsh language in particular online groups precisely because such language is the norm of that group (O'Sullivan and Flanagin 2003). Thus, flaming is not just specific message characteristics but is rather driven by a lack of motivation to meet the norms of a particular online space. Indeed, motivations may provide a key explanatory variable for flaming as anticipated future interaction often precludes the use of hostile behaviors in computer-mediated settings (Walther 1994).

Trolling and flaming are two communicative instances where we can see how a lack of motivation to be appropriate is likely to lead to perceptions of incompetence. The anonymous nature of some online spaces may encourage this type of online disinhibition. However, the majority of communication facilitated through technology is not anonymous and occurs between interpersonal network members. In order to build and maintain connections within one's social network, people should generally be motivated to be competent users of communication technologies. However, motivation is not enough to establish competence. Knowledge and skills regarding communication technology are also important components of being a competent communicator through mediated channels.

KNOWLEDGE

Digital Literacy

In order to competently navigate the online world, communicators must first possess various digital literacies. Scholars have developed a variety of terms for literacies needed for online communication including media literacy, information literacy, digital literacy, internet literacy, and technical literacy (Livingstone and Helsper 2010; Park 2012; Rainie and Wellman 2012; Koltay 2011). Other literacies related to digital literacy include graphic literacy, navigation literacy, context and connections literacy, focus literacy, multitasking literacy, skepticism, and ethical literacy (Rainie and Wellman 2012).

This multitude of literacies coalesce around two main themes: operational literacies and information literacies. Operational literacies address a user's ability to actually use the tools and hardware necessary to use a computer or other devices and get online (Gui and Argentin 2011; Brandtweiner, Dontat, and Kerschbaum 2010; Litt 2013a; Park 2012; Van Dijk 2005). Literacy terms such as technical, graphic, and navigation fall under this idea of operational literacies.

People who possess operational literacies are able to operate a computer or mobile device, download applications that they need, type well enough to send messages, navigate the internet, identify appropriate links, have sufficient password protections, and other functional aspects of using computing technology, mobile devices, and internet-based media. These literacies exist on a continuum rather than a dichotomy. For example, one individual may have some level of operational literacy with using a mobile phone in that they can make phone calls and send text messages whereas another person may be able to use a phone for calls, messages, checking social network sites, monitoring health information, finding entertainment and more. Still others might be able to use their phone to set up internet hot spots for other devices or create mesh networks which allow for the transmission of information outside of a centralized internet organization (de Fillipi 2014).

People may also possess different types of operational literacies. Theoretically, an individual may understand the physical construction of computers well enough to build their own but struggle navigating through hyperlinks to get the information they are seeking. Another individual might have a good idea of both how to get information into online-based repositories (commonly called the cloud) and keep other information out of the cloud and yet have very little idea of other operational issues such as how to create and post videos.

The second theme, termed information literacy, refers to the ability to obtain and understand the *content* that is delivered through online channels (Livingstone and Helsper 2010, Gui and Argentin, 2011). This theme is similar to the traditional definition of media literacy: the ability to read and understand mediated messages (Park 2012). At a basic level this requires a certain reading level ability needed to navigate the primarily text-based online environment. At another level, these types of literacies refer to the ability to assess the credibility of message sources (Rheingold 2012). As online sources of varying quality can be made to look the same, this is no easy task for the average person. The ability to assess information online may require a healthy dose of skepticism (Rainie and Wellman 2012) as well as the wherewithal to be able to use triangulation methods to assess information found online with other sources (Rheingold 2012).

The ability to place information received online in its proper contexts also contributes to information literacy (Rainie and Wellman 2012). The ability to assess the likelihood that a photograph has been photoshopped or that an image belongs to another story helps communicators make better decisions about the world around them. The difference between reports of information based in evidence and observation and communications that are misleading, propaganda, and even satire can be difficult even for experienced internet information consumers. For example, recent stories from the *Daily Currant,* a satirical website whose Google listing reads "The Global Satirical Newspaper of Record" has regularly been mistaken by journalists as actual news (Weigel, 2013).

CMC Competencies

Operational and informational literacies are necessary components of the knowledge needed to competently navigate networks using mediated channels. However, these literacies are not sufficient components of a communicator's ability to competently craft and send messages through computer-mediated channels (Wrench and Punyanunt-Carter 2007). Knowledge of computer hardware and software is very different than knowledge related to competent message crafting (Spitzbert 2006; Wrench and Punyanunt-Carter 2007). Forming, maintaining, and communicating with network connections requires an understanding of interpersonal processes related to CMC. Similar to offline communication, competent online communication requires reducing uncertainty about one's co-communicators and following social norms. Competent communicators have the ability to combine their knowledge about generalized communication conventions and idiosyncratic information about fellow communicators to produce messages that will be viewed as appropriate by our fellow interactants and help us effectively reach our communication goals.

Unfortunately there is a dearth of literature regarding knowledge of particular communication concepts required for competent CMC. There is far more research examining operational literacy rather than skills related to CMC message construction (Litt 2013a). Of course, much of what we know from decades of research on interpersonal communication offline, also applies to online communication. There are, however, two particular areas where CMC can be very different from non-mediated communication. One, CMC requires communicators to choose an appropriate medium, whereas non-mediated communication occurs face-to-face by default. Two, CMC can distort the sender's perception of the message audience and simultaneously greatly increase the potential receivers for any given message.

Medium Choice

One of the first decisions an individual must make when considering using communication technology is which medium will be the most acceptable (Keaten and Kelly 2008). People have a wide variety of choices that they can make regarding mediated communication. They can voice call, video conference (e.g. Skype or FaceTime), text, instant message, email, or communicate via SNS. Even within an SNS individuals can choose different ways to communicate (Burke, Kraut, and Marlow 2011). Individuals can engage in direct communication with friends through private or public channels, or passively browse connections' accounts for news or broadcast their own updates.

Individuals should choose media based on how appropriate or effective they think a medium is for a particular task (Spitzberg 2006). In addition, while people may choose channels based on how appropriate they view that channel for their intended message, they might also choose a channel because they feel more comfortable communicating with that particular medium. Knowledge of how to use communication technology is a critical component of CMC competence (Sherblom, Withers, and Leonard 2013). For example, someone might choose to call and leave a voice mail even if they know the receiver doesn't like checking their voice mails because the sender lacks knowledge of how to send a text message. In this case, an operational literacy would help a message sender have more options for sending appropriate messages. However, beyond understanding how to send messages through a particular medium, senders must also understand social norms regarding particular media.

Norms may develop within social groups regarding the appropriate use of technology. For example, Fulk et al. (1995) found that people were more likely to use CMC channels the way their immediate co-workers used the channels. Poole, Holmes, and DeSanctis (1991) discovered that different groups develop different ways of using technology. We can still see the emergence of different norms across age cohorts and population segments today. For example, teens and young adults may view Facebook as a "basic" component of one's social media portfolio (McEwan 2013a) and choose to use other platforms to send messages to more clearly delineated segments of their social network. On the other hand, young parents in their 30s may use the same platform to share pictures of their children with wide-flung network members. Those children's grandparents may use SNS to see those pictures and reconnect with long-lost family members.

Media Richness

The choice of an appropriate medium may also take into account the "richness" of the medium (Daft and Lengel 1984). The term media richness incorporates four different constructs: the number of verbal and nonverbal cues that can be transmitted through the medium, the speed at which feedback can be made available, the range of meaning that could be conveyed with symbols, and how well messages can be adapted to the current and changing needs of the receiver (Daft and Legel 1984, 1986). Daft, Lengel, and Trevino

(1987) argued that communicators should choose rich media for more ambiguous messages whereas relatively straightforward messages could be communicated via less rich channels. Essentially, the more cues a medium can make available and the faster rate of back-and-forth communication between interactants, the more equivocality a medium can handle. In early media richness studies face-to-face interaction was considered as the richest channel and mediated channels were defined as less rich. However, it is important to remember that much of this early research was conducted when the media landscape looked very different. Email was available but not common. Intraoffice text systems could be found on a limited basis (Markus 1994). When early media richness scholars considered "less rich" forms of media they were discussing the difference between a written memo distributed to the entire office and a letter addressed specifically to the recipient (Daft and Lengel 1984).

Nonetheless, different forms of communication technology can also be classified as more or less rich. However, communication technologies may not fit richness typologies as neatly as scholars might like. For example, email could be considered low in richness because it is primarily text based (Walther 2010). However, email could also be considered high in richness in terms of feedback speed if the emailers respond to each other quickly. Texting or instant message programs might also be low in available cues but high in the rapidity of feedback and the adaptation to the receiver. Other channels might be considered low in cues but can be "hacked" to provide more information. For example, Twitter restricts users to a 140-character limit for individual tweets, but users use their allotted characters to provide a link to a longer story, an image, or a video.

Furthermore, simply adding richness does not always make a medium more effective or appropriate (Walther 2010). Although people often say that they prefer to communicate via rich channels, observational studies suggest that this is not actually the case (Fulk, Schmitz, and Ryu 1995; Markus 1994). There are times when people would like to communicate but cannot choose a more immediate channel such as face to face or a phone conversation due to other constraints. Perhaps they are not yet dressed appropriately, are engaged in a separate activity, or simply cannot meet due to being geographically removed from their chosen receiver (Rabby and Walther 2002). People might also choose a less rich medium, such as texting, precisely because the medium affords less immediacy (McEwan 2013a). For example, a teenager might choose to send a parent a text instead of a phone call or Skype as the audio or visual information available from more rich technologies might reveal a forbidden location. A job candidate might prefer a phone interview that can be completed while wearing pajamas instead of Skype interview that requires full interview dress and a neat background.

Theory of the Niche

As particular communication technologies become more prevalent, the social norms and structural components of a medium influence the *niche* that that technology inhabits in the communication environment. Niche theory proposes that media may fulfill specific niches where a medium's characteristics may "amplify or attenuate the opportunities for deriving gratification from the medium" (Dimmick, Kline, and Stafford 2000, 230). The theory is based on a uses and gratifications approach. Particular media may be more or less effective choices for helping people reach particular communication goals, such as fulfilling particular gratifications (Dimmick et al. 2000; Palmgreen 1984; Katz, Blumler & Gurevitch 1974). There are gratifications specific to each medium but media may also share gratifications (Ramirez, Dimmick, Feaster, and Lin 2008). In these cases media may "compete" against each other to fulfill a specific societal niche. For example, both email and text messaging can fulfill the niche of keeping information from a short message for later use. However, email tends to fill this niche in professional settings whereas text messaging fulfills this niche for interactions between friends (McEwan 2013a).

Thus, in a given interaction people may gravitate toward one medium or another based on the potential gratifications that medium can effectively fulfill as well as their comfort level with a specific medium. Competent communicators likely weave a variety of medium choices through their daily interactions and relational communication (Ruppel and Burke 2014). When choosing media, competent communicators must also be cognizant of the expectations that their receiver likely holds for that medium. An understanding of both general social norms as well as the idiosyncratic preferences of a specific receiver can be useful for the task of competent media selection. In order to hold these understandings message senders must also have some idea of the likely receiver(s) and audience(s) of their mediated messages.

Audience

The intended and actual target(s) of a message can affect choices that communicators make regarding how to deliver their messages. Communication technologies can facilitate one-to-one, one-to-many, or many-to-many communication (Morris and Ogan 1996; Shirky 2008). One-to-one communication includes channels such as emails or texts where the sender is targeting a specific receiver. One-to-many communication is mass communication. Traditional mass communication channels include television and radio programming. The internet can also facilitate one-to-many communication in the format of mass emails, lectures or vlogs (video diaries), public blogs, streaming traditional media, or webinars.

The introduction of networked technologies has also facilitated the ability to engage in many-to-many communication (Stevens 1981). Many-to-many communication can be asynchronous as in the case of message board communities or social network sites or it can be synchronous as in the case of video conferencing (Morris and Ogan 1996). O'Sullivan argued that communication technologies, particularly those that support many-to-many communication, create a new form of communication called *masspersonal* communication. Masspersonal communication describes the intersection between interpersonal communication and mass media. Masspersonal communication may incorporate one-to-many channels such as people using traditional mass media for interpersonal purposes (e.g. a marriage proposal on the evening news), or using one-to-one channels to attempt to diffuse messages to larger groups (e.g., using text messaging to send emergency messages). However, often masspersonal communication takes place in the many-to-many contexts when people engage in mass and interpersonal communication simultaneously. Many-to-many masspersonal communication includes using platforms like social network sites or message board communities. These communication technologies allow individuals to send and receive messages that we might consider interpersonal but the audience for those messages can be scaled up considerably.

Mediated messages in many channels can have persistence, meaning that they last longer and can be revisited, and are searchable and shareable (boyd 2011). These message features introduce slippage between the nature of the intended receiver and the intended audience. A message which seems completely appropriate for one receiver might be viewed by others who deem the message to be inappropriate. This can happen for a number of reasons. Privacy settings on a social network site might not be set properly or may change without warning. Messages may be seen by members of the message sender's network that the sender forgot about. Texts and emails could be forwarded or shown to others.

The ability to send appropriate messages is based on being able to take the perspective of the message receiver. When there is a discrepancy between the intended receiver(s) and the actual audience of the message this introduces new challenges to competency. In order to address these challenges senders may need to think more deeply about the potential audience for their messages. Individuals might choose from several strategies in order to create messages that are appropriate for both their receivers and wider audiences, including being cognizant of their most conservative potential audience members, choosing channels with less persistence such as the phone when information is sensitive, or negotiating privacy boundaries with co-communicators. These strategies will be discussed more in depth in chapter 4; however, the point here is that having knowledge that there are potential differences between intended receivers and possible audiences is an important component of CMC competence.

SKILLS

As noted above, competent communication via computer mediation may rely more on skills related to message production than technical knowledge related to computers and the internet (Wrench and Punyanunt-Carter 2007). Spitzberg (2006) proposed four skills related to CMC message production: attentiveness, interaction management, expressiveness, and composure.

Attentiveness

Attentiveness refers to showing concern and making sure that CMC messages are uniquely adapted for specific receivers. Messages sent through computer-mediated channels may be viewed as more appropriate and effective when the messages are crafted in such a way that recognizes the receiver as a unique individual. For example, Facebook messages directed toward a specific Facebook connection may have a more positive impact on the relationship than Facebook messages that serve as broadcasts to a larger group (McEwan 2013b; McEwan, Fletcher, Eden, and Sumner, 2014). Learning the customs and culture of a particular virtual community will make one a more effective communicator within that community (Rheingold 1998). Violations of norms on social media can lead to network members ignoring the violator or even removing the network member from their social media connections (McLaughlin and Vitak 2011).

Interaction Management

People skilled in *interaction management* know how to open and close topics in computer-mediated dialogues as well as understand the timing of particular mediums (Spitzberg 2006). On message boards people may be more likely to get a response if they keep their posts on topic and ask relevant questions (Arguello, Butler, Joyce, Kraut, Ling, and Wang 2006).

The timing component of interaction management may be particularly important for CMC as different channels may be thought of as synchronous or asynchronous. In synchronous channels communicators may expect return messages very quickly. Indeed, receivers may even be aware of how long it takes senders to compose text or chat messages due to functions that show when the sender saw the message and if the sender is currently writing. In asynchronous channels, senders may need to adjust to the norms of a particular medium. For example, one may want to respond to email quickly but not too quickly. People may find each other to be incompetent texters if they have different ideas about how long it should take to respond to a text message.

Another component of interaction management is how often people send messages via various media. Autistic adults interviewed by Burke, Kraut and Williams (2010) reported struggling with this aspect of CMC competence. One participant reported scaring away a potential romantic partner by sending her far too many text messages (a few hundred) within a few days. Another participant reported overcoming their difficulty understanding the appropriate amount of messages to post on Facebook by calculating the average number of posts his network members made and then making that number of posts. Non-autistic adults may be more likely to simply intuit the normative number of texts to send or posts to make rather than calculating the average, but any individual who violates the norm within their network may be viewed as less competent.

Expressiveness

Expressiveness refers to how articulate and convivial individuals are in their online communications (Spitzberg 2006). The items Spitzberg used to measure expressiveness include how individuals use humor and emoticons. In face-to-face interaction much of the meaning in humorous or emotional interactions is carried in nonverbal channels (Mehrabian 1971). Those who use CMC often may be better able to compensate for the lack of nonverbal cues (Wright, 2000). Online communicators may convey nonverbal meaning in text-based CMC environments through paralinguistic and chronemic cues.

Paralinguistic cues in CMC are typographical marks and textual features that have shared social meaning beyond the literal meaning of the typed words (Lea and Spears 1992). Examples of online paralinguistic cues include vocal spelling (e.g. spelling out a word to express intonation such as "heyyyy gurl" or "hey! grrl" instead of "hey girl"), lexical surrogates (e.g. writing out a spoken tone such as "hmmmm" or "ummm"), emoticons (e.g. using text to create facial displays such as :-( ), and manipulating grammatical markers (e.g. using punctuation such as ellipses (…) to express a pause or speechlessness) (Carey 1980; Lea and Spears 1992; Riordan and Kruez, 2010).

Time may also carry nonverbal meaning in computer-mediated environments. Chronemic signals such as when messages were sent or time-stamped or how quickly receivers respond to messages may also carry interpersonal meaning in CMC (Walther and Tidwell 1995). Individuals who respond to messages quickly may be seen as more immediate communicators. The ability to engage online in an immediate and expressive manner may lead to online communicators being viewed as more competent.

Composure

Composure is a matter of how assertive and confident a communicator comes across in the messages they send online (Spitzberg 2006). People who are able to communicate confidence may be seen as more credible online communicators. Certain paralinguistic cues may be useful in being viewed as an assertive and confident communicator. For example, a very simple component of composure could be standard spelling and grammar. Participants in Metzger, Flanagin, and Medder's (2010) study noted that misspellings in online reviews, message board posts, and websites make them feel uneasy about the information within misspelled messages. Online communicators who avoid misspellings may appear more confident and credible. On the other hand some types of misspellings and shorthand may serve as idioms which can communicate in-group status and shared social norms to receivers (Bell and Healey 1992). The difference is that the misspellings need to be strategic rather than random. Random typos and grammatical mistakes are more likely to communicate a lack of composure whereas consistently using a term like *pwned* (a term relevant to online gamers) or *teh* (originally a misspelling of the—*teh* now serves as a colloquialism in certain blogging and message board communities) may provide one with in-group cache within the right online group. Of course as these examples show, different ways of being expressive and communicating composure may be perceived differently by different groups of receivers. In order to be competent computer-mediated communicators individuals may need to be adept at sussing out the norms of the particular platform, community, and receivers.

CHALLENGES TO COMMUNICATION COMPETENCE

CMC Apprehension

One challenge to communication competence is when individuals experience communication apprehension specifically related to CMC. Communication apprehension is "an individual's level of fear or anxiety associated with either real or anticipated communication with another person or persons" (McCroskey 1977, 78). Individuals who are highly communication apprehensive anticipate negative outcomes from communication, suffer anxiety if forced to communicate, and tend to withdraw from social situations (McCroskey 1970).

Previous research has shown a negative correlation between communication apprehension and social abilities such as self-disclosure (McCroskey and Richardson 1977) and approaching peer strangers (McCroskey and Sheahan 1978). General communication apprehension has been proposed to affect CMC competence in two competing ways. One, communication apprehension for face-to-face communication situations may spill over into the online environment, causing individuals with high communication apprehension to also avoid CMC. Two, individuals who have high communication apprehension might embrace CMC as a way to have more control over an interaction and less message channels to be concerned about than in a face-to-face interaction (Wright 2000c). However, studies examining how communication apprehension predicts orientations to and motive for CMC have not found support for either of these hypotheses. Communication apprehension has not been found to correlate with either CMC use (Patterson and Godycz 2001) or satisfaction with CMC (Campbell and Neer 2001). The motive for using CMC may be associated with levels of communication apprehension; people with high communication apprehension may be more likely to choose a mediated channel when they need to give negative or critical feedback (Campbell and Neer 2001).

In order to more fully capture the influence apprehension might have on CMC, CMC researchers have expanded the definition of communication apprehension to incorporate feelings of apprehension specifically regarding communicating via communication technologies (Ledbetter 2009a). Flaherty, Pearce, and Rubin (1998) defined CMC apprehension as "anxiety associated with using the computer to interact with others" (263). Ledbetter (2009a) measured CMC apprehension by asking participants if communicating online made them feel uncomfortable, awkward, tense, and nervous. Individuals who are apprehensive about communicating via CMC may experience trepidation and fear regarding communicating via CMC and may exhibit avoidance toward CMC (Wrench and Punyanunt-Carter 2007). CMC apprehension is a separate construct from simply being apprehensive about computers or one's writing abilities (Scott and Timmerman, 2005). Although computer apprehension is related to avoiding the use of new communication technologies, CMC apprehension is a stronger predictor for avoiding email, chat, and instant messaging than either computer apprehension or writing apprehension (Scott and Timmerman 2005). In addition, people who rated themselves as more apprehensive about online communication also perceived themselves as less competent communicators in general (Ledbetter 2009a).

Individuals with higher CMC apprehension seem to be less likely to use CMC to achieve interpersonal goals. Flaherty et al. (1998) found that people high in CMC apprehension were less likely to use the internet for motives such as pleasure, inclusion, affection, and meeting new people. Individuals high in CMC apprehension are also less likely to use Facebook for interpersonal communication (Hunt, Atkin, and Krishnan 2012). Furthermore, individuals who were high on CMC apprehension were also more likely to avoid the interactive features of social network sites and online discussions (Hunt et al., 2012; Sherblom et al., 2013) and more likely to choose asynchronous forms of online communication (Ledbetter 2009a). In addition, individuals who are apprehensive about communicating online are more likely to use the internet compulsively and feel unable to control or reduce their online behavior (Mazer and Ledbetter 2012). However, CMC apprehension is not an insurmountable problem. People generally experience social anxiety when they are not confident in their social skills (Leary and Kowalski 1990). Providing education and training on digital literacies as well as CMC competence may help reduce CMC apprehension. Indeed, Wrench and Punyanunt-Carter (2007) found a negative relationship between CMC skill and CMC apprehension, suggesting that if CMC skills can be improved for individuals their apprehension may lessen as well.

CMC and Social Skill Deficits

There is an argument in the popular literature that engagement in CMC may lead to the reduction of interpersonal communication skills (Bindley 2011; Ludden 2010, Mastre 2010, Titcomb 2012; Young 2012). Early research in this area suggested that internet use was associated with lower levels of extroversion and smaller local social networks (Engleberg and Soberg 2004; Kraut et al. 2002). Researchers and pundits alike were concerned that heavy internet use might displace other more social activities (Kraut et al., 2002; McPherson et al. 2006; Turkle 2011).

However, more recent data do not support this assertion. In the last decade, internet usage has increased. As of May 2013, 85% of all American adults were online, up from 64% in 2003. However, the activities that individuals engage in on the internet are primarily social. In an average 2013 day, 88% of internet uses will send or read e-mail, 67% will use an SNS such as Facebook, 46% will send instant messages, 46% will upload photos to a website to share with others and 32% will read someone's blog (Pew 2012). Individuals with higher social communication skills have more Facebook friends and engage in more one-on-one mediated communication than those with lower levels of social communication skills (Burke et al. 2011). Furthermore, engaging in online interactions can actually improve offline communication competence. Lonely adolescents who engaged in internet use and identity experiments were able to increase their overall social competence (Valkenburg and Peter 2008).

An issue affecting perceptions of CMC use and communication competence is that people who are less skilled at face-to-face communication may choose mediated channels (Caplan 2005; Ruppel and Burke 2015; Valkenburg and Peter 2007). Lonely individuals may be more likely to use the internet, feel more comfortable communicating online, and report feeling addicted to the internet (Bonetti, Campbell, and Gilmore 2010; Engleberg and Soberg 2004; Kraut, Patterson, Lundmark, Kiesler, Mukophadhyay, and

Scherlis, 1998). Less competent communicators might choose these channels because less rich media provides them more time to edit messages and has fewer overall communication cues to worry about managing. People who are uncomfortable with disclosure in offline settings and fear the negative evaluations of others may be more likely to use mediated online channels (Caplan 2003; Keaten and Kelly 2008; Ledbetter 2010b).

Several studies have found that individuals with lower social skills might choose less rich channels. Caplan (2005) found that people with low self-presentation skills were more likely to prefer communicating online than offline. Engleberg and Soberg (2004) found that individuals reporting higher internet use were found to also have lower emotional intelligence. McEwan (2009) found that individuals who rated themselves as less skilled at interpersonal communication were more likely to attempt to make new friends via social network sites than more socially skilled individuals. Ruppel and Burke (2014) found that people with lower communication competence were more likely to make choices to consistently use less rich media than to supplement less rich media with face-to-face or phone interactions.

In addition, individuals with lower communication skills may choose to engage in more broadcast-type strategies than one-to-one online communication (Burke et al. 2011). Children who were taught to suppress emotions and opinions were more likely as young adults to say that they preferred online to offline communication (Ledbetter 2010b). Use of this type of mass messaging may make it more difficult to achieve relational goals than when individuals use online communication channels to craft messages that are directed toward specific individuals (McEwan 2013b). Undirected messages may not help people develop relationships (Burke et al. 2011). Thus, individuals who are not terribly competent communicators may choose the mediation that online communication offers. Early internet studies that found correlations between low social skills and sociability and internet use may have been picking up on individuals with low communication skills desire to communicate through less immediate channels. In other words, lower-skilled communicators adopted online communication earlier in greater numbers than more highly skilled communicators. As the reach of communication technologies has expanded, CMC options have attracted a wider range of individuals in terms of skill level.

CONCLUSION

Living in a society based on technologically networked individualism requires the individual to put forth individual effort to form and maintain network connections. One's ability to build sufficient networks is dependent on the ability to communicate competently. As mediated channels play a greater and greater role in the maintenance of network ties, the ability to communicate competently via CMC becomes increasingly important to the individual. The basic principles of communication competence apply; communicators must have the motivation to gain the knowledge and skill necessary to send effective and appropriate messages. However, the motivations, knowledge, and skills may vary in mediated environments. This chapter has provided an overview of general literacies and skills needed to engage in communication via technology. However, as a communicator's goals vary, their motivations and the knowledge required to be competent may vary as well. Further understanding the interpersonal processes people engage in using communication technology can help communicators become more competent at building and maintaining networks. The remaining chapters of this book focus on specific communication challenges that individuals must surmount in order to be competent and successful networked individuals.

Chapter Three

Identities in Networked Locations

Communication technologies affect the enactment of identity by modifying the way that we perceive and are perceived by networked audiences. A greater understanding of how different networked spaces can create different opportunities and challenges for self-presentation can help people to successfully navigate these spaces. Although mediated spaces have created modern changes to how some aspects of identity are performed, basic principles derived from classic theoretical work can help us understand these changes.

THE PROCESS OF IDENTITY PERFORMANCE

The term identity refers to performances of the self, tailored for a specific audience (Altheide 2000). The process of identity performance is akin to impression management which is "the process of controlling how one is perceived by other people" (Leary 1996, 2). Managing impressions and or identity performances is a complex cycle where aspects of the self are selected, presented, and adjusted to meet the gaze of a specific audience (Cunningham 2013; Papacharissi 2013). Scholars from a variety of social scientific perspectives have theorized about identity and self-presentation (e.g. Mead 1934; Goffman 1959; Leary 1996; Tracy and Trethewey 2005). Many scholars work from the framework that identity performances are collaborations between the self and the audience or network. This framework is deeply rooted in the perspective of symbolic interactionism. Symbolic interactionism and related perspectives such as the dramaturgical perspective and the crystallization of self are useful frameworks for understanding mediated identity production and interpretation.

SYMBOLIC INTERACTIONISM

Symbolic interactionists argue that the self is communicated to us through the actions of others. One of the first symbolic interactionists, Cooley (1902), created the concept of "the looking glass self." This concept suggests that identity performances attempt to reflect back to others the messages that those others provide about the self. What people believe about themselves is derived from the messages of the network members. Mead (1934) posited that people perceive a generalized other which is the presumed attitude of their entire community. The self is then an amalgamation of how a generalized other views the individual. People can then use their perceived knowledge of what the generalized other expects to both understand their selves and craft their identity performances.

The Dramaturgical Perspective

The dramaturgical perspective stems from the earlier work of these symbolic interactionists. Similar to symbolic interactionism the dramaturgical perspective also argues that the self is performed according to the expectations of a generalized audience. Specifically, Goffman (1959) argued that the self is a performed character, a dramatic representation constructed from any activity on the part of the actor that influences others' opinion of that individual. Goffman refers to these identity performances as the lines that we take, as if we are actors on a stage performing our identities for a specific audience. Furthermore, he argues that people strive to achieve and maintain a *well-received* performance or face. People maintain their face when they are able to present impressions that are consistent with their own view of themselves and agreed upon by other network members (Goffman, 1967).

The dramaturgical perspective is one of the most popular theoretical treatments for the study of identity performance via communication technologies (for examples of applications of Goffman see Bargh, McKenna, & Fitzsimons 2002; Cunningham 2013; Donath 1999; Hogan 2010; Kuznekoff 2013; Miller 1995). Goffman's work has been influential for researchers interested in the performance of identity on social online spaces because these spaces provide a "stage" for the management of identity performances.

Crystallized Selves

Performances of the self are not static representations of a singular identity. Given that identity performances are given for particular audiences, a self may articulate different facets of self for different segments of their network. As characteristics of the perceived audience fluctuate, so do self-presentations. The idea that the self is composed of many facets is not a new one

(James 1890). More recently, Altheide (2000) argued that how we are known to others "crystallizes the essence of identity" (4) and invokes a metaphorical idea of identity as a growing, multi-faceted entity. Tracy and Trethewey (2005) continued this line of argument and argued people have varied facets of their crystallized selves. Each facet of the crystallized self is both as real and as performative as the next. One may be a mother, a daughter, an editor, a friend, a volunteer, and so on. However, the crystallized self is in some ways tied to the different contexts in which one can enact the self. The way one performs "friend" for an audience of friends on a Friday night may be somewhat incongruous as the way one might perform daughter at Saturday's family brunch.

Online venues for identity performance can modify the process of performing specific facets of self. At times performances may become constrained due to different network segments converging into a single audience (Marwick and boyd 2011; McEwan and Mease 2013). At other times, online communication can allow people to experiment with facets of the self that they may not have introduced to their existing offline network.

CONSTRUCTION OF MEDIATED IDENTITY PERFORMANCES

In many ways processes related to identity performance are similar whether they occur on- or offline. We create presentations of ourselves for specific imagined audiences. The image that is reflected back to us by those audiences informs our sense of self. We present certain facets of ourselves to network segments that we deem appropriate to receive those facets. However, in other ways the structure of communication technologies can influence the way identity performances are expressed and received or as Goffman (1967) would phrase it, the way performances are *given* and *given off.*

Performances Given

Goffman (1967) defined *performances given* as the way performance cues are transmitted through verbal and nonverbal messages. Online communication can give us the opportunity to give very refined performances of our identity. The asynchronous nature of some communication technologies can facilitate strategic, asynchronous collaborations between performers and audiences by providing time for senders to construct the best possible versions of their selves. Furthermore, the reduced cue environment of some communication technologies allows receivers to form idealized perceptions of the senders' identities (Walther 1992, 1996).

The persistence of some forms of online communication can also change the way performances are given. Hogan (2010) has argued that markers of online identity, while performative, are less like staged scenes and more like artifacts displayed in a museum rather than a performance on stage. Hogan noted "everyone can have his or her exhibit, as long as the relevant information can be displayed with some coherence" (382). People select particular artifacts to be displayed in particular spaces in order to present their identity to others. Posts, pictures, and comments are presented and archived to provide others with a sense of the personality of the curator (the self). The audience either nullifies contributions through rejecting identity bids or reifies authenticity through likes, comments, and other communication that confirms the networks' perception of the veracity of identity performances.

Performances Given Off

Goffman's (1967) concept of performances given off refers to how identity performances are received by the audience, other members of the social network. Communication technologies can affect the way performances are given off in multiple ways. First, mediated versions of verbal and nonverbal cues may differ from face-to-face settings. Second, communication technologies can greatly expand who potentially receives these cues. Third, audiences may receive cues differently in mediated settings than they might in face-to-face interaction.

Cues

Identity performances may be interpreted differently due to the number and scope of the potential message cues that are available. CMC environments vary greatly in the number and type of cues provided (Culnan and Markus 1987). Some provide only text, some allow for small avatars and pictures. Some, such as Twitter, restrict the amount of text that can be provided at any one time. Others, such as Facebook, allow and encourage longer posts, pictures, and even video. Although cues can be limited, performances are still *given off* by these cues. Receivers of limited cue messages still make powerful attributions regarding the identities of their co-communicators. Impressions formed in text-based CMC environments may be less detailed yet more intense than impressions formed in face-to-face meetings (Walther 1992). For example, Jacobson (1999) found that people may create online impressions based on very limited information. For example, one of Jacobson's participants created a detailed person based solely on screen names. The screen name of JoshSamBob became to her, a white southerner, a stereotypical frat boy, who is 6 feet tall, particular about what he wears and is very neat. In her mind, JoshSamBob also fidgets and likes sports and horseplay.

Audience

Identity performances are so deeply grounded in the concept of audience; thus changes communication technology makes to the scope and structure of our networked audiences changes identity performance processes and outcomes. The concept of an audience in a networked society, particularly a society networked through technology, is a fluctuating premise. Audiences for identity performances refer to co-members of a network that might view a particular identity performance. Through technology these audience members might vary greatly along two dimensions. One, audiences could be made up of ties of varying strength. Two, audiences could possess varying levels of cognition regarding corresponding offline identities of the online communicator. In certain mediated spaces selves perceive anonymity and audiences that have little to no connection with other components of that self's network. In other mediated spaces, various segments of the self's networks collapse, (Marwick and boyd 2011) bringing a certain rigidity and need for congruency to identity performances. The construction of the network serving as audience for a particular identity presentation creates differing challenges and opportunities for the performer.

FIXED AND FLEXIBLE NETWORKS/FIXED AND FLEXIBLE SELVES

There have been previous attempts to define differences in networked spaces and audiences. Often these attempts ascribe the differences as related to interacting online versus offline and even conflate online with real and off line with fake. However, the terms "real" and "fake" are inappropriate as networks based primarily online are just as "real" as networks based in corporeal connections. The terminology "online" and "offline" are weak placeholders for different network types as so-called "offline" networks often engage in online communication. Indeed, often there are network members co-networked with other "offline" network members who communicate primarily online. Zhao et al. (2008) provided an attempt to stop characterizing online has anonymous and non-real by providing the terms "nonymous" spaces and "anchored" identities. Their term "nonymous" refers to spaces that are online but not anonymous spaces. In contrast, anchored identities are identities connected to the corporeal world. While these are useful starting places, modern online spaces are more likely to be nonymous than not and the idea of anchored and non-anchored identities suggests online spaces exist as a dichotomy. A better terminology might take into account a continuum of online spaces rather than dichotomies and focus perceptions of the availability of identity performances on particular types of network members rather than categories based on modality.

Identities exist as perceived entities in networked spaces. Whether we base our identity performance on bodies or user names – within our societal space we are what we perform for others. These performances are supported by networked audiences that demand some level of consistency in individual performances (Ross 1977). Perceptions of our networked audience and those audiences' influences on our identity performances are based on how *fixed* or *flexible* we view particular networked spaces to be. The idea of *fixed* and *flexible* represent two endpoints of a continuum. The fixedness or flexibility of a network is based on varying degrees of corporality, anonymity, and the stability of identity performances.

The Flexible—Fixed Continuum

On one end of the continuum are flexible networks. Fully flexible networks are marked by identity performances divorced from both the embodied self and stable connections between network members. Within these spaces communicators come and go with little social repercussion. Socially, such spaces are still networked—communication patterns are formed between network members. However, the individual can easily present different identities and perhaps even multiple identities. In pure flexible spaces there is less concern about who a network member "really" is and more engagement with whom they happen to be.

On the other end of the continuum, networks based on corporeal connections tend to be fixed. Members of fixed networks might choose multiple modalities for communication; however, the position of the communicator is fixed to their particular network position regardless if communication happens face to face, via the phone, or through an SNS. Communication technologies, particularly SNS, can actually introduce more rigidity to identity performances than existed in networks prior to the introduction of SNS. Prior to SNS, the position of an identity might be fixed within the network, but individuals may still present different facets of self to others or may change their specific identity performances based on their position relative to their expected audience. Communication technologies based on bringing network ties from various segments of one's social world together make it necessary for the individual to create congruent performances (Robinson 2007; Zhao et al. 2008). To not do so is to invoke social consequences as other members may struggle to understand who a fellow network member "really" is. In addition, fixed network spaces make it more difficult for people to fabricate identity performances that would be viewed as unauthentic to segments of the network. Take, for example, attempts to use a false name on Facebook. People do attempt to do so in order to be less searchable online even though it is against Facebook's terms of service. However, because most of the rest of their network is using "real" names, the network usually brings into sharp relief the corresponding corporeal identity of the pseudonymous Facebook user.

Both "pure" flexible and "pure" fixed networks represent extreme ends of a continuum. Most networks whether formed through online or offline communication will rest somewhere along the continuum rather than at one of two ends. However, this continuum provides a way to organize different internet spaces. For example, SNSs facilitate communication in highly fixed networks. Communication and its consequences on SNS may be structured based on this fixedness. Sites like YikYak provide an extremely flexible space as communicators are considered anonymous and do not retain stable identities from message to message. However, YikYak also introduces some fixedness in that messages are grounded in co-location and shared place norms. For spaces like Twitter, which has been difficult to categorization due to different ways networks form for different users, we can express the users' experiences based on fixedness or flexibility. Users who form small groups with other users are quite fixed within that small network. Users who attempt to engage with larger audiences containing people they are previously acquainted with and new connections are able to incorporate some flexibility into their identity performances while still being fixed into a particular role. Users who create pseudonymous accounts are in a flexible network position.

Changing network variables can change the level of fixedness and flexibility of a network position, regardless of communication modality. Some online spaces may provide for great flexibility but over time gain rigidity. For example, when joining an online game, people may experience a great amount of flexibility; they use an avatar, a pseudonym, and no one yet knows who they are. However, as people gain stable connections with others they gain a fixed position in the network. Indeed, even as people maintain alternative characters (alts), they may seek their fixed position in their network with messages like "Hey, It's Oikoo. This is my new alt, Zokaug." Yet, neither "Oikoo" or "Zokaug" point to an identity performance external to the game.

Challenges in Flexible Networks

Networks that are on the far end of the flexible continuum are typically online communities where individuals give off identity performances either anonymously or pseudononymously. Identity in a fully flexible network is dissociated from both the embodied self as well as network connections that know other identity performances of the embodied self. These are the type of online spaces that people describe as places where one is free (Donath 1999) or one can be "anyone you pretend to be" (Turkle 1995, 12). Any coherence in flexible network identity performances is due to the communication provided by the self.

This flexibility and associated anonymity gives people the chance to experiment with different self-presentations (Turkle 1995; Valkenburg et al., 2005). People may use these spaces to move beyond the limitations of the offline social environment and experiment with new identities and characteristics (Miller 2013; Valkenburg et al., 2003). Concerns exist that the anonymous side of the internet provides spaces where deviant or suppressed identities can be enacted. Another concern is that people can take advantage of flexible network positions to maliciously deceive others about their identity. However, the type of deception that most (but not all) people engage in within flexible networks is more subtle shadings of their offline personas. For example, people might enact their most-hoped-for-possible self (Zhao et al., 2008). "Hoped for possible selves are socially desirable identities an individual would like to establish and believe that they can be established given the right conditions" (Zhao et al., 2008). The existence of flexible network spaces may allow people to seek out conditions where they can present this "best" version of their self, a version that may not be possible in fixed networks due to relational constraints or pre-existing attributions.

Some people feel that online identity performances in flexible spaces are actually closer to their "true self" than performances in fixed network spaces (Bargh et al. 2002; Miller 2013). People might be able to express a version of self that they feel is more in line with their "true self" due to a lack of gating features in text-based CMC. Gating features such as body size, race, attractiveness, dress, or dialect can create barriers in creating diverse offline relationships. The reduced cue environment of flexible online environments can help people move beyond gating features and allow communication with a more diverse set of co-communicators. Another way that people may find their online performances to be more authentic than offline performances is if they feel able to disclose information about themselves that they might be reluctant to share with their fixed social networks (Newman, Lauterbach, Munson, Resnick, and Morris 2011; Shaw and Gant 2012). Flexible networks allow connection with others with less risk of serious reprisal if one's disclosures are not well received.

However, it is important to remember that while communicators may perceive greater network flexibility in anonymous online spaces, this does not mean that a particular space is or will remain flexible. Consider the case of a member of the online forum reddit: *Violentacrez*. Violentacrez was the moderator of several incredibly offensive Reddit boards. The one he was most widely associated with was a board called "jailbait" where redditors would post pictures of women and girls who either were or appeared to be underage in revealing clothes. Violentacrez was also associated with other boards such as "r/rapejokes" (CNN), "r/rapebait," and "r/Jewmerica" (Chen 2012a).

Reddit's message board community represents an extremely flexible network. People can move in and out of the various communities easily, have multiple handles, and generally remain pseudonymous. For Violetnacrez, however, there eventually came a day when someone considered his communication within the flexible Reddit community so offensive that they brought forth his redditor identity artifacts to his fixed network.

Violentacrez turned out to be the online persona of a computer programmer named Michael Brutsch. Brutsch's fixed network identity was connected to his Violentacrez persona by a reporter writing an expose for Gawker (Chen 2012a). In subsequent interviews with Gawker and CNN Brutsch attempted to separate his fixed network identity performances of father, husband, and computer programmer from the identity artifacts he'd presented in the flexible Reddit networks. In spite of this effort, Violentacrez's actions had serious ramifications for Brutsch and he was fired from his job (Chen 2012b). There are multiple lessons to be learned from Violentacrez's downfall, but for the purposes of understanding identity performances within networks there are two that are particularly important. One, anonymity or pseudonymity is a key component of flexible network spaces. If an identity assumed in a flexible space becomes associated with a non-anonymous entity in a fixed network space any incoherencies in the identities will need to be reconciled in order to avoid sanctions. Two, while flexible networks can impose some social sanctions—for example ceasing communication or banning a username from a group, fixed networks have far greater sanctioning power. One aspect of the fixedness of fixed networks is that it is difficult to fully exit fixed social networks. While one could imagine an individual becoming a hermit to escape fixed networks, communication technologies that tie together fixed networks can create further rigidity in identity performances. Even if a person moves from one town to another, the fixed network can easily follow through online social networks. Thus, social sanctions imposed by fixed networks can be long-lasting and difficult to overcome.

Challenges in Fixed Networks

In online fixed networks such as SNS, people are embedded in a network of people that also know their embodied identity (boyd and Ellison 2007). People may feel pressure to present identities their audience will see as authentic representations of the self even if those performances are mundane or negative (Rosenbaum, Johnson, Stepman, and Nuijten 2013). The creation of authentic online performances may be difficult because online identity artifacts may be viewable by multiple segments of the social network. People must present a self that has coherence, continuity, and authenticity for multiple audiences (Ellison 2013, Stutzman, Gross, and Acquisiti 2012; Papacharissi 2013).

The need to perform a coherent self for multiple audiences can create rigidity in identity performances and discourage people from presenting multiple facets of self (Hogan 2010; Marwick and boyd 2011; McEwan and Mease 2013). The online environment can flatten or compress the multiple facets of a crystallized self (McEwan and Mease 2013). The structure of online social network sites may mean that individuals restrict their identity artifacts to those facets of their self that can be stably represented across multiple segments of their network.

It may be partly due to the need to form an image appropriate to these collapsed, time-divorced, audiences, that people often choose to create a positively valenced identity online (Day 2013; Zhao et al., 2008). The norm on Facebook is to post positive information. A large-scale linguistic analysis found that almost half of Facebook posts contain positive words while less than a quarter contained negatively valenced words (Kramer, Guillory and Hancock, 2014). In general, people tend to play up positive characteristics and downplay negative characteristics in public (Leary 1996) so it is consistent that people would also tend to produce socially desirable online presentations.

SNS users are in the position of being able to create optimal self-presentations because they can take the time they need to craft their identity messages, control and monitor identity information left by connections, and they can concentrate on the construction of their Facebook identity without having to consider other cognitively demanding communicative actions (such as monitoring nonverbal cues or considering the setting) that are necessary in face-to-face interactions (Toma 2013). SNS users appear to use this extra cognitive ability to attempt to present themselves as current, positive, or interesting (Rosenbaum et al. 2013).

However, although people may strive to put forward their best possible face, performances of self are also based in the perceptions and judgments of the audience. If the network views a communicator's online performances as overly out-of-sync with offline performances they may be likely to judge the performance as inauthentic. Audiences may react negatively to exaggerations, contrived presentations, or identity performances that are inconsistent with other identity information they hold about the poster (Rosenbaum et al. 2013). People may be surprised or upset by finding online material about a friend that is "out of character" (Davis 2012). Such inconsistencies in self-presentation may lead audience members to view the individual as inauthentic and less credible. Some may even feel betrayed by the inconsistencies (Davis 2012). In order to strike a balance between positivity and authenticity, people attempt to make their own presentations authentic by making sure their profile is current and accurate, sharing candid photos, and writing up-to-date status updates (Rosenbaum et al. 2013).

Warranting Theory

Another complication for identity presentation in fixed networks is that other members of the network contribute to the identity artifacts of the self in ways that are not fully within the self's control. An SNS user may clear their page of untoward activity and post only carefully tilted head shots in good lighting only to have an acquaintance tag him or her in an unflattering badly lit bar photo. Deepening this complication is that people may be more likely to believe information that others post about us than information we post about ourselves. This is a central tenant of warranting theory first proposed by Walther and Parks (2002). People may be suspicious of our online performances because they are aware that such performances can be deceptive and that people are likely to manipulate their online identities in order to be seen in a positive light (Donath, 1999; Zhao et al. 2008). People may find identity cues provided by others less able to be manipulated by the sender and thus more credible.

A warrant or warranting cue is "any cue that authenticates or legitimizes an online self-presentation" (DeAndrea 2014, 187). Where or who a warranting cue comes from has warranting value because it is thought that the target has less control over warrants from external sources (DeAndrea 2014). "Warranting value is a psychological construct that is predicted via the warranting principle to moderate the effect of information on impressions" (DeAndrea 2014, 188). "The warranting principle posits that the less information is perceived to be controllable by the person to whom it refers, the more weight it will carry in shaping impressions" (DeAndrea, 2014, 188, see also Walther Van Der Heide, Hamel, and Shulman 2009).

Support for warranting theory has been mixed. Walther et al. (2009) found little support for the warranting principle in relation to claims about extroversion although they did find support for claims regarding attractiveness. Other studies have found third-party comments affect perceptions of popularity (Hong, Tandoc, Kim, Kim, and Wise 2012) and social attractiveness (Antheunis and Schouten 2011).

It may be that the warranting value of others' warranting cues are more influential to the receiver when the identity component in question is something that is determined by the network rather than the self. Utz (2010) argued that the warranting principle is more important when the trait in question is an interpersonal one rather than a personal one. Attractiveness and how one engages communally are not fully determined by the self so others' understandings of these identity claims are seen as more credible. For extroversion and other internal traits, the self may be seen as the most credible source. On the surface, Utz's findings contradict this argument; she found that self-claims are seen as more influential for how others rated the individual on popularity, an external characteristic. However, the popularity scale used included items such as "unsocial-social" so the measure may have been a better indicator of internal feelings about being social rather than a measure of external views of popularity.

Who provides the identity artifact may also influence the warranting value of the warranting cue. A cue from a close friend might actually have less warranting value than a cue from a weak tie because the target may be thought to have more influence over the postings of a close friend. In addition, the presence of networked others as an audience may serve as a warranting cue in and of itself. People may be more likely to believe self-claims if they assume that the sender is constrained by the network to tell the truth (DeAndrea 2014).

Of course, people still control who is allowed to post to their profile (DeAndrea 2014). Rosenbaum et al., (2013) found that people do try to control what others post about them by monitoring and deleting wall posts. The more diverse the online network is, the more likely people are to engage in protective self-presentation regarding unwanted identity information others provide (Rui and Stefanone 2013). However, if people are perceived to be filtering the contributions of the network, the audience will find network contributions in general less valuable (DeAndrea 2014).

Navigating Fixed and Flexible Networks

People may manage identity presentations through managing the makeup of their networks (Zhao et al. 2013). The ability to consider specific audiences is an integral component to the production of self (McEwan and Mease 2013). One strategy is to develop multiple profiles in order to fragment the audience (Drushel 2013). An SNS user might have one profile that is intended for close friends and another profile that they use for professional connections. Others, particularly youth, might fragment their audience by using different forms of social media with different network segments (boyd 2014). One might have a catch-all Facebook page, a professional Twitter account, and an Instagram that is open only to close friends.

Although technologies allow for this negotiation of audiences, audience segmentation can also be a cumbersome task. People report Facebook's segmentation tools are difficult to use (Zhao et al. 2013). In addition, due to the replicability of online communication we may never fully know who is viewing our identity artifacts (boyd 2011). Hidden audiences may have access to identity information they were not intended to see (Hogan 2010). Posters may forget about the presences of silent audience members—such as infrequent posters, third-party applications, and the SNS itself (Stutzman et al. 2012). When people are not fully aware of the makeup of the audience it is difficult for communicators to perform appropriately and adjust online identity performances (boyd 2011).

Another concern is that the fragmentation of identity performances may lead to a self that is incoherent (Turkle 1995). However, other scholars have noted that the self is "surprisingly resilient" (Lifton 1993, 1). Miller (2013) argued that people flow between "a multiplicity of online and offline identities without any clear break between these." Indeed, the self may benefit from presentations in multiple venues. For example, after experiencing ego-threatening messages people may like to reassure themselves of the positive aspects of their self by viewing their Facebook profiles (Toma 2013). In addition, the profile viewing was associated with increases in self-esteem scores on a subsequent self-esteem task. The ability to experience more diverse identities may ultimately contribute to a growing, changing self.

CONCLUSION

Identity performances are a negotiation between a particular self and a given audience. Communication technologies, specifically those that facilitate networked communication, change the dynamics of this negotiation. Some internet-based spaces allow for greater fluidity in the presentation of self that is available in corporeal settings; other internet-based spaces introduce increased rigidity. Understanding differences in networked spaces beyond online/offline, real/fake dichotomies can help people make appropriate choices regarding identity performances that are appropriate for each space and the opportunities that are available in both fixed and flexible spaces. A deeper understanding of these differences may also help communicators deftly fragment their networked audiences in order to perform different facets of self and fully realize potential identities.

Chapter Four

Privacy Management in Collapsed Contexts

As people continue to find new ways to express themselves and perform identities through communication technology, they must also navigate how to appropriately manage and maintain privacy boundaries. The tension between forging interpersonal ties through disclosure and protecting privacy through concealment is not a new one (Baxter and Montgomery 1998; Petronio 2002). People have always needed to disclose information in order to build and deepen interpersonal relationships (Altman and Taylor 1973). At the same time people may develop privacy boundaries to keep certain information from certain people (Petronio 2002). These boundaries may be constructed to keep information that might be out of sync with the identity a person is trying to perform in a given context away from that particular audience. Thus, the tension between disclosure and privacy is complicated by communication technologies that collapse the contexts of our social life (boyd 2011). In particular, fixed networks such as social network sites can collapse contexts by bringing together disparate segments of one's network (boyd 2011, Marwick and boyd 2012). Thus, the very tools that people may use to enhance their management of expanding network ties can also negatively interfere with relational processes.

People often add individuals to their SNS that come from a variety of social contexts. Facebook, in particular, can serve as a catch-all rolodex. These contexts might include friends, family, work colleagues, and acquaintances gathered from a variety of social venues. However, the creation of this undifferentiated audience collapses social contexts. Context collapse makes it difficult to direct communication on social media to particular sub-segments of our total network (boyd 2009, 2011). Twitter, for example, "flattens multiple audiences into one" (Marwick and boyd 2012). Often social media

47

users are not fully aware of the entire audience and all of the contexts in play (boyd 2011). When messages that are intended for a particular audience segment are transmitted to multiple segments of our networked audience problems can occur. Collapsed contexts lead to people having to make different types of strategic decisions regarding privacy than they might make when considering their offline communication choices.

One problem is that online messages can be easily replicated from audience member to audience member. One individual might tweet a message that subtly criticizes another network member without mentioning their target by name (this phenomenon is called a *subtweet*) and other members retweet the message until it is seen by the message target. A parent might take a video of their kid singing a pop song or talking back in an amusing way and their network connections share the video and their network connections' connections share the video until it has gone viral. Due to the ease of replication of online messages (e.g. retweets, sharing, or cut and paste) the actual audiences for our social messages may be far different than our envisioned audience. Individuals find themselves having to prepare their communication for invisible audiences and attempting to craft messages that will be viewed as appropriate by a potentially far-flung audience of network ties (Marwick and boyd 2011; McEwan and Mease 2012; Rainie and Wellman 2012).

Another issue is that communication technologies blur the lines between private and public spheres (boyd 2009; Rainie and Wellman 2012). An email may feel like a private medium until someone forwards your message to an unintended recipient. SNS posts may feel like announcements at a private party until someone uninvited accesses your page. A text seems to exist in a closed system unless the text is shared on a more public website (e.g. textsfromlastnight.com) or a screen shot is posted to a social media page.

The structure of the medium and the coordination issues inherent in the collapsed nature of the audience must both be taken into account when examining privacy management in online spaces. Indeed, Litt (2013b) argued that when managing privacy in SNS, individuals require both the technical skills to negotiate how the structure of various platforms affect privacy as well as the social skills needed to be aware of privacy issues and manage privacy within their audience(s).

PRIVACY AWARENESS

Most people are aware of some level of need for privacy management. Warnings from the media and one's social community regarding the implicit threat of social media postings to our personal privacy abound (McEwan and Mease 2013). For example, one of Debatin et al.'s (2009) young adult participants noted that "everybody knew someone who got in trouble for underage drinking pictures" (98). While disclosure is important for building network connections, disclosures that are viewed as inappropriate can lead to employment difficulties and conflict with network members. A recent report by Stutzman et al. (2012) found that over time Facebook users have become increasingly protective of their personal information by limiting data shared with strangers.

However, although users are aware of the need for privacy, Debatin et al. (2009) also found that participants were more likely to find this issue more salient for *other* people than themselves. Participants generally found that respondents were more likely to perceive risks to other users' privacy than their own. Furthermore, stories of privacy failures for others did not spur participants to take additional steps to protect their own privacy; only privacy breeches of their own profiles led to increased attentiveness to privacy options. Debatin et al. (2009) also found that the majority of Facebook users claimed to be familiar with privacy settings and claimed to have restricted access to their profile. Users who felt comfortable with their ability to restrict access to their profiles through privacy setting were then likely to disclose personal and private information on Facebook. However, people may overestimate their ability to use privacy settings effectively. Social media platforms often change privacy settings, requiring additional opt-ins or reverting settings back to defaults. Also, others who have access to the posts may replicate them for audiences outside of the original poster's online privacy boundaries. Overall, this evidence paints a picture of Facebook users who are concerned about privacy, engage in limited ways to protect their information, convince themselves that they have protected their information, and then blithely go about posting interpersonal messages to various social media outlets without fully recognizing the influence of audience, context, and boundary coordination.

PERCEPTION OF AUDIENCE

One issue relevant to privacy management is our perception of our audience. The ability to understand both audience and context is important for managing online privacy (Litt, 2013b). Who we think will be the recipient of our messages has a great impact on both the messages we send and how we choose to frame those messages (Bernstein, Bakshy, Burke, and Karrer 2013). Anticipating and negotiating social media audiences is difficult even for the most competent communicators.

One reason for this difficulty is that often at least a portion of the audience is invisible (boyd 2009). In order to be competent at presenting information via social media we need to be aware of the makeup of our invisible audiences (Rainie and Wellman 2012). These invisible audience members could include lurkers, individuals who view our content but do not comment or provide other feedback. They could be people who we might have considered would see our message but who viewed our content at a different time and in a different context than originally intended. Bernstein et al. (2013) argued that social media is *socially translucent* as opposed to being socially transparent because "posting to a social network site is like speaking to an audience behind a curtain" (para. 1). We know that there is an audience and we may even have some idea of who our audience is; however, we regularly fail to grasp the full scope of the receivers of our social media messages.

As users cannot clearly perceive the full scope of the audience, social media users must manage messages for "imagined audiences" (Marwick and boyd 2012). How one imagines one's audience may determine the messages and artifacts that one puts forth on social media sites. The question is: how good are social media users at imagining these audiences?

One answer, provided by recent work by Bernstein et al. (2013), is not very. Bernstein et al. found that Facebook users consistently underestimate the size of their audience in terms of how many audience members saw their content. Bernstein et al. asked people to provide estimates for how many of their Facebook friends saw a particular post and how many Facebook friends saw any of their content in a particular month. They then compared this report to actual Facebook logs reporting users who saw specific content. Bernstein et al. found that people underestimate who sees any specific post by an approximate factor of four—user estimates of audience size was approximately 27% of the total actual audience size. People underestimated their general audience (the number of people who would see at least one item they shared over the course of a month) by an approximate factor of three. The data for actual views revealed that around 34% of people on one's friends list will see any given post and 60% of users' friends see at least one item they share a month. However, it is incredibly difficult for any given user to estimate how many people and which people will view any specific piece of content. The data for the percentages given isn't normally distributed, so more people may see one post and less people may see another.

Actual audience size for posts was widely variant and the feedback cues that people are provided with on Facebook (such as likes and comments) simply do not provide enough information for people to derive accurate estimates of their audience (Bernstein et al., 2013). Perhaps it should be unsurprising that people regularly underestimate the size of their social media audience as previous research has shown that people generally underestimate the size of their total social network (Sudman 1985). In addition, the audience of Facebook messages varies considerably from day to day, thus we can never be entirely sure who is receiving a particular message (Bernstein, et al., 2013). Furthermore, even when we think content is restricted to our friends lists, the feature of replicability of online content means users can never be entirely sure who the content has been reproduced for (Hogan 2010).

The inability to deduce our total audience may lead to expectancy violations. Such an expectancy violation may occur when there is a discrepancy between our intended and expected audience (Stutzman and Kramer-Duffield 2010). However, this expectancy violation is not necessarily negative. Bernstein et al. (2013) noted that about a quarter of their sample wished that they had a larger audience than the one they perceived. These individuals may actually have the larger audience than they desire. Although it is somewhat unclear if people are literally wishing for more views of their posts or if they wish their posts would garner more interaction with friends, having a larger audience doesn't always mean users clamp down on information either. Vitak (2012) found that individuals with larger audiences tended to disclose greater amounts of information. This finding may point to a gregarious effect in some social media users. Those who are outgoing and gregarious collect larger audiences to communicate with and spend more time actually communicating with that audience. These gregarious users might be less concerned with keeping messages private and more concerned with disseminating their thoughts and posts to many network members.

There are, however, additional audiences that may concern SNS users. This audience is the SNS itself and third-party applications (apps). Facebook, itself, is a social entity, and is responsible for the distribution of all individual-level information (Hogan 2010). Although we may think of this information as protected, there are cases of law enforcement gaining access to social media information through warrants (Roberts 2011). Third-party apps may also harvest information from Facebook pages (Stutzman et al. 2012). Perversely, as people feel that they have increased control over their privacy settings, they may increase their disclosures. At the same time that individuals feel that they are locking down their profiles to strangers, they have opened up quite a bit of private information to what Stutzman et al. termed "silent listeners"—Facebook itself, advertisers, and third-party apps.

MANAGING BOUNDARY TURBULENCE IN COLLAPSED CONTEXTS

The technology that facilitates networked societies can also create instability in social norms as networked individuals strive to negotiate the conflicting demands of multiple contexts and networks (boyd, 2011; Rainie and Wellman 2012). Individuals need to make choices regarding appropriate levels and amounts of self-disclosure (Rainie and Wellman 2012). Much of our previous research on communication competence is based on meeting appropriateness norms by gauging the social norms of various groups and/or contexts (Spitzberg and Cupach 1984). Preparing messages for venues that collapse contexts may be more demanding of individuals in terms of crafting appropriate and effective messages because of the changes in the makeup and perception of the social media audience.

Boundary Coordination

In order to successfully use social media for the purpose of developing and maintaining social relationships, SNS users may find themselves needing to regulate disclosures and coordinate boundaries around private information. Boundary coordination refers to when people negotiate rules regarding the further dissemination of disclosures so that it is understood how the information is to be managed in future interactions (Petronio 2002). One example is a woman might disclose her pregnancy to a friend but ask that her confidante not share the information with others until she is ready to tell. This instruction constitutes an explicit privacy rule as the confidante is specifically asked not to share the information. In another case, a couple might discuss intimate aspects of their relationship with the understanding that the information is to be kept between the two of them. This would be an implicit privacy rule as it relies on the partners having a mutual understanding of what can and cannot be shared outside of the relationship. In order to successfully regulate privacy, individuals must also navigate boundary turbulence (Petronio 2002). Boundary turbulence occurs when confidants either have not agreed upon or break rules regarding privacy. In an SNS, boundary turbulence can occur in at least two ways – first, people may not explicitly coordinate with all of their ties regarding what can be shared from their profile. Second, people may not explicitly coordinate what can be shared from their offline communication to the SNS (see McEwan and Mease 2013).

Replication Boundary Coordination Issues

As noted, individuals might share information from one's profile with audiences the information was not intended for. Unintended audiences may lack the ability to appropriately interpret reproduced messages. Replicated messages may also not be deemed appropriate for the unintended audience. As noted earlier, one of Debatin et al.'s (2009) participants stated "everyone" knew someone who had gotten in trouble for drinking pictures. It is likely that the pictures in question were intended for the view of one segment of the underage drinker's social network such as peers, and were later shared with segments of the social network that did not approve of such behaviors— perhaps parents or school administrators.

This type of privacy violation regarding moving social information beyond the boundary of the SNS to unintended audience members might be most likely to occur on the periphery of one's social network (Stutzman and Kramer-Duffield 2010). As noted in chapter 1, SNSs may be particularly useful for maintaining weak ties, which in turn is useful for accessing greater diversity of social information and resources. The trade-off is that it may be particularly difficult to coordinate boundaries with weak ties. Weak ties may be the weak links in controlling boundary coordination (Stutzman and Kramer Duffield 2010). Debatin et al. (2009) found that young adult users did understand the need for caution in terms of weak ties, but still accepted large numbers of weakly linked friends. One reason for the discrepancy between the professed understanding of the need for caution and actions regarding adding weak ties may be that individuals make these privacy-related decisions at different times. When they choose to add a new weak tie connection, the potential benefits of the tie may be most salient in their decision making. Later, when individuals are considering information that they are sharing, they may no longer be cognizant of the full audience. Of course, this implies that individuals are mindful at all when they share messages. It may be that given the opportunistic nature of social mediums and the fact that they are increasingly available fairly continuously via mobile that people do not put much thought at all into the messages they post or the audience.

Offline to Online Boundary Coordination Issue

A second concern regarding boundary coordination is in regard to information coming into the social network. It isn't only one's own disclosures that may prove problematic, it is also the disclosures of network connections (Donath and boyd 2004). Individuals cannot fully control the messages coming in from their network ties. Although much of the content posted about one on Facebook is self-posted, others can contribute to one's SNS identity through comments, tagged posts, photos (tagged and untagged). For example, a participant in a study by Wessels (2012) study noted that "offline and online issues of privacy overlap as you are conscious not to tell people information that you don't want on Facebook, information travels so much faster now Facebook is so widespread" (1264). As discussed in chapter 3, due to the warranting principle people may be even more likely to believe messages and photographs posted by people who are not the profile owner (Walther and Parks 2002; DeAndrea 2014).

McEwan and Mease (2013) argued that this boundary coordination issue is particularly problematic. To successfully negotiate privacy issues in collapsed contexts requires a careful eye to what identity artifacts are exhibited via social media (Hogan 2010). When others are able to post information that creates our identity performances without our vetting the information, we may find ourselves in the position of needing to perform for conservative "lowest common denominator" audiences both online and offline.

STRATEGIES FOR PRIVACY MANAGEMENT

Although the difficulties of managing privacy outlined above remain, great numbers of individuals are still choosing to participate in social media. In part, some individuals may simply be willing to accept the tradeoff of less privacy for greater social interaction. Some individuals are naturally more socially motivated and may have larger friendship networks, greater amounts of disclosure, and greater risk-taking proclivities (Fogel and Nehmad 2009; Vitak 2012). In addition, while users recognize that identity performances via social media can never be fully private (Wessels 2012), identity performances in general were never meant to be private. The tension between seeking social connection through communicative acts and disclosure and concealing aspects of self through privacy management is not a new one (Altman and Taylor 1973; Petronio 2002; Baxter and Montgomery 1988). However, the occurrence of context collapse may be more prevalent and public since the advent of social media (boyd 2009, 2011).

Scrubbing

Perhaps the simplest strategy for the management of privacy disclosures is self-censorship (Marwick and boyd 2009). Individuals may choose prior to disclosure to only disclose certain types of information (Vitak 2012). Individuals may also engage in what Stutzman and Kramer-Duffield (2010) called discursive privacy and Child et al. (2011) termed *scrubbing*. This strategy refers to deleting things that are already posted. Child et al. found that individuals were likely to engage in *scrubbing* for a variety of reasons. One, individuals might scrub information because they later realized that the initial information was inconsistent with how they wanted to be perceived. For some participants, this occurred when entering a new context, such as leaving college and entering the professional labor force. For others this occurred when they realized that network ties not previously on social media, such as family, had now joined and might be able to access particular types of information. A second reason for blog scrubbing was concern regarding identity safety. Some scrubbers realized that information they had posted might contribute to identity theft or allow someone to stalk a profile owner. In these cases scrubbers removed the information for self-protection. A third scrubbing reason was relational triggers. In this category participants referred to removing information regarding former relational partners after a break-up, removing information to avoid conflict with friends, and removing information that might displease their family, particularly parents. Participants also removed information due to fear of legal or disciplinary action. For example, participants reported removing negative disclosures regarding their work or posts that could be considered threatening or libelous to others.

Compartmentalization

Individuals may attempt to circumvent context collapse by compartmentalizing their identity presentations (Rainie and Wellman 2012). One way people might attempt to do this is by creating multiple online persona and performing a different identity for different groups (Marwick and boyd 2011). In some platforms, this is acceptable usage. Twitter, for example, allows a person to have a professional account, a personal account, a humorous account, and more. Other platforms attempt to drive individuals toward a single identity, utilizing the misnomer, "real" identity. Google+ created a kerfuffle when they insisted that people use their "real" name (Gaudin 2011). Facebook's terms of service require that "Facebook users provide their real names and information—"You will not provide any false personal information on Facebook," and "You will not create more than one personal account. However, Facebook does allow users to divide their Facebook friends into specific groups. Individuals who choose to do so may be more vigilant about privacy overall as such individuals also were more intentional in regard to their disclosures (Vitak 2012).

Others may attempt to maintain privacy by resorting to anonymous and pseudonymous presentations of self. People may feel more comfortable disclosing when their online identity is separated from their embodied offline identity. Of course, it is important to realize, as noted in the discussion of *violentcruz* in chapter 3, anonymous and pseudonymous online communication is also not fully private either. Online communication can be traced in a variety of ways. Regardless, people may use anonymous accounts even though they realize that such accounts are potentially traceable (Wessels 2012). In addition, as noted above, the use of non-legal names may be against some social media sites' terms of service.

Conversant Privacy Practices

Another attempt to handle context collapse and boundary coordination issues may be to engage in conversant privacy practices (Stutzman and Kramer-Duffield 2010). Stutzman and Kramer-Duffield used this term to describe the practice of asking others in your social network to change their profile, remove photos, or make specific elements private. Due to the persistence and replicability of social media, the cat may be out of the bag regarding the specific artifact that spurred the conversant privacy attempt. However, engaging in such attempts may result in an education for one's network connections regarding what one is comfortable with having posted online. Conversant privacy practices may increase the saliency of privacy issues and make the network more aware of their responsibilities to each other (Stutzman and Kramer-Duffield 2010).

Targeting the Lowest Common Denominator

Hogan (2010) suggests that when gauging the appropriateness of a message, people may choose an individual or group that is "the lowest common denominator" (such as a boss or mother-in-law) and craft their messages according to the appropriateness standards for that person or persons. The lowest common denominator (LCD) might be someone like a boss or a mother-in-law. The LCD is someone with whom a person has established the thickest, least porous privacy boundaries (Hogan 2010; Petronio 2002). Hogan argues that an individual's choice to even join an SNS may be driven by "whether his identity can be effectively represented by the lowest common denominator of the people who view content in his absence" (384).

Vitak tested Hogan's contention by examining whether an increase in size and diversity of one's Facebook audience led to restricted postings. The size and diversity of Facebook users' potential audience does not necessarily lead to restricted postings. However, concerns regarding privacy did lead to both lower amounts of postings and use of features that allow individuals to segment their audiences (e.g. utilizing Facebook features such as making lists of specific friends). These results suggest that individuals who are concerned about appearing competent on social media may engage in privacy strategies that appeal to the lowest common denominator.

McEwan and Mease (2013) made a similar argument in their work on compressed identity presentations on social network sites. Although we did not use the term "lowest common denominator," we did argue that savvy individuals would likely privilege the most conservative and powerful discourse communities such as employers and governments. We argued that privileging these audiences may lead individuals to attempt to compress their identity expressions (McEwan and Mease 2013). We argued (as does Vitak 2012) that the problem with approaches that privilege conservative gazes or lowest common denominators is that restricting information to that level may make it difficult to forge relational connections with others. As shown in part by Vitak's (2012) gregarious participants, the purpose of social network sites is to communicate with members of our social network. When individuals clamp down on the information that they present to the network they may also be restricting their opportunities to connect with a broader social network.

Assuming the Vulnerabilities

Another communicative choice individuals might make is simply to assume the risks of online disclosures. Users may recognize that online disclosures can never be fully private. However, identity performances are not meant to be private. Individuals have long wrestled with managing the tension between wanting to be open and self-disclose to others and desiring some level of privacy and wishing to avoid the vulnerability inherent in self-disclosure. The structure of online communication, particularly social media, may create new challenges for managing these tensions. However, some combination of the above privacy techniques may help individuals balance the trade-offs between the risks of disclosure and the potential benefits of creating and maintaining network connections via social media and other forms of CMC.

CONCLUSION

Many online communication channels, particularly social media, can collapse contexts and introduce new challenges into the age-old practice of negotiating the tension between disclosure and privacy. These challenges can arise due to a need to either perform an identity that is consistent across contexts or compartmentalize identity performances so that specific messages reach specific subsets of the overall social network. Online disclosers need to coordinate privacy boundaries just as offline disclosers do but may be met with challenges unique to the online environment such as not being able to fully control the public replication of online disclosures or the additional information that network members may post online about them. Individuals may use a variety of strategies to manage this tension including managing disclosures, coordinating boundary rules with network members through conversant practices, scrubbing information that is no longer deemed appropriate, or posting through anonymous accounts. These privacy strategies represent attempts to garner diverse network ties and the resources associated with such networks while still providing performances that are appropriate for different network segments.

An additional privacy concern for networked citizens should be noted but is beyond the scope of this chapter. This chapter's focus has been on negotiating privacy issues that arise in interpersonal relationships due to the use of networked technologies. However, internet-based communication lends itself to bulk-data collection by governmental and corporate entities as well. Although this type of privacy invasion is not directly linked to interpersonal privacy processes, it is concerning for the networked citizen. As will be addressed in subsequent chapters, networked individuals rely on internet-based technology to form and maintain network ties. Privacy invasion and data amalgamation by outside entities run the risk of impeding these social processes and hindering the communication a networked society needs to stay connected and dynamic.

Chapter Five

Forming New Network Connections through Communication Technology

An underlying assumption of the idea of networked individualism through communication technology is that people are in fact able to create quality relationships via internet-based communication. In networked individualism the pressure is on the individual to handle the communication work necessary to form new network connections. Although some scholars have expressed concerns about the nature and quality of relationships formed online (Turkle 2011), research gathered over time has shown that people can and do engage in social communication and form interpersonal connections through CMC (Tidwell and Walther 2002; Walther 1992, 2010). Although in many ways the processes of online relationship formation and development are similar to relationships that germinate offline, communication technologies do introduce some changes to these processes. This chapter outlines theoretical explanations related to communication processes related to forming online relationships. The following chapter explores specific internet-based spaces where people may find and create new network connections.

CUES FILTERED OUT

Early research suggested that forming interpersonal relationships in text-based environments could be difficult due to the lack of nonverbal cues (Short, Williams, and Christie 1976; Siegel, Dubrovsky, Kiesler, and McGuire 1986). Both social presence theory (Short et al. 1976) and media richness theory (Daft et al. 1987) posited that media are more or less rich, that people gravitate toward richer media for interpersonal communication, and that the transmission of equivocal or ambiguous information requires a rich medium. This perspective is labeled the *cues-filtered-out* perspective (Culnan and Markus 1987).

Social presence theory (Short et al. 1976) predicted people would choose media that allowed for the transmission of a greater number of nonverbal cues for interpersonal communication. According to social presence theory this preference should occur because the more nonverbal cues that can be transmitted, the more communicators might feel as if they are co-present with their co-communicator. Face-to-face communication, where communicators can experience voice, facial displays, gestures, body language, and even the touch and smell of their fellow interactant allows for the greatest amount of co-presence as individuals actually are co-present with each other in the same time and space. Other forms of media may facilitate perceptions of varying amounts of co-presence. Short et al. theorized that a medium like the phone which allows for the transmission of vocalic information including tone, pitch, pauses, and hesitations may let co-communicators feel greater co-presence with each other than a medium such as a written memo. If social presence theory were to be applied to today's technologies, media that allows for greater transmission on nonverbal cues such as Skype should theoretically create greater feelings of co-presence than a medium that transmits reduced nonverbal information such as text messaging.

Media richness theory makes a similar argument but posits that the availability of nonverbal cues is just one component that makes up the *richness* of a particular medium. Daft et al. (1987) argued that media that transmits less nonverbal feedback is less rich than media with more nonverbal feedback. However, richer media also offer greater speed of feedback, greater language variety, and allow the sender more adaptability to the receiver. Within the framework of media richness, a face-to-face conversation would be seen as richer than a phone conversation. A phone conversation would in turn be seen as richer than an email and email would be richer than a posting to a bulletin board.

Early work on media richness took place in the 1980s prior to the explosion of different types of communication technologies. Daft et al.'s (1987) theory made comparisons between face-to-face communication, the telephone, letters or notes to a specific receiver, and memos written to multiple receivers. Since that time communication technologies that vary in richness have come onto the scene. For example, text-based communication such as instant messaging or texting might be seen as less rich than a phone conversation due to reduced verbal cues. Instant messaging and texting might also be perceived as less rich if feedback is not provided right away. Text messengers might also experience reduced language variety as they attempt to punch words in with a single finger or adapt messages to a reduced number of characters. On the other hand, some new technologies could be seen as conveying more richness. The advent of internet-based video calling such as the afore-mentioned Skype or Face Time could introduce greater richness than is available in phone calls due the greater number of nonverbal cues available to the receiver. Instant messaging might be seen as richer than, say, an email, given that instant messaging is more synchronous than an email. However, an email written from a computer with a standard keyboard might be richer than an email or text composed on one's phone due to the potential of greater language variety. An email sent to a single receiver could be seen as richer than a posting to an online message board due to the sender's ability to adapt to the specific recipient of the email.

Media richness posed that people should choose richer media when attempting to communicate messages that could be high in ambiguity. Communicators should reserve leaner media for simple tasks of information transmission (Daft and Lengel 1984; Daft et al. 1987). Similar to social presence theory which argued that more social messages should be saved for media that could more easily transmit nonverbal cues, media richness theory also expressed concern that text-based communication was too lean for task-related communication (Daft and Lengel 1984)

Although these theoretical perspectives provided useful typologies for the way that we think about mediated communication channels, text-based communication such as instant messaging, email, and text messaging have proved useful for both task and relational communication purposes. In some cases individuals may even show a preference for text-based media for relational goals (Walther 2010). Researchers have found that communicators regularly use CMC for relational purposes (Walther 1992; Baym 2010). Even very early CMC research by Rice and Love (1987) found that CMC can facilitate messages that express emotions and social information.

EARLY STUDIES OF MEDIATED ONLINE INTERPERSONAL RELATIONSHIPS

Rice and Love's (1987) work showed that individuals could adapt media that was low in interpersonal richness for the pursuit of interpersonal goals. Through these adaptations, individuals could communicate social presence and form relationships. Even in the early days of the internet, online communicators using text-based systems were able to overcome the paucity of nonverbal cues and use online text for interpersonal purposes (Finholt and Sproull 1990). For example, email carried social information to those whom we already knew from offline interaction (Stafford, Dimmick, and Kline 2000). Some turned to online dating in order to reach beyond their offline social network to find new romantic connections (Sprecher, Schwartz, Harvey, and Hatfield 2008). Newsgroups, chat rooms, and MOOs (multi-user object-oriented spaces) were online venues that helped people form relationships with individuals whom they might never have met offline (Parks and Floyd 1996; Parks and Roberts 1998). Twenty years ago, Parks and Floyd (1996) found that newsgroup users quite often formed personal relationships with other users. Parks and Floyd (1996) posited that "personal relationships [online] are commonplace and evolve naturally as a function of time and experience in the on-line environment of newsgroups" (Parks and Floyd 1996).

Online relationships come in a variety of formats, including close and casual friends and romantic relationships (Parks and Roberts 1998). Relationships formed online can be quite stable. Two-thirds of the relationships in a study of internet friendships lasted for at least two years. These friends characterized their relationships as being just as real, important and close as their offline friends (McKenna, Green, and Gleason 2002). It seems that whether communicating offline or online people are driven to maximize interactions and seek out satisfying communication (Baym 2010). Walther (1992, 2008) argued that humans are driven to affiliate and construe relational meaning from a variety of message types, including text-based CMC. This axiom forms the basis of social information processing theory.

SOCIAL INFORMATION PROCESSING THEORY

Social information processing theory (SIPT) proposed that people do communicate interpersonal and relational messages online although the process of relational communication online may vary from face-to-face communication in two important ways (Walther 1992, 2008). First, individuals may need to substitute linguistic and paralinguistic cues for nonverbal cues. Second, due to the longer transmission time relational processes may simply take more time in an online environment than an offline environment.

Even though many CMC environments are reduced-cue environments, SIPT, in contrast to media richness theories, posits that individuals are able to substitute different processes to perform the relational functions that nonverbal communication serves in offline environments (Walther 1992, 2008). Despite the lower amount of nonverbal information available individuals still find ways to send and receive social information. For example, in an offline environment interactants might gather how much a co-interactant is enjoying the interaction through decoding a collection of nonverbal cues such as smiling, eye contact, head nodding, and body orientation. To communicate the same message online interactants may need to verbally state their feelings and emotions toward each other. Online communicators might also simulate nonverbal messages by writing something like "sigh" in place of the actual exhalation of breath that would communicate frustration in a face-to-face setting.

There are other stylistic choices that communicators might make in order to convey relational information (Knapp, Vangelisti, and Caughlin 2014). For example, individuals might choose less formal forms of address (for example, an email addressed to "Bree" instead of "Dr. McEwan"). This informality might extend to informal language choice or phonetic spellings that can make online spaces feel casual and conversational (Baym 2010). More first-person plural pronouns, such as "we," than first-person singular pronouns, such as "I," can also show affiliation.

Online groups might also develop and use idiomatic communication (Knapp et al. 2014; Parks and Floyd 1996). Idiomatic communication refers to inside jokes and slang that are known only to a small group of communicators (Bell, Buerkel-Rothfuss, and Gore 1987). Idioms help signal group and relational belongingness. The emergence of idiomatic communication within an online space can signal a sense of camaraderie among group members and learning the lingo of a particular online group can indicate one's membership in that community. For example, those using online message boards related to wedding planning learn that FI means fiancé and FMIL means Future Mother-in-Law. In online parenting boards common acronyms include family role designations such as DH, DS, DD (Dear Husband, Dear Son, and Dear Daughter). Online video games often have their own language as well. For example, in a popular massive multiplayer online game, *League of Legends,* players can go "jungling" through one setting in order to avoid the "lanes" where the "creeps" move.

Each of the above communities employs different types of idiomatic language to distinguish it from other groups. It is likely that such idioms provide greater feelings of cohesiveness for in-group members (Bell and Healey 1992; Dunleavy and Booth-Butterfield 2009). Making these linguistic choices can show a deepening or a desire to deepen online relationships, whereas resisting these choices could indicate a lack of desire for closer online relationships.

Interactants might also convey the sentiments encoded in nonverbal messages through a series on paralinguistic cues. Paralinguistic cues are nonverbals that provide context for the interpretation of verbal messages. In a face-to-face setting, paralanguage might be tone of voice, facial displays, and/or hand gestures that help message receivers understand verbal messages. Different types of paralinguistic cues exist in text-based communication (Lea and Spears 1992). For example, online paralinguistic cues might include using an ellipsis to indicate a pause or silence or an exclamation point to show a forceful tone (Lea and Spears 1992). Interest might be expressed through italics or through quick responses to the co-interactant. Excitement might be expressed through all caps. Emoticons of "smiley" faces or sad such as :-) or :-(can help communicators convey emotional affect and message valence (Baym 2010, Walther and D'Addario 2001).

Due to the reduced ability to encode multiple nonverbal signals in a CMC environment, the transmission of social information is slower than in a face-to-face setting (Walther 1993, 1996). Thus, SIPT posits that relational communication and the formation of meaningful online relationships is most certainly possible but social tasks may take longer when occurring over CMC than in face-to-face settings. In line with this claim, Parks and Floyd (1996) found that the longer that an individual had been a member of a particular newsgroup the more likely they were to have formed personal relationships.

Despite needing to work around a lack of nonverbal cues and take more time to develop relationships, research has shown that people are able to develop relationships and engage in interpersonal communication online (McKenna et al. 2002; Parks and Floyd 1996; Parks and Roberts 1998). People may be motivated to transmit the relational information needed for interpersonal communication for a variety of reasons including the anticipation of future interaction (Walther 2008).

THE HYPERPERSONAL EFFECT

As shown, people do engage in relationship formation and interpersonal communication online. Furthermore, there may be cases where "leaner" media might actually be the better facilitator of interpersonal communication and relational development than face-to-face communication. For one, the lack of richness might actually help people self-disclose more due to a lack of gating features. McKenna et al., (2002) defined these gating features as "easily discernible features such as physical appearance (attractiveness), an apparent stigma such as stuttering, or visible shyness or anxiety" (10). When these features are not present, as they are not in a primarily text-based environment, people might communicate and form relationships with individuals that they might not approach offline.

A second reason CMC might better facilitate relationships is that people might be able to form relationships that would be more difficult to form and maintain offline. For example, Parks and Roberts (1998) found that individuals in their study were more likely to form cross-sex than same-sex friendships. Their finding is unusual because generally people have more same-sex than cross-sex friendships. However, in the online setting of the MOO, people may be able to form social relationships with the opposite sex without worrying about how the network will perceive the relationship.

For these reasons, CMC environments may be optimal for creating *hyperpersonal* relationships (Walther 1996). Hyperpersonal communication occurs when interaction via CMC is viewed as more socially desirable than similar face-to-face interaction would be considered. People in hyperpersonal relationships form connections that feel deeper and closer than they would have formed had they met the same fellow communicator in an offline setting. Walther (1996) argued that hyperpersonal effects occurred due to three characteristics of online communication: *strategic message production* on the part of the sender, *idealized perceptions* on the part of the receiver, and intensification of these strategic messages and idealized receptions through an ongoing *feedback loop*.

Strategic Message Production

CMC environments allow message producers more dexterity in selecting and editing messages than is afforded in a face-to-face conversation. Due to the reduction of physical cues, senders can choose to create messages that present them in the best possible light (Walther 1996). Asynchronous channels allow senders to create thoughtful presentations of self and competent messages. Even CMC environments that are considered synchronous such as chat applications still allow for more lag between messages than is available in face-to-face settings. Communicators can use that extra time to think carefully through their messages and consider the effect particular message content and design may have on their intended audience. They may also further edit messages during and after message composition. Communicators may manipulate a variety of cues that would be less malleable in an offline setting such as appearance or interest via CMC. People may also be able to engage in greater conversational planning online. The end result of these strategies is an online conversational partner who has the opportunity to present themselves in the best possible manner. For these reasons, online communication may feel less awkward than face-to-face interaction (Henderson and Gilding, 2004).

Idealized Reception

In text-based environments the interpretation of the reception of messages is more strongly determined by the sender than it would be in offline interactions. For example, in an offline conversation imagine the sender makes a joke and receives a weak smile in return. The receiver has multiple channels available—a groan, an eyebrow raise—to let the sender know the joke just wasn't that funny. However, if online that same sender might make that same joke, the receiver might send back a cursory, "lol" or "ha"—the receiver has a quite a bit of leeway in their interpretation of the response. If the sender thinks their original joke was hilarious they may assume the "lol" indicates the receiver is in agreement.

On the other side of the interaction, receivers are presented more limited information from senders than they might receive in face-to-face conversation. Regardless, communicators are driven to reduce uncertainty (Berger and Calabrese 1975). Thus, in the absence of cues, receivers may make attempts to fill in the missing social information (Lea and Spears 1992, Walther 1996). Walther and Tong (2014) argued that the receiver is the primary driver of their perceptions of their online co-communicator. The heuristics the receiver applies to their perceptions of the sender may drive their concept of the co-communicator far more than the actual sent messages. Furthermore, receivers have a tendency to fill in missing social information with positive idealized perceptions (Bargh et al. 2002). These idealizations may lead receivers to overestimate both liking and similarity in their online communications.

Feedback Loops

Strategic self-presentation and idealized perceptions combine in dynamic feedback loops to create *hyperpersonal* impressions. Senders strategically self-present an ideal self. Receivers fill in the cues that are missing in text-based interactions to create an even more positive image of the sender. As the communicators respond to each other, the strategic sending and idealized perception reconfirms their positive perceptions of each other. For example, Jiang, Bazarova, and Hancock (2013) found that people perceive initial disclosures as more intimate in CMC environments than in face-to-face contexts (the disclosures were actually exactly the same). Feeling that someone had provided a more intimate disclosure to start with leads receivers to reciprocate with more intimate disclosures of their own. As individuals spend more time sharing these reciprocal and increasingly intimate messages, the more overall intimacy and positivity they are likely to feel regarding their fellow online communicator and the more likely the relationship will become hyperpersonal.

Walther and Tong (2014) argued that in CMC environments, people likely do not realize the power of this feedback loop. Messages sent online may affect the subsequent communication of the receiver more than face to face messages. Yet, online communicators think their messages have less effect on each other than offline messages. Thus the online communicator finds their co-communicators responses that they have influenced to be similar or positive, to be spontaneously serendipitous. The feeling of just happening to find such a similar, positive, co-communicator may also drive the hyperpersonal effects.

The existence of hyperpersonal effects explains several research findings. One, people who met on the internet might develop greater liking for each other than those who meet up face-to-face (McKenna et al. 2002). On message boards, communicators have been seen to engage in deeper and higher quality relational development than might occur in a similar offline relationship (Henderson and Gilding 2005). Self-disclosure has a greater effect on perceptions of intimacy in CMC contexts than face-to-face conditions (Jiang, Bazarova, and Hancock 2011, 2013).

Hyperpersonal effects may pose little to no problems for relationships that the communicators intend to keep online. In this case the communicators can enjoy a relationship that feels closer and more satisfying than it might if the communicators met up offline. However, there is evidence to suggest that if communicators in a hyperpersonal relationship meet offline, the meeting may have a negative impact on their relationship (McEwan and Zanolla 2013; Ramirez and Wang 2008; Ramirez and Zhang 2007). The effect of modality switching on hyperpersonal relationships is discussed in more detail in chapter 6.

SELF-DISCLOSURE

If communicators are to form any type of relationship online, be it interpersonal or hyperpersonal, they must feel comfortable disclosing to others online. Internet users' ability to self-disclose is important because confiding information and emotions through self-disclosure sets the stage for a continuing, close relationship (Derlega and Chaiken 1977, McKenna et al. 2002). Typically, online communicators who find themselves making new acquaintances are doing so within flexible network spaces. There are three facets of the online flexible network spaces that may make people feel more comfortable with online disclosures. One, communication in these spaces, particularly in the early stages of relationships, tends to be anonymous. Two, flexible networks, while easily joined, are also easily exited. Three, co-members of flexible networks are less likely to have ties to fixed network members and are less likely to be able to impose sanctions if disclosures are viewed as taboo or inappropriate (Baym 2010).

Anonymity

The anonymity of interactions in internet-based flexible network spaces can reduce the perceived risks of self-disclosure (Baym 2010; McKenna et al. 2002, McKenna and Bargh 1998, 1999). Experimental studies have found that people are more likely to disclose personal information when interacting with a new acquaintance anonymously via CMC than when engaged in a face-to-face discussion (Joinson 2001, Tidwell and Walther 2002). As noted above, people are more likely to perceive that the messages they receive via CMC are more intimate than those received via face-to-face communication (Jiang et al. 2011, 2013). When online communicators attribute a desire to be more intimate to received message they may reciprocate by opening up more deeply in turn (Jiang et al. 2011; 2013).

Ability to Exit

People may feel free to disclose more online because online relationships and communities are easily exited (Miller, Fabian, and Lin 2009). If an individual feels embarrassed or hurt because of the depth or valence of their disclosure they can more easily leave the online community. Conversely, if an individual experiences embarrassment within their corporeal network these relationships are more difficult to exit quickly and other repair strategies may be needed. Of course, the ease of exiting an online community does depend on if the community is separate from or intertwined with the network that is anchored to one's physical self.

Separation from Fixed Networks

People may also self-disclose more online when their online co-communicators are not connected to members of their more fixed social networks. People may be less likely to experience social repercussions regarding potentially sensitive disclosures when confessing thoughts and feelings to people unconnected to their fixed networks (Henderson and Gilding 2004; Joinson 2001). These perceptions may make people more likely to engage in deeper disclosures to online audiences than to close network members who are known offline (Qian and Scott 2007). People may feel that they can more easily disconnect from flexible network connections if the disclosure is received poorly. For example, if an individual tells a friend an embarrassing story they lose some of their ownership of that story (Petronio 2002). The friend may tell another friend or an entire network of friends. Telling the same story online runs the same risk of loss of ownership regarding the story but the online co-communicators may not have access to shared offline network members to whom they can repeat the story. Thus, while the individual experiences the same issue with boundary ownership, they may experience far lower boundary turbulence and less social consequences from having their disclosure retold.

Interestingly then, the more engaged a person becomes with a flexible online network, the greater the potential repercussions of disclosure become. A newcomer loses very little if a disclosure is not received well, but a longstanding member of an online community may experience greater social losses if a disclosure is taken badly. When individuals become an integrated part of an online community, the cost of deceiving others in the community becomes higher (as the cost is being kicked out of the community if the deception is discovered). Higher punishment costs within a CMC setting does not mean that people are unable to deceive, but it does make receivers more likely to trust the messages that others send (Donath 1999).

TRUST

Although people new to online communities may feel free to engage in profligate disclosures, people seeking to establish relationships will need to develop some level of trust with potential relational partners. Due to the anonymity afforded by text-based interactions, communication processes related to interpersonal trust online may be different from interpersonal trust offline. In fixed social networks, other network members may vet and vouch for new acquaintances. When entering a flexible network, all of the other network members may be new acquaintances. In addition, the media provides sensational warnings about trusting individuals you meet online. Shows such as NBC's *To Catch a Predator* or MTV's *Catfished,* provide the message that trusting others on the internet can have results ranging from dangerous to embarrassing.

Yet, everyday people log in and communicate with individuals that they only know from their online presences. Parks and Floyd (1996) found people have moderate to high levels of disclosure with their online friends. People who do disclose their inner self online will be more likely to form close relationships online (McKenna et al. 2002). Indeed, in some cases people may be even more likely to trust others that they meet online with interpersonal self-disclosures than people they know offline (Baym, 2010). Factors that can lead to greater trust in flexible network spaces include reciprocity in the community, the stability of identities, and the competence of communicators.

Reciprocity

The norm of reciprocity (Gouldner 1960) may be at work in online groups. For one, if people believe that others in the community are also confiding personal information, people may be more likely to disclose in return (Henderson and Gilding 2004). People may also feel more connected to the group if someone in the group has done them some type of favor (Joyce and Kraut 2006). Finally, feeling that we have personal dyadic bonds with other individuals within the community also ties us to the larger group and may make us more likely to trust other group members (Joyce and Kraut 2006).

Identity Stability

Due to the lack of connection to an embodied self, people may be less certain about the truthfulness of fellow communicator's representations of identity. Not being certain of people's identity online may lead to less confidence in the information online communicators provide (Green 2007). Due to the limited cues in some online environments, people have noted that they enjoy the ability to play with their identity performances. However, playing with their own identity means they realized that others could also be engaging in identity play (Henderson and Gilding 2004).

How much people trust others' online may be in part due to the stability of others networked identity. The stability of an online persona is a continuous construct, not a dichotomous one. On one end of the continuum we might imagine an individual who creates a handle (or uses the ever common "Anonymous") to post once within a community and then disappear. On the other end, we could imagine something akin to a Facebook profile when an individual uses the name on their driver's license, a picture of their physical self, and are connected to a plethora of individuals who know that person both on and offline. The space in the middle is vast and allows for all kinds of different choices regarding stability even within flexible networks. Stability is not about "real" names or "real" avatars. Rather, it is about how the community perceives the consistency of the identity performance of that individual. An individual could use a cartoon avatar and a pseudonym and be considered one of the most stable, trusted group members. Another member could use their physical self as their avatar and their actual name and still be treated with caution if they have not yet established themselves as a constant presence in the community. Another indicator of identity stability might be if an identity appears in multiple fora. For example, if an individual is an active member in a blog community, and is also known as that identity in a twitter network, and perhaps appears in certain message boards, the consistency across boards might make that person appear more trustworthy.

People may be more likely to trust others who were known either by their offline identity or a consistent pseudonym (Henderson and Gilding, 2004). Perceived stability in identity performances may make us more likely to believe we could establish a relationship with that individual. Expectation of future interaction motivates people to communicate in a social manner (Rice and Love 1987). Parks and Floyd (1996) found the best predictor of developing personal relationships was how long and how frequently an individual participated in a news group. The longer someone participated in a newsgroup they more likely they were to form personal relationships. This finding may be because individuals could acquaint themselves with the stable identities that others were presenting over time. The more vocal individuals were, the more status they had in the group. Just like in offline relationships, the more time we spend with an individual the closer we rate our relationships with that person (Parks and Roberts 1998). Constant participation means that you are better known and perhaps better trusted. (Donath 1999).

Competence

Perceived interpersonal characteristics of fellow online communicators may also make them more likely to be perceived as trustworthy, such as similarity and perceived expertise. When discussing online reviews, people seemed to trust those who they perceived to be similar by seeking out the opinions of similar others. (Metzger et al. 2010). Granitz and Ward (1996) found that people were able to establish status in online communities if they were seen as experts on a particular topic. In contrast to offline communication, participants rarely mentioned other status indicators such as occupation, income, residence. Granitz and Ward's findings suggest that online communities do potentially provide a means to move beyond traditional status markers.

Certain message characteristics may also be related to perceived trustworthiness. Messages that use standard spelling and grammar may be seen as more credible and trustworthy (Metzger et al. 2010). Those who consistently introduce spelling and grammar errors may be viewed as incompetent or careless (Lea and Spears 1992). Interestingly, idiomatic communication, which may include nonstandard spelling and grammar, seems to help signal community cohesiveness and becomes an in-group marker once you are in a community (Bell and Healey 1992; Dunleavy and Booth-Butterfield 2009). However, proper spelling and grammar is needed at first to help posters to seem credible. The right mix and timing of idioms and standard grammar is probably key to being perceived as a credible community member.

BENEFITS TO ONLINE FRIENDSHIP

Although Walther and others' research shows that individuals *can* engage in social communication and create friendships online, there is also a question of *why* individuals might do so; what benefits are there to creating and maintaining online friendships? In a networked society, individuals experience greater pressure to form their own new relationships as they cannot rely as heavily on social groups to provide new experiences and interaction partners. Reaching out through online channels can help people identify potential new connections based on shared interests and other similarities.

Online interaction may provide access to interpersonal benefits. Approximately half of the internet users in McKenna et al.'s (2002) study reported that using the internet had made them feel less lonely. Those who were lonely prior to making online friends reported making more online friends and greater satisfaction with those friendships (McKenna et al 2002). Individuals who are shy might turn to CMC to overcome this limitation (Myers 1987). Interaction in CMC may be attractive because interactions in flexible networks have fairly low stakes. As discussed above, people can exit easily and do not have to stake their offline identity performance on their online messages. Walther (1992) argued that due to the low social presence and reduced social context cues, messages in the early stages of CMC relationships should be low in relational dominance and high in equality. Initial interactions may be less arousing and allow people to have and show more composure (Walther 1992). Then, just as occurs in face-to-face interaction, greater cohesiveness, solidarity, and affiliativeness should occur over time (Walther 1992).

Online communication may be particularly useful for finding others who enjoy similar interests, particularly if such a community is not available locally. People who find themselves isolated from others with similar interests might turn to online communication to locate others with similar proclivities. For example, some of Henderson and Gilding's (2004) participants discussed making online friends to help with problems encountered while experimenting with different identities online. One respondent noted that he might discuss problems that he has as a wizard in on online role-playing game with other online community members rather than offline network members who do not play the game. The internet also allows individuals to search for and explore interests that might have been more difficult to pursue prior to the advent of an easily searched internet. For example, if a person in the US developed an interest in Japanese anime, prior to the internet they would have needed to search out anime comics and tapes that were available in the United States on a limited basis. Now, individuals can download a wide range of anime from a variety of internet-based sources. Then, if no one in the immediate vicinity is interested in discussing plot lines or critiques of anime, the individual could choose to go to forums devoted specifically to the discussion of anime and look for new network connections that share this specific interest.

While people might seek out others with similar interests, individuals might also be more likely to form relationships with different types of people than they might otherwise because of the lack of gating features previously discussed (McKenna and Bargh 1999). People might be less likely to form prejudices about others as status markers and gating features (including race, gender, age, national origin, and physical appearance) are not immediately salient online (Rheingold 1998, Sproull and Kiesler 1986). In the absence of these social context cues, individuals may feel freer to communicate with others they might not choose to communicate with offline. Thus, online communities can provide a broader network of weak ties and wider variety of support (Baym 2010; Steinkuehler and Williams 2006). The more bridging social capital an individual has through their weak ties the greater access they have to a diverse set of information and knowledge (Putnam 2000).

Online communication may be particularly beneficial for individuals with both social and physical disabilities. People may choose to form relationships online as a way to overcome obstacles they face in offline settings. In some cases people who are on the autism spectrum might choose to communicate online as the time delay and lower stakes may make social communication less daunting (Burke, Kraut, and Williams 2010). Individuals on the autism spectrum report that although the lack of nonverbal information can make it difficult to interpret social messages online, the asynchronous nature of CMC can still make it more comfortable to pursue social interactions online than offline (Burke et al. 2010).

Others with physical disabilities say they appreciate the leveling ability of online spaces which allow others to get to know them first "without attaching a wheelchair to it" (Wiginton 2014). In other cases, the disability may make it difficult to communicate offline, but the asynchronous and text-based online world is more easily conquered. Rheingold (2001) relays a story of a severely disabled young man with nearly unintelligible speech. Although only his mother could understand his verbal communication, through pecking out messages on a keyboard with a stick, he can communicate and socialize with a larger network.

CONCLUSION

Forming new network connections online may be a challenging undertaking as individuals navigate reduced cue environments, concerns regarding interpersonal trust, and illusionary perceptions of their co-communicators. However, individuals are still able to form relationships and share relational messages and self-disclosures through communication technologies. Given the right circumstances these relationships can provide valuable interpersonal outlets for disclosure that may not be available from other segments of the social network. Networked communication technologies can help people engage with others with similar interests, overcome barriers to forming new relationships, and ultimately build less constrained social networks.

Chapter Six

Where New Connections Are Formed

Networked individuals utilize the internet and associated communication technologies to build networks of choice made up of members who share common interests and goals. The internet frees people from only being able to form ties in co-geolocated groups and kinship networks. These potentially far-flung new network members can provide valuable information, resources, and social support. In order to meet potential new connections, internet users have built various gathering places that people can move in and out of, seeking social interaction. In some ways these online spaces are akin to Oldenburg's (1989) idea of *Third Places.* Oldenburg argued that brick-and-mortar spaces such as coffee shops and taverns serve the function of allowing individuals to establish casual, free-form communities. The characteristics of third spaces, accessible neutral places where the main activity is conversation and membership is fluid, also apply to many digital spaces such as message board communities or online video game worlds (Rheingold 2001). Although these spaces are characterized by weak ties and generally represent extremely flexible networks, the existence of online third spaces provides a valuable social resource for networked individuals who seek to expand their network.

CONNECTING ONLINE

Many internet users use CMC to communicate with current acquaintances, not to make new ones; however, the amount of people who do form new online acquaintanceships and friendships is not zero or even near zero. For example, a study of British internet users found that 20% of internet users had met a new friend online (Di Gennero and Dutton 2007). Typically, new dyadic relationships emerge from existing online communities (Baym 2010; Tang 2010). However, not all online venues are the same and different types of CMC may provide better or worse environments for forming new friendships (Walther 1992). Certain online venues lend themselves to making new friends whereas other venues lend themselves to maintaining connections with individuals known to us offline. For example, Ellison and colleagues (Ellison et al. 2007; Lampe, Ellison, and Steinfield 2006) found that college students are more likely to use an SNS like Facebook for the purpose of cataloging fixed network connections made offline rather than making new friends. Indeed, using spaces such as Facebook to try to meet new connections may be seen as socially incompetent (McEwan and Guerrero 2010). However, online groups and communities that are formed around shared interests as opposed to pre-existing networks may prove fruitful places for the formation of new networks and dyadic relationships (Baym 2010). For example, many people who used MOOs in the 90s reported forming at least one personal relationship through the MOO (Parks and Roberts 1998). Indeed, people have been forming new interpersonal relationships with others they meet online since the debut of Usenet groups in 1979.

SEEKING ONLINE COMMUNITY

When people first access online communities they are often seeking information exchange (Ridings and Gefen 2004). The internet, of course, has information available on almost any topic under the sun—and yet people still gravitate toward interpersonal sources of information rather than document-based answers. Communication researchers have long known that individuals find messages more credible and persuasive if they come from an interpersonal source (Rogers 2003). These message perceptions appear to transfer to online spaces as individuals continue to seek out information from online community members (Metzger et al. 2010).

Some people come to an online forum once, ask a question and then never return. Others, however, may stay for the social interaction and companionship (Ridings and Gefen 2004). Individuals might also seek out an online community specifically to find additional social support. Those who join health and wellness or professional oriented communities are particularly likely to be seeking out support from others who have gone through similar experiences (Ridings and Gefen 2004). Some researchers have argued that as less real-world outlets are available for community and social interaction (Putnam 2000), people might turn to virtual spaces in order to meet their needs for social interactions (Williams 2006a). Others argue that due to our social nature, humans are simply prone to adapt task and information spaces for social purposes (Baym 2010).

Joining online communities may lead to increased social capital, particularly increases in bridging social capital (Blanchard and Horan 1998). As discussed in chapter 1, large numbers of weak ties in an individual's social network are known to increase the diversity of information available to that individual. Online communities are spaces where individuals can seek out existing networks of weak ties in order to tap into expertise and knowledge that might not be available in that person's existing personal network. Online communities tend to be flexible networks. Oldenburg (1989) noted that a certain level of flexibility is part of the charm of third spaces. Having a large collection of weak ties, he argued, can occur "*only* if people do not get uncomfortably tangled in one another's lives" (22). Online communities can serve as digital third places where people can come and go, meet others casually, and come into contact with new network members.

Online communities have various definitions. These definitions cohere around five principles. The first two are inherent in the term online community: online communities are aggregates of individuals, who communicate primarily thorough mediated means. Online communities are organized around shared interests, community members engage in relational communication, and membership is tenuous.

Aggregates of Individuals

First, online communities are aggregates of individuals (Porter 2004; Rheingold 1998, 2001). Internal social structures are fairly egalitarian. Although message boards may have some moderator or individual or company who is responsible for the technical infrastructure of the board, this entity serves a role that is akin to the local bartender or coffee shop owner in an offline third place. Within the social community of an online message board individual commentators may be afforded different statuses by the community based on expertise or longevity but these commentators are not in charge of the group, nor can they issue formal invitations or restrictions to group members. Individuals can log into the community when they please, stay as long as they like for any particular session, and be away from the group for various times. The social leveling created by online third spaces allows people to interact with a more diverse set of co-communicators than those they are structurally bound to offline. Online fora allow individuals from different statuses, both in socioeconomic status and in topic expertise, to communicate.

Mediated Means

Online communities communicate primarily through mediated means (Ridings, Gefen, and Arinze 2002; Bagozzi and Dholakia 2002; Li, 2004; Rheingold, 2001; Porter, 2004). Communication technologies serve to break the connection between communication and shared space (Baym 2010). Many online communities can be accessed simply by following a link. Message boards are probably the most common means of hosting an online community but other forms exist. For example, an email list serve can facilitate interaction or the comment section of a blog may develop into a community. The asynchronous nature of CMC means that people can respond to posts at different times, and no longer does one have to be present for an initial utterance in order to join a conversation. In addition, community members may expand their communication beyond the original community space. Dyads or subgroups might send each other emails or join related groups on SNS. Community members might also choose to meet each other face-to-face (McEwan & Zanolla 2013), but the home of the community is the shared online space.

Shared Interest

Online communities are organized around some shared interest or interests held by the community members (Li 2004; Ridings et al. 2002; Rheingold 2001; Porter 2004). These interests can be wide ranging—from origami enthusiasts to soccer fans to feminist theory. Regardless of the type of interest, some coherent theme is necessary in order to attract new members. Seeking or exchanging information on some topic is often the primary motivation for newcomers to find and return to the online community (Ridings and Gefen 2006). Attracting newcomers is an important process for online communities as these members help even out the loss of exiting members and provide new energy to the group (Lampe and Johnston 2006).

Communities for almost any topic can be found on the internet. These shared interests serve as foci around which communities can coalesce (Feld 1981). In the 1980s, Feld argued that the joint activities that foci are organized around would depend on existing social structures such as workplaces, organizations, hangouts, or families, However, the internet allows people to move beyond offline social structures and organize their network connections around shared interests (McKenna et al. 2002; Rheingold 1998).

Relational Communication

Fourth, although individuals are drawn to the communities for instrumental reasons (to discuss a shared interest), communication in online communities also encompasses the relational goals of interpersonal bonding and the development of shared culture (Etzioni and Etzioni 1999). Having an online space where people can discuss some topic is not enough to create a community. Interpersonal communication is a key component of why some communities thrive and persist and others fade away (Preece 2001). Online communities simply do not exist without interpersonal conversations (Ridings et al. 2002). The exchange of socioemotional information (Bale 1950) helps keep the community in place and the information flowing. Community members engage in communication that develops and maintains relationships such as self-disclosure and humor. This type of phatic communication can help maintain a sense of community. Interpersonal communication can also help create, negotiate, and share group norms (Baym 2010; Wise, Hammon, and Thorson 2007). Group members may even engage in meta-communication where they discuss the appropriateness or inappropriateness of other members' postings.

Tenuous Membership

Membership in an online community is somewhat tenuous (Li, 2004). Online communities are flexible networks based on a large number of weak ties rather than strong ties. The fluidity of the network and relationships allows people to both enter and exit easily. Membership in online communities is voluntary and group members can generally enter and leave the group at will. However, the fluid nature of online community membership means that the networks can sustain even as people exit and dyadic relationships dissolve (Castells, 2001).

The flexibility of online communities is not necessarily a negative quality. Online community members may feel more able to communicate opinions that they might suppress in more fixed network spaces. In some cases, online communicators may be seeking out this type of community space precisely to engage in less inhibited communication. Another potential benefit is that the weak ties a person can connect with in an online community may be a more diverse set of individuals than are available offline. Finally, although the connections that make up networks in online communities may consist of weak ties, online groups often develop a strong sense of group membership (Baym 2010). This sense of membership can persist outside of the flow of exiting and entering members (Castells 2001).

MESSAGE BOARD COMMUNITIES

Message board communities are sometimes referred to as bulletin boards, electronic bulletin boards, or newsgroups. The main purpose of message board communities is to engage in conversation regarding a particular topic (Arguello et al. 2006). One of the largest message board communities is reddit which spans sub-reddits on almost any topic imaginable. Other message board communities may be more topic-specific, such as boards on parenting, particular sport teams, exercise and wellness, or particular illnesses. The visible communication of online communities is typically a series of threaded conversations with each thread containing a short, focused conversation. Message board communities require members and potential members to actively seek out the community space online rather than passively receiving the messages as one might on an email list serve (Ridings and Gefen 2004). People who use message boards are more likely to make online-only friends than internet users who do not use message boards (Di Gennero and Dutton 2007).

People join different types of message board communities for different reasons. Ridings and Gefen (2004) found that information exchange and friendship were important motivators for all of the board types that they studied. However, health or professional related boards are more likely to be joined for social support (Ridings and Gefen 2004). Boards related to hobbies, pets, or recreation were more likely to be joined for entertainment purposes.

Board Characteristics

The asynchronous nature of online message boards allows for fluidity in the community in that all members do not have to be online at the same time. On the other hand, the board must be populated by at least some members (not necessarily the same members) most of the time so that others find communication waiting for them when they log onto the message board. There are four interrelated concepts that help determine the success or failure of message board communities: stability, cohesiveness, sociability, and interactivity. Message board communities with higher perceived sociability and interactivity will have greater stability and cohesiveness. The moderation of message board communities may help communities experience greater stability, cohesiveness, sociability, and interactivity.

Stability

For virtual communities to help people find friends, information, or resources, the community must have some level of stability. The stability of an online community depends on how willing individuals are to stick with the group over time (Arguello et al. 2006). Message board communities must be stable enough for individuals to feel that it is worth seeking out and returning to the community. The specific network relationships may change over time, but the overall network should remain.

Cohesiveness

Cohesion is a multi-construct recursive process based on group members' desire to socialize with other group members and the pervasiveness of shared goals within the group (Casey-Campbell and Martens 2009). The more individuals are attracted and committed to being members of the group the greater the cohesiveness of the group (Festinger 1950, Lott and Lott 1965). The more cohesive the group is the more group members will want to contribute to the communication, goals, and vision of the group. In addition, the more cohesive the group, the more likely current and new group members will be attracted to the community. The more current and incoming message board members see the group as having some shared interest or vision, *no matter how mundane*, the more likely the members are to view the group as cohesive.

Sociability

Message board communities are more likely to be cohesive and stable if that community has a higher level of sociability. Sociability is how members of a community interact with each other (Preece 2001). The tone of communication in sociable communities is generally open and friendly. The sociability of a message board community is likely what leads an online community to persist or wither away (Wise et al 2006). Predictors of sociability in online communities include the number of participants in a community, the frequency of messages and on-topic messages, how satisfied members are with a community, reciprocity between community members, and how much members trust each other (Preece 2001).

Interactivity

Perceived sociability could be driven in part by the level of interactivity on a particular message board (Preece 2001). Increased interactivity may also be related to greater cohesiveness in online groups. On message boards interactivity refers to how much messages relate to each other. Interactivity is sometimes measured as thread depth (Preece 2001). Message board communities that have threads that typically receive multiple responses are seen as more interactive than a community where the average thread receives few responses. This measure of interactivity is likely tapping into the construct of responsiveness. A community is more responsive when community members are more likely to respond to postings. Getting a reply to a post increases the likelihood that a poster will post again (Arguello et al. 2006; Joyce & Kraut 2006). Community responsiveness to messages is an important component of engendering stability and cohesiveness in a message board community (Arguello et al. 2006).

Another aspect of interactivity is the average length of time between posting a message and receiving a response. If there is too much lag between posting a message and getting a response, community members may drift away and/or find other sources of information and communication. On the other hand, when messages come too fast, community participants may feel a need to quickly comment before their thoughts lose relevance and thus might not participate if they think that a particular conversation is over or is moving too quickly (Wise et al. 2007).

Moderation

Quality moderation of message board communication is an important factor in keeping sociability and interactivity high. At first the idea of providing structured rules for interaction and possibly censoring messages that do not meet community rules may seem antithetical to keeping conversation on a message board free and flowing. Indeed, some of Tang's (2010) participants noted that the polite civility of their message board sometimes kept people from disclosing negative or contentious feelings. In turn, they felt this civility kept them from really getting to know other board members. However, other research suggests that moderation is key for maintaining a quality message board environment. Messages correcting members for violations of group norms can be a sizable (McLaughlin et al. 1995) proportion of messages in an online community (McLaughlin et al. 1995). While moderation may create barriers to strong tie relationships by restricting the depth of disclosure, message boards need moderation, or at least strong community appropriateness norms, to provide a space for the large networks of weak ties that they support.

Anonymous flexible network spaces can facilitate negative behavior if individuals feel they are less responsible to a community. The anonymity may allow people to experience toxic disinhibition (Suler 2006). As noted in chapter 2, people may feel safe to be more rude and hateful than they would be offline. This feeling of safety might embolden online communicators to engage in the riling behaviors of a an internet troll or to communicate in a hostile fashion know as flaming (Lea, O'Shea, Fung, and Spears 1992). Unfortunately, flaming and trolls detract from sociability (Preece 2001), making the community a less pleasant place to stay. The presence of moderators has a strong positive impact on online message board communities (Yeow, Johnson, and Faraj 2006). Moderation can help reduce the presence of harmful and repetitive messages. People are more likely to want to participate in communities that are perceived to have some type of moderation, whether that is a professional editor or corps of volunteers (Wise et al. 2007). Moderation can help bring online communication in line with offline politeness norms and counteract the negative effects of anonymity.

Leaders and Lurkers

Leaders

Online communities can be either member driven or organization sponsored (Porter 2004). Who ultimately owns or controls the community can impact both the interaction on and ethics of any particular online community space. Web communities may seem ephemeral but they require server space, software, and people with the expertise to provide the coding necessary for the online community. The owner of the community also can set the tone or moderation rules for the community. For some online communities the ownership seems nearly invisible. For example, the online community, reddit, is owned by Advance Publications, part of media giant CondeNast, but there is little evidence of this in the reddit forum. For other communities the corporate sponsorship is very visible. TheKnot provides a variety of message boards for brides to be and newlyweds, but it is also very clear they intend to advertise and sell wedding-related merchandise. For better or worse, corporate sponsorship of online community turns the community and its communications into a commodity (Rheingold 2001). One alternative is for communities to create and host their own online spaces. However, besides just providing the necessary technical aspects, homegrown or grassroots online communities must also negotiate with each other regarding how to best govern their online spaces (Rheingold 2001). Such negotiations can be tension filled and contentious. For communities that exist simply for casual social connection, the costs of creating such spaces may be more than community members wish to undertake.

Lurkers

Online message boards are important for those who visit these online places to socialize, exchange information, or seek support. However, the majority of people who visit an online community only browse or "lurk" the postings—they do not comment themselves (Donath 1999; Baym 2010; Granitz and Ward 1996; Nonnecke, Preece, and Andrews 2004; Nonnecke and Preece 2000). In some communities, the presence of lurkers is known to other community members. Some message boards give readers counts of both the number of replies to a message as well as the number of views. A large discrepancy between the number of views and posts indicates the presence of lurkers. In communities that do not post page views, the presence of lurkers might go undetected by the average reader.

Lurkers do not necessarily lurk all of the time. Nonnecke and Preece (2001) found that lurkers were more likely to lurk at two times. First, individuals report lurking the most when they first join a community. Newcomers-as-lurkers then sometimes move from the silent lurking role in the community to a more active one—a process called "de-lurking" (Nonnecke and Preece 2001). Lurking as a newcomer may also lead to "satisfied discontinuance." Satisfied discontinuance occurs when a lurker decides that that particular community is not for them and stops browsing in the community without ever having posted (Yeow et al. 2006). Satisfied discontinuance may also occur if a lurker is simply seeking information, finds what they need in the community postings, and then does not return. Second, community members may begin to lurk when they are in the process of leaving a community (Nonnecke and Preece 2001). Individuals may not choose to leave online communities all at once but may de-intensify their relationship with the community by posting less and less until they realize they are simply viewing messages but not contributing their own communications (Nonnecke and Preece 2003).

Lurking involves two communication choices. First, lurkers choose to visit a particular online community and receive messages. Second, lurkers choose not to send messages. There are multiple reasons an individual might make either of these choices (Nonnecke and Preece 2001). Lurkers stated that they chose not to send messages because they wanted to preserve their own privacy or safety or were shy about public postings. Other lurkers did not post because they thought that they would receive poor quality responses or that they would end up with either too many messages or too few messages to deal with. Finally, some lurkers said they did not contribute because they had limited time to create postings for a group.

Lurkers chose to follow online communities for a variety of reasons. Lurkers might attend to the online community for entertainment purposes, to gather information, to access others' expertise or experience, to feel a sense of community, and to connect with other individuals (Nonnecke and Preece 2001; Yeow et al. 2006). The last two reasons may seem counterintuitive as lurkers are not directly helping to build the community or reach out to individuals. Nonetheless, lurkers did feel that they developed a sense of community and knowing others in the community through lurking, although their sense of belongingness was lower than non-lurkers (Nonnecke, Preece, and Andrews 2004). New group members may lurk in order to learn community norms to prepare for when they de-lurk (Yeow et al. 2006). Through viewing others messages and learning community norms they may come to feel more integrated in the community even though they have not yet posted to the group (Nonnecke and Preece 2003).

Since lurkers are silent, it may appear that their presence in an online community is ineffectual. However, lurkers may have both positive and negative effects for online communities. Lurkers can create a much larger audience for posts than the membership that is salient to posters. This can be damaging to communities who are concerned about control regarding their messages (Donath 1999). The motivations of lurkers may not be amenable to the posters. Lurkers might be reading for sensationalism, they may be using the posters feelings as entertainment or they may simply be tourists of sensitive subjects. Yeow et al. (2006) found that high amounts of lurking contributed to decreases in the number of total community members and postings. On the other hand, for groups trying to disseminate a message to a wider audience lurkers can help extend the reach of the group. For example, some lurkers may lurk in some communities but be active in others. These lurkers may carry topics of discussion in a lurked group to other online and offline conversations (Nonnecke and Preece 2003).

VIDEO GAMES

Another online location where individuals might make online friends is various versions of online gaming. Games can also serve as virtual third places (Steinkuehler and Williams 2006). Online games that lend themselves to community formation are typically massive multiplayer online games (MMOs or MMOGs). A sub-type of MMOs includes massive multiplayer online role-playing games (MMORPGs). The demographic makeup skews heavily male, but not entirely so (studies have reported demographics between 80% and 85% males) and young, but not overly adolescent. (Griffiths, Davies, and Chappel 2003, 2004; Kolo & Buer 2004; Yee 2006b, Williams, Yee, and Caplan 2008). Although many gamers are in their late 20s and early 30s, Williams et al. (2008) found that the amount of hours logged per week by a gamer increases steadily with age such that gamers under 18 logged just over 22 hours/week and gamers in their 50s played just over 30 hours/week.

MMOs and MMRPGs are set in online worlds where players log in to the game and interact both with non-player characters (NPCs) as well as other individuals who are playing the game. Many MMOs or MMRPGs encourage or require gamer interdependence (Teng, Chen, Chen, and Li 2012). Success or failure in the game is dependent upon interacting with other members of the online game community. Thus, the creation and maintenance of social ties is not just an added bonus of playing MMOs, social communication is a fundamental component of the game play (Ekland and Ask 2013). These games range in the number and type of cues presented. A text-based game might provide only linguistic and paralinguistic cues. Other online games might provide individuals with choices (albeit typically limited) regarding gender, species, and appearance. Regardless, fewer cues are available in game worlds than in face-to-face.

A cues-filtered-out approach would suggest that online video game players would focus on the game and tasks related to the game and thus engage in very little socio-emotional communication. However, research has suggested that communication in online games is rife with socio-emotional messages (Pena and Hancock 1996). Players do communicate social information and report enjoying social aspects of the game. Early online games, such as the primarily text-based *Bolo,* became spaces for the development of social communities formed through informal conversation before and after the game sessions (Moore, Mazvancheryl, and Rego 1996). Today's MMOs and MMORPGs include text-based interaction between players as well as visual information provided by choices made regarding one's avatar and dress and various nonverbal behaviors that the avatar can engage in (such as hugging or dancing). Within these immersive MMORPGs, the majority of messages include socio-emotional content (Pena and Hancock 2006).

Many MMORPG players report choosing to play a MMORPG *because* of the social nature of the game (Griffiths et al., 2004; Williams, 2006a). People report wanting to play games for a variety of communal reasons including to socialize by engaging in conversation and making friends, build relationships through self-disclosure and support, and contribute to teamwork through collaboration and contributing to group achievements (Yee, 2006a). Game players may meet individuals on their own through the chat function that is included with most MMORPGs or they might join a guild or clan within the game. Most MMORPGs contain some type of formal group structure (often called a guild or clan) where individuals can socialize, organize team game play, and share items. These groups often have a more formal social hierarchy with a specified leader and then sub-leadership roles. Status within the guild might also be denoted through providing labels or titles for certain players. The more social online gaming an individual engages in, the more likely they are to meet exclusively online friends (Domahidi, Festl, and Quandt 2014). Social gamers use games to maintain relationships with old friends and create new online connections (Domahidi et al. 2014; Ledbetter & Kuznekoff 2012).

The immersive nature of MMOs and MMORPGs helps facilitate the formation of new social network ties. Individuals playing MMORPGs were more likely to acquire new friends than individuals playing arcade, console, or solo computer games (Smyth 2005). People experience differing levels of social cohesion in online games. Game environments that provided greater social cohesion were more likely to induce players to stick with both the game and the social groups that they formed (Pahnila and Warsta 2012). Both individual players and game context can influence the cohesiveness of any particular online game. Games that necessitate greater gamer interdependence facilitate greater gamer loyalty (Teng et al. 2012). This increase in loyalty likely occurs because individuals feel a greater sense of responsibility and positive affect to the community with a particular game. The more loyal to a game an individual player is, the more likely it may be that they will take on the communicative work needed to form and maintain both dyadic and network connections within the online game world. Players with more experience, who are typically higher status players within the guild or clan structure of a particular game, may be more embedded within the game community and have a larger vested interest in taking on the communication work necessary to maintain group cohesion and satisfaction (Pena and Hancock 2002).

MMORPGs may provide an online venue where individuals are able to circumvent gating characteristics (Cole and Griffiths 2007). A third of gamers in Cole and Griffiths (2007) study reported they felt they could "be more themselves" in the game than real life and some reported being able to discuss issues that they felt were too sensitive to share with offline friends. Players in online games make multiple friends and some report that online games have helped them become more sociable (Cole and Griffiths 2007; Domahidi et al. 2014; Kolo and Bauer 2004). Social game players report lessened feelings of loneliness over time and an increase in feeling that everyone is connected (Williams 2006). Interestingly, women, although they make up a smaller proportion of gamers, may be more likely to utilize the social features of games. Both men and women express interest in socializing during game play but women may be more likely to try and form relationships with fellow players (Yee 2006b) and arrange to meet their online game friends offline (Cole and Griffiths 2007).

Disadvantages of Online Games

Although games can allow players to reach new network connections, these connections may come at the cost of spending less time with offline social network connections. Lo, Wang, and Fang (2005) found that the quality of offline relationships decreased as the time playing online games increased. Communication with offline network connections may become more sporadic as time spent in-game increases (Kolo and Bauer 2004). Williams (2006a) called this phenomenon cocooning. Cocooning occurs when playing an immersive online video game leads to lower levels of face-to-face interaction. Multiple studies have found that online video gaming can be associated with lower quality offline relationships. Heavy players may feel that their online relationships are more important than offline relationships (Kolo and Bauer 2004). In other cases, the online socialization in the video game may be compensating for poor offline relationships. People with lower quality networks might choose to play immersive games for the social life that such games offer. However, experimental and longitudinal studies suggest that immersive online games may directly contribute to lower quality offline networks. One-fifth of gamers in Cole and Griffiths's (2007) study thought playing a MMORPG had a negative effect on their relationships outside of the game. In an experiment, Smyth (2007) found that individuals who were assigned to play a MMOPRG (as opposed to other types of video games such as an arcade game or stand-alone console title) were more likely to report that the game interfered with their offline social life. Williams (2006a) found over time people who were social online experienced drops in their perception of having offline individuals that they could turn to for advice and help with personal problems. They had friends over less and visited relatives less.

Of course, gamers may simply value online connections more than their offline connections. Like other networked individuals, gamers make choices both on- and off-line regarding which network connections they spend time with and which relationships they choose to maintain. However, the more hours an individual spent in a game the less overall diversity they had in their friendship network. The reduced diversity is not entirely unsurprising given that online video game players tend to be more white, more educated, and more wealthy than the US average. Thus, playing online games may provide a social outlet but these online worlds might actually be less diverse than players would encounter offline (Williams et al. 2008).

Networks composed of online game friends may also be more fragile than offline networks as well. Creation of bonding social capital in MMOs is rare (although not non-existent) (Steinkuehler and Williams 2006). When gamers choose to leave a particular game setting, they often find that quitting the game means quitting the friendships (Eklund and Ask 2013). People find it difficult to carry friendships with them outside of the game environment unless another foci can be found to help carry on the relationship (Eklund and Ask 2013).

Moving Online Connections to Offline Spaces

Individuals who meet in online communities sometimes choose to meet their online friends in offline spaces (Rheingold 2001). Parks and colleagues (Parks and Floyd 1996; Parks and Roberts 1998) found that people used a variety of channels including the phone, letters, and face-to-face communication to stay in touch with online friends. Other research has found that individuals who meet on message boards may occasionally try to meet up in offline settings (McEwan and Zanolla 2013). Shifting interaction from one type of communication channel to another is called "modality switching" (Ramirez and Zhang 2008). Women may be less likely than men to meet online friends offline, but in general the longer people use the internet the more likely they are to have met a friend they first met online, offline (Di Gennero and Dutton 2007).

There can be benefits to switching modalities with online friends: for example Tang (2010) found that the more communicative spaces a friendship expanded into, the closer and more intimate the friendship was. McEwan and Zanolla (2013) also found that in general moving an online friendship into an offline space leads to greater relational satisfaction and closeness. However, there are some caveats. Individuals who form hyperpersonal or overly close relationships online may be disappointed when they meet with their friend offline (McEwan and Zanolla 2013). The hyperpersonal effects enabled by CMC may be detrimental for relationships if individuals decide to take their online relationship offline (Ramirez and Wang 2008, Ramirez and Zang

2007). When people build up over-idealized expectations of their online friend, the physical interaction with the friends can fall short of the idealized friend. When expectancies are negatively violated in this fashion, an offline meet-up with an online friend can be detrimental to an individual's perceptions of closeness and satisfaction in the friendship (McEwan and Zanolla 2013). Ramirez and colleagues found that switching from CMC to face-to-face conditions after six weeks of interaction led to reductions in social attraction, predicted outcome value, intimacy, and social orientation (Ramirez and Wang 2008; Ramirez and Zhang 2007).

CONCLUSION

Rheingold (2001) posed the question, "How many people flee the idylls of small towns because they look or think or act differently than the local norms?" (361). Online communities allow individuals the freedom to escape geographically linked networks and form relationships with others who might understand them better. This phenomenon can be problematic if individuals seek out only homophilous or similar others, but it can also provide support, encouragement, and companionship to individuals who find some lack in their offline communities. However, a question for future research is how close and how stable are these connections. Individuals can slip in and out of online communities easily. One of the benefits of these spaces is that anyone with access can join. On the other hand, individual members can drop out of communities as easily as they joined. Some individuals, the lurkers, may never even contribute to a community. Others may form hyperpersonal relationships which can disintegrate when individuals meet up offline. Despite these concerns, the internet can provide spaces for persistent networks and communities that are stronger than any particular dyad or small group relationship that is part of that network (Castells 2001). These persistent spaces may provide touchstones for individuals seeking information, resources, or social support. Although in networked individualism it is incumbent upon the individual to develop relationships, online communities, much like offline third places, present a starting point for people to form and build new network connections.

Chapter Seven

Maintaining Network Connections

Not only do internet-based technologies help networked individuals find new network connections, these technologies can also help maintain existing connections. Technology can help relationships continue despite barriers of space and time. Communicative tasks for maintaining relationships are important for both weak and strong tie relationships. Communication technologies, particularly SNS, are well-suited to assisting people maintain their relationships (Walther and Ramirez 2003). Advances in communication technologies have allowed people to maintain larger numbers of network ties and quickly send relational maintenance messages at almost any time of day or night.

RELATIONAL MAINTENANCE

Relational maintenance is the strategic and routine behaviors that individuals engage in to maintain their relationships (Canary and Stafford 1994). There are four main definitions of relational maintenance (Dindia and Canary 1993). The first is to simply keep a relationship in existence. The second definition goes further than that and examines maintenance as a way to keep a relationship in a "specified state or condition" (p. 163). The third definition considers that relational partners might want that specified state or condition to be a satisfactory one and the fourth definition considers keeping a relationship in repair. Much of the relational maintenance research examines maintenance as a way to keep a relationship satisfactory or in a high-quality condition (Oglosky and Bowers 2013). However, a few studies have also examined ways that individuals might keep platonic or romantic partners at a preferred distance (Goodboy and Myers 2010; Hess 2000).

All relationships require some level of maintenance or else they will deteriorate (Canary and Stafford 1994; Stafford and Canary 1991). Thus, relational maintenance scholars have explored relational maintenance in a wide variety of relationships including married relationships (Canary and Stafford 1993; Canary, Stafford, and Semic 2002; Stafford and Canary 1991), dating relationships (Dailey, Hampel, and Roberts 2010; Dainton 2000, 2013; Maguire and Kinney 2010), and friendships (Canary, Stafford, Hause, and Wallace 1993; McEwan and Guerrero 2012; Messman, Canary, and Hause 2000; Oswald and Clark 2006, Oswald, Clark, and Kelley 2004).

CMC AND RELATIONAL MAINTENANCE

When work on relational maintenance strategies began CMC scholars were just starting to recognize the importance of CMC for interpersonal and relational communication (Stafford and Canary 1991; Walther 1992). Thus, it is unsurprising that early relational maintenance measures privileged face-to-face communication. In 1993, Canary, Stafford, Hause, and Wallace culled a variety of communication messages that might be useful for maintaining a variety of relational types (friends, family, romantic partners) from an undergraduate essay assignment. These strategies primarily included specific message types (Openness, Positivity, Assurances, Humor, Avoidance, Antisocial) or activities one might share with a relational partner (Task Sharing, Joint Activities, Social Networks) for the purpose of maintaining that relationship. The message types included openness (direct conversation with the other person), positivity (attempts to be cheerful or upbeat), assurances (affirming the importance of the relationship), humor (jokes and attempts to be funny), avoidance (staying away from certain topics), and antisocial (behaviors that seem unfriendly or coercive). The activities included task sharing (sharing routine tasks and chores), joint activities (sharing fun or enjoyable activities), and networks (spending time and communicating with other members of one's shared network). In addition to these messages and activities, Canary et al. also included one strategy that is reflective of specific channels more than specific types of messages or activities. This strategy, labeled *Cards, Letters, Calls,* indicated that mediated communication could also be useful for maintaining relationships.

As CMC usage becomes a part of daily life, scholars are increasingly interested in how people might utilize mediated channels for the purpose of relational communication (McEwan 2013b; McEwan, Fletcher, Eden, and Sumner 2014; Ramirez and Broneck 2009; Spitzberg 2006; Stafford et al. 1998; Rabby and Walther 2002). CMC may represent a practical choice for relational maintenance (Rabby and Walther 2002). Communication technologies may be easily accessible to the message sender and do not require the receiver to be simultaneously available (Rabby and Walther 2002; Walther and Ramirez 2010). As communication technologies allow people to easily send maintenance messages throughout their day as well as keep track of contact information of a large quantity of network members, CMC, particularly social network sites, can allow people to maintain larger social networks.

Concern has been expressed that CMC might be too impoverished a medium for the purposes of interpersonal communication (Daft and Lengel 1987). Yet, people often communicate with friends and family via electronic means. Rabby and Walther (2002) argued that while people might indicate that they prefer rich media for interpersonal goals, they actually are fairly opportunistic in their media choices. Sending a message through SNS or text can be a quick and easy way to send relational maintenance messages. Using Internet-based communication channels to send relational messages is even easier as people already spend a considerable amount of time using computers for a variety of relational, task-based, or entertainment purposes (Tong and Walther 2011). When we are already at the computer, we may be able to fluidly move from working on a project to sending a friend a quick note. Tong and Walther (2011) argued that CMC represents what they call a "lightweight" method for people to maintain their relationships. CMC is "lightweight" because we are often already at the computer, on our smartphones, and using the internet. Thus, it takes a low amount of effort to "look up, initiate a connection to, and create messages for, another person" (p. 110). So, while people might say they would prefer to have face-to-face interactions with friends, they often actually choose to send a quick Facebook message or text since those choices are more readily available than arranging a face-to-face meeting.

Different types of relationships may be maintained through different CMC choices. Close or strong ties are typically sustained through communication via lots of different channels, a portion of which might be CMC channels (Baym, Zhang, Kunkel, Ledbetter, and Lin 2007; Miczo et al. 2011). One-to-one CMC channels that require direct contact information (such as a phone number or email address) are more likely to be used for closer connections. Communication technologies that allow for one-to-many communication and allow individuals to amass contacts within the application may be used for both strong ties and weak ties. SNS in particular may be well-suited for this as the number of weak ties that can be maintained through SNS versus traditional means is greatly increased (Donath and boyd 2004). Individuals might use Facebook for maintaining relationships with distant contacts (Joinson 2008) or to solidify relationships with others they have recently met offline (Ellison et al., 2007).

At minimum, CMC allows network connections to stay in touch with each other (Rabby and Walther 2002) and be reminded of others' existence or presence in the social network (Tong and Walther 2011). The ability to stay in touch and remind others of one's existence is an important building block for relational development (Radovanovic and Regnedda 2012). However, it is also important to note that many relationships may stay just at this level of being aware of the other's presence. Remember, one of the definitions of relational maintenance is keeping the relationship at a desired state (Dindia and Canary 1993). Individuals might have various reasons for wanting to keep a presence within the social network of others but not want to engage in a more involved relationship. Rawlins (1994) argued that over the lifespan some friends become dormant. Dormant friends do not maintain regular contact but there is an expectation that the friend could be called upon if needed. Such "just present" network members might be ones that you consider useful for providing future resources or for sending information your way. They might also be individuals that you stay connected to because other network members are more closely connected to them and to become unconnected would be disruptive to the greater network (Hess 2000). CMC, particularly SNS, provides a lightweight way to maintain relationships one does not wish to deepen or intensify and keep track of dormant friendships.

In keeping with this line of thought—that CMC can be used to keep relationships in a specified, but not close state—CMC could also be used to regulate the amount of interpersonal distance between friends. Using CMC may allow you to maintain a basic connection, perhaps with an acquaintance or a closer friend that has grown more distant, while avoiding more involved friendship activities (Miczo et al. 2011). Johnson and colleagues (Johnson and Becker 2011; Johnson, Haigh, Becker, Craig, and Wigley 2008; Johnson, Haigh, Craig, and Becker 2009) have argued that friendships are flexible relationships in that friend dyads move through phases of closeness and distance in a nonlinear fashion. Thus, at times friends may be interested in communication strategies that maintain the tie but minimize the current level of investment.

Individuals might also use CMC to maintain relationships with those who have become geographically distant (Adams 1998; Johnson et al. 2008). In these cases, maintaining relationships through face-to-face communication may have become overly difficult. For example, for high school friends transitioning to college, while all types of communication dropped, face-to-face communication dropped the most (Dainton 2013). Due to their tenuous and voluntary nature (Bliezner and Adams 1992), friendships may be particularly sensitive to decreases in contact frequency (Roberts and Dunbar, 2011). Increasing time since last contact decreases the emotional intensity of a friendship in a way that does not happen in family relationships (Roberts and Dunbar 2011). Long-distance family relationships are held together through the communication work by the family network in a way that is less likely for friendships. However, various types of CMC have introduced a method for people to at least maintain an awareness of the presence of their long-distance friends.

Email

Although early uses of electronic mail or e-mail were work- or task-related (Markus 1994), in the early 2000's, Bargh and McKenna professed the main reason people used email was to maintain interpersonal relationships. Indeed, one of the earliest studies on using CMC for relational maintenance found that people used their home email to keep in touch with friends and family (Stafford et al. 1999). Email helps relational maintenance strategies overcome both distance and time, allowing people to share daily interactions and receive support (Johnson et al. 2008; Stafford et al. 1999).

Although, some researchers have investigated friendship strategies via email (Johnson et al. 2008), email appears to now be the mainstay of long-standing, close relationships such as family. Relatives communicate via email more than friends do (Houser, Fleuriet, and Estrada 2012). This finding may be because family relationships often involve inter-generational contact. Older adults might be more likely to use email for social purposes than younger adults, thus both older and younger family members may choose email to communicate with each other. Houser et al. (2012) found that using email was significantly related to using positivity in a relationship, suggesting that individuals who are interested in being pleasant and friendly in a relationship are also likely to choose email to communicate.

Instant Messaging and Texting

A few studies have investigated the use of instant messaging and texting as a relational maintenance activity. The one-to-one nature of instant messaging and texting may lead people to use these channels to maintain close relationships such as romantic partners and close friends (Ishii 2006; Ramirez and Broneck 2009). Instant messaging has been shown to be used primarily to engage in the maintenance strategy of positivity (Ramirez and Broneck 2009). Texting has been found to be used to make plans, send assurances, and engage in social network maintenance strategies (Brody, Mooney, Westerman, and McDonald 2009). In addition, the more a person feels that text messaging is intended to be a synchronous medium, the more likely that person is to use text messaging to maintain friendships and romantic relationships (Brody et al. 2009).

Text messaging may have different relational outcomes in friendships and romantic relationships. Brody and Pena (2015) found that only texting positivity and social network strategies to friends was significantly related to relational satisfaction, whereas for romantic partners, both Brody and Pena

(2015) and McEwan and Horn (2015) have found similar findings for positivity, but also that texting assurances and task management were the drivers
of relational satisfaction rather than social network strategies. It may be that
friendships are influenced more strongly by belonging to the same social
network than romantic partners. Romantic partners, on the other hand, may
be more likely to share tasks and engage in communication that assures each
other about their feelings for the relationship.

   Houser et al. (2012) found that both texting and the use of instant messaging were related to the maintenance strategy of openness. Both of these
channels may facilitate discussion and disclosure. However, openness may
not always have positive effects on relationships. Brody and Pena (2015)
found that communicating openness through texting had a negative effect on
relational satisfaction for romantic partners. This finding is in line with work
on face-to-face maintenance strategies which has also found that once positivity and assurances are controlled for, increased openness in a relationship
may be tied to lower relational quality (Ramirez 2008).

Social Network Sites

The majority of research conducted on using CMC for relational maintenance focuses on social network sites. SNS makes it easy to maintain a large
number of diverse network ties (Bryant and Marmo 2012, Ellison et al. 2007;
Walther and Ramirez 2009) Although early online communication channels
were often used to communicate with previously unknown communication
partners, the most popular of these, Facebook (Hampton, Goulet, Rainie, and
Purcell 2011), is primarily used to maintain relationships with people whom
one has previously met offline (Cowden 2012; Ellison et al. 2007). The most
commonly reported motivation for using Facebook is a desire to keep in
touch with friends (Wilson, Gosling, and Graham 2012). Indeed, friends
communicate via SNS more than family or romantic partners (Houser et al.
2012), although Dainton (2013) did find that positivity communicated via
SNS can help maintain romantic relationships. SNS can be particularly helpful for maintaining connections that were once proximally close, but are now
more geographically distant (Bryant and Marmo 2012).

   To return to Tong and Walther's (2011) terminology, social network sites
are likely a very lightweight way to engage in relational maintenance. SNS
reduce the various costs of maintaining relationships by allowing users to
essentially keep an online rolodex close at hand (Bryant, Marmo, and Ramirez 2010; Ellison et al., 2007). Features such as Facebook's NewsFeed allow
users to stay up to date with a variety of people throughout the day. Users can
quickly like posts or comment on statuses in order to connect with far-flung
network connections. In addition, one can update large portions of one's
network in regard to major events such as an engagement, prosaic moments

such as your lunch, or whatever whimsy might be floating through your head. These updates go rapidly out to your network whereas without the SNS you might have to call friends and relatives one by one to announce your engagement and for better or worse your lunch and whimsy might simply go uncommunicated.

Another way we might maintain network connections is by engaging in surveillance through social network sites (Joinson 2008; Bryant and Marmo 2010). Surveillance allows us to keep in touch at the most minimal level. Through surveillance we can stay abreast of the big life events of people that we might otherwise have very little contact with. Monitoring friends through SNS may be related to greater relational satisfaction, liking, and closeness (McEwan 2013b).

Of course, people post updates for our surveillance in hopes that others will respond (Cowden 2012). Posting updates for the purposes of seeking responses is one way that people attempt to maintain relationships via SNS (McEwan 2013b; McEwan et al. 2014). Sometimes these types of updates take on the role of broadcast small talk or *phatic* communication (Radova-novic and Regnedda, 2012). Phatic communication is communication simply for the purpose of social upkeep (Malinowski 1923). These small-stakes posts may help users maintain relationships by maintaining presence in others' SNS and show a desire to connect with others (Cowden, 2012; Radova-novic and Regnedda, 2012). Other times these posts will announce big life events such as engagements, new jobs, pregnancies, and births. Big events are more likely to get big responses from one's Facebook network (Cowden, 2012).

In addition to response-seeking strategies and surveillance, McEwan and colleagues (McEwan 2013; McEwan et al. 2014) identified a strategy called social contact. This maintenance strategy involved people using Facebook to send specific and tailored messages to their friends. The social contact main-tenance strategy included behaviors such as offering congratulations and support, wishing a friend happy birthday, sending cheerful messages, and tagging network ties in Facebook statuses. Social contact maintenance be-haviors correlate with higher friendship quality (McEwan 2013, McEwan et al. 2014).

SNS users might also maintain their relationships through participating in social network games (Wohn, Lampe, Wash, Ellison, and Vitak 2011). Al-though online games exist in many formats, social network games are unique in that individuals must have an established connection within the SNS be-fore they can play games with them. However, players for any given game might cut across wide swaths of one's social network. Wohn et al. (2011) found that social network game players were very diverse and included close and casual friends and family members. Games can serve as way to keep these diverse network connections salient and help geographically distant friends and family members maintain their relationships.

Romantic relational partners might also use Facebook to engage in *tie-signs* (Walther and Tong, 2011). The definition of *tie-signs* comes out of nonverbal research. *Tie-signs* are nonverbal signals such as holding hands that allowed others to perceive those engaging in tie-signs were part of a relationship (Guerrero and Anderson, 1991). On an SNS when we comment on or like others' status updates or tag them in a post or photo, part of the message we are sending is that we have a relationship with this individual. Thus, these behaviors serve as digital tie-signs reinforcing the relationship between network members.

Tie-signs through SNS may work to help maintain romantic relationships. For example, Facebook has a mechanism that allows members to state if they are dating, engaged, or married to another Facebook member. Today's colloquialism refers to this public statement of a romantic relationship as going "Facebook Official." Going Facebook Official serves as a substantial tie-sign by making the relationship salient to the network. Going Facebook Official carries important maintenance information directly to the members of the couple as it communicates assurances to the commitment to the relationship (Fox and Warber 2013). Having network support for the relationship may help reinforce the importance of the relationship to the relational partners and also introduce an additional barrier to exiting that relationships as changing the Facebook Official status will require explanations to the larger group.

Finally, simply being part of the social network may help us to maintain additional weak and latent ties. Communicating maintenance strategies to one friend may help maintain larger groups of friendships, as friends of friends can see various comments and postings that we have made with others (Ellison, Vitak, Gray, and Lampe 2014). Postings to and from others may highlight relationships that are collegial but based more in network structure than actual feelings. People may maintain connections to others they are not particularly invested in having a relationship with simply because that other is part of their other network members' network.

These types of relationships are structural friends. Structural friendships are friendships where the relationship is maintained through mutual connections to others rather than any strong friendly feelings toward the other. Structural friends might come about when there is a network member who is not as well-known other members of the network. In other cases, active dislike for a structural friend might exist but the connections maintain a level of *stasis* in the relationship so as not to upset the friendship network. Such individuals might stay connected on Facebook due to the potential negative effects of de-friending a current Facebook connection (Bevan, Ang, and Fearns 2014).

Gender Differences

A few studies have suggested that women may be more likely to use CMC for relational maintenance. Houser et al. (2012) found that women use CMC in general for relational maintenance more than men. Ramirez and Broneck found that women reported using instant messaging for relational maintenance slightly more than men. Boneva and Kraut (2002) found that relational maintenance via email was more likely to be conducted by women than men. When it comes to technology use, men are traditionally thought of as being the more stereotypical user (Bimber 2000), however it appears when those technologies are used for the purpose of relational communication women are the more likely users.

Does Mediated Maintenance Work?

Scholars have argued that CMC may be an important channel for relational maintenance and that relational maintenance may be the "greatest utility" for social networking sites (Walther & Ramirez 2010). Yet, there is still the question of if and how CMC helps maintain relationships. As noted earlier in the chapter, SNS might be useful for simply maintaining a long list of network connections that are inactive or latent relationships. This strategy is in keeping with at least one definition of relational maintenance—that maintenance is simply to keep the relationship in existence. However, there are also some assumptions in the relational maintenance literature that maintenance behaviors should be associated with some level of friendship quality (McEwan 2013b; McEwan & Guerrero 2012; Oswald et al. 2002). There are still important research questions regarding the effect CMC relational maintenance may have on relationships.

Research on CMC use for relational maintenance has produced mixed results. Baym et al. (2007) found that CMC neither improved nor impoverished relational satisfaction and closeness. However, Ledbetter, Mazer, De-Groot, Mayer, Mao, and Swafford (2011) found that Facebook communication did predict relational closeness. Ledbetter (2010a) found that while face-to-face maintenance strategies were related to both interdependence (feeling connected and reliant on the other person) and control mutuality (feeling that both you and your friend have some say in the direction and quality of the relationship as well as the right to influence each other (Canary and Stafford, 1994)), online maintenance strategies were only related to interdependence and did not predict control mutuality. Later work by Ledbetter and Mazer (2014) continued to find that Facebook communication was associated with greater relational interdependence in friends. However, they also found that if a communicator holds a positive attitude regarding online communication in general, then Facebook communication will lead to even greater interdependence between friends. Ledbetter and Mazer's (2014) work suggests that how an individual approaches a particular channel may have implications for the effects of relational maintenance strategies performed through that channel. If someone attempts to maintain their friendship through Facebook, but their friend does not enjoy communicating through Facebook or dislikes online communication for social purposes, then the effects of the maintenance strategy on the relationship will be diluted.

Similar to Ledbetter and Mazer, Craig and Wright (2012) found that the more people self-disclosed on Facebook the more interdependent they were with their Facebook friend and the less uncertain they felt about their Facebook friend. However, disclosure on Facebook may have its limit. Too many status updates and too much self-disclosure are viewed negatively by Facebook friends (Cowden 2012). Posting information regarding Facebook games risks annoying those who do not play (Wohn et al. 2011). Broadcast-style Facebook messages may lead to lower relational quality in friends (McEwan 2013b). Unfortunately, it is difficult to estimate what counts as "too much." Indeed, different people likely have different thresholds for how much information they are interested in seeing. McEwan (2013b) found that posting a lot of information on Facebook can lead to negative relational outcomes for friendship dyads unless both friends are the type of people who like to post a lot of information on Facebook. Furthermore, this threshold probably varies not only by person but also by each relationship that person is considering. An individual may be thrilled to see a bevy of baby pictures from a long-distance close friend, but be less enamored with repeated viewings of the mug of a former high school acquaintance.

Another issue is that some behaviors might be perceived as maintenance behaviors but may not actually do the work of "sustaining desired relational characteristics" (Dainton 2013). People appear to appreciate the SNS role in keeping relationships that would otherwise just not exist. As one of Bryant and Marmo's participants stated, very weak ties don't really interact on Facebook but remain connected because, "It's kind of nice because you know that if you ever wanted to talk to them you could." The weak tie is kept in a sort of relational limbo just in case you ever did want them or need them for some purpose. The relationship is maintained but only at a very superficial level. For relationships where people desire higher quality interactions, Facebook is considered only supplemental; close relationships rely on a variety of channels for relational communication (Ledbetter and Mazer 2014).

In terms of romantic relationships, use of the internet to help maintain a long-distance relationship was associated with both the use of positivity and social network strategies (Dainton and Aylor 2002). These results indicate that individuals who attempted to keep things pleasant and upbeat and also make plans and communicate with the couple's shared social network were also likely to report using CMC to help maintain the relationship. Dainton and Aylor (2002) also found that communicating via the internet led to greater trust in these romantic relationships, perhaps because the more frequent contact reminded relational partners that they were thinking of each other even when they could not be physically co-present. In any romantic relationship (long-distance or otherwise), tagging each other in photos, status, and notes appears to be associated with greater relational closeness (Carpenter and Spottswood 2013).

CONCLUSION

Communication technologies provide convenient and *lightweight* ways for people to keep in touch and maintain relationships with a wide variety of network ties. Email, instant messaging, and texting all provide ways for people to reach out to each other and communicate maintenance strategies. SNS allow for various maintenance strategies to be directly communicated to network ties as well as allow individuals to more passively maintain relationships by simply using the SNS to keep a record of their network relationships. As the shift to networked individualism puts greater pressure on the individual to maintain network connections, communication technologies can help relieve this pressure by providing simple ways to reach out and tools to help keep more distal ties salient. However, although SNS certainly allows users to maintain a greater number of network members, the effect of maintenance via an SNS on relational quality may be limited. For close relationships, SNS and other communication technologies may represent just one component of an overall approach to relational maintenance that involves multiple channels.

Chapter Eight

Reaching Support through Fixed and Flexible Networks

One of the great advantages of building increased and varied network connections is the ability to access and acquire greater amounts of social resources. An important social resource is social support. Computer-mediated communication can also be a way that individuals can access greater social support. Increased access to social support is a popular reason for joining online communities, particularly communities focused on health and wellness or professional and occupational topics (Ridings and Gefen 2004). National surveys conducted by the Pew Internet and American Life Project have found that 16% of American internet users say they have gone online to seek out others with similar health problems (Fox and Duggan 2013). Forty percent of people have posted some comment or story about their personal health experiences online (Fox and Duggan 2013). While joining online support groups is an obvious source of social support, Shaw and Gant (2002) found that even just chatting anonymously online without joining a particular group leads to increases in perceived social support. The perception of increased network support may be due to increased abilities to communicate easily with larger weak tie networks.

SOCIAL SUPPORT

Social support is "perceived or actual instrumental and/or expressive provisions supplied by the community, social networks, and confiding partners" (Lin 1986, 18). Social support can be needed for a wide variety of stressors such as transitioning from one location and/or life phase to another (Mikal, Rice, Abeyta, and DeVilbiss 2013), the break-up of romantic relationships

(High, Oeldorf-Hirsch, and Bellur 2014), illness (Davison, Pennebaker, and Dickerson 2000; Wright 2002), aging (Wright 2000a), parenting (Drentea and Moran-Cross 2005), disability (Cummings, Sproull, and Kiesler 2000), addiction recovery (Wright 2002) and more. Benefits from social support include increased mental health, self-esteem, feeling a sense of belonging, a greater ability to cope with stressful situations, and improved psychological well-being (Antonucci 1990; Schiffrin, Edelman, Flakenstern, and Stewart 2010). Social support may also provide a buffer from the negative effects of stress (Cohen 1988; Dean and Lin 1977; La Rocca, House, and French 1980).

Types of Support

While there are many typologies of social support available, one of the most commonly used comes from work by Cutrona and Suhr (Cutrona and Suhr 1992, 1994). These support types include emotional support (sometimes called socio-emotional support), esteem (which has also been called validation support (see Mikal et al. 2013)), network support (sometimes called embedded support, see Mikal et al. 2013), informational support, and instrumental support (sometimes referred to as tangible support).

Emotional support is defined by Burleson (2003) as "specific lines of communicative behavior enacted by one party with the intent of helping another cope effectively with emotional distress" (552). Emotional support takes many forms including reminding the participant of the love and care the supporter has for them, providing physical affection and encouragement, promising confidentiality, expressing sympathy, listening and empathizing (Cutrona and Suhr 1992). Emotional support is the most common and effective type of support (Braithwaite, Waldron, and Finn 1999; Burleson 2003).

Esteem support can "enhance how others feel about themselves and their attributes, abilities, and accomplishments" (Holmstrom 2012, 78). Esteem support includes compliments, validation (agreeing with the recipient's perspective), or trying to relieve feelings of guilt (Cutrona and Suhr 1994). Esteem support can validate a person's worth, make the receiver feel better about him/herself, increase self-efficacy and reduce stress (Mikal et al. 2013).

Network support refers to reassurances of connections to the greater network (Cutrona and Suhr 1994). This type of support includes connecting the recipient with new connections, spending time with the recipient, and reminding the recipient about others in the shared social network that may have similar experiences (Cutrona and Suhr 1992). Increased amounts of online network support, also called embedded support, can increase one's network and perceptions of community with others who are experiencing similar stressors (Mikal et al. 2013).

Informational support is about providing information that is relevant for coping with the stressor (Cohen 2004). Informational support includes giving suggestions and advice, providing referrals to other sources of help, providing information that helps redefine the situation or explains skills needed to deal with the situation (Cutrona and Suhr 1992). Informational support could be advice, facts, or feedback (Walther and Boyd 2002).

Instrumental support refers to providing tangible assistance. Instrumental support is the "provision of material aid" (Cohen 2004, 676). This type of support includes providing loans or offers to help, offering to perform tasks directly related to the stressor or taking over some of the recipient's other responsibilities to alleviate some of the stress (Cutrona and Suhr 1992).

These types of support can occur through both offline and online network connections and communication. Internet use may be correlated with greater perceptions of informational and emotional social support (Leung and Lee 2005). However, many types of support including embedded support, informational and socio-emotional support, instrumental support, and validation/esteem support are available through online groups. (Mikal et al. 2013). Informational and emotional support may be the most common types of online social support while instrumental support is the least common type of support provided by online groups (Leung and Lee, 2005; Mikal et al. 2013).

Support Processes

Social support has been studied from a variety of different perspectives including sociological, psychological, and communication perspectives. (Burleson and MacGeorge 2002, see also MacGeorge, Feng, and Burleson 2011). These different perspectives bring together three types of processes that help individuals perceive, seek, and receive social support: network, cognitive, and communication. Network processes provide access to connections that can potentially provide support. Cognitive processes affect how individuals perceive social support. Communication processes allow individuals to encode and decode messages of social support.

Network Processes

Individuals interested in studying social support from a sociological perspective are likely interested in social support in terms of integration into a social network. Increases in the size of an individuals' social network can affect the amount of social support that is available to an individual (Israel and Antonucci 1987, Wellman and Gulia 1999). However, the type of support that is available from each network connection is also an important variable as different sources can provide different types of support (Agneessens, Waege, and Lievens 2006).

From the sociological perspective, access to a wide range of types of support is important. Although strong ties provide the majority of our social support (Agneessens et al. 2006), having access to diverse networks of weak ties can increase the total amount of accessible social support. Communication technology helps increase the number of others that we can access at any given moment. People can access greater amounts of social support either through tapping into network connections via SNS or joining online groups that help us to expand our weak tie networks (Ridings and Gefen 2004; Vitak and Ellison 2013). Individuals who engage with online support communities may feel that they are enmeshed in a flexible network with people who understand their issues and stressors. People can also potentially access greater social support by belonging to social network sites that allow individuals to expand their weak tie network may make them feel more socially integrated.

The internet can also help people find potential sources of support more quickly. Wellman and Wortley (1990) argued "If social support is specialized [different types of support coming from different types of network members], people may have to spend much time and effort shopping among their network members for aid" (560). Using communication technologies to locate social support could reduce these costs of seeking social support. Individuals seeking informational or emotional support can post a query on a specialized message board rather than seeking out a specific network member who might have that piece of information or be able to provide that level of emotional support. Individuals could also reach out to a wide swath of their network at once through social network sites.

In an example from my own network, a friend recently had a problem with their electric meter and received a $1200 bill. In her frustration, she literally posted to Facebook, "HEEEELLLLPP!" and then described the problem. She received a fair amount of emotional support in return. However, what was probably most useful was that a cousin who was an electrical engineer saw her post and was able to provide informational support. He recommended shutting off the main breaker and then watching the meter. Sure enough the meter continued running even with no power to the house and my friend was able to document this and received a full refund from the power company. Without access to an SNS, my friend may still have been able to access the same information, but she would have had to remember that her cousin was the right person to ask, find the contact information for this distant cousin, and actually get into contact with that person. Even if she did remember that this was the appropriate tie, the process would have taken much longer than the 10 minutes between when she posted her request for help and her cousin responded.

Cognitive Processes

Researchers interested in social support from a psychological perspective are interested in the individual's perceived availability of social support (Feeney and Collins 2014; Lakey and Orehek 2011). Perceived social support is likely rooted (although certainly not perfectly correlated with) network size, diversity, and previous interactions. Individuals with larger, more diverse networks, who have received support from these network connections or network connections like these in the past, may be more likely to perceive that they have greater amounts of social support available to them now. Maintaining larger or more diverse online networks might also lead individuals to perceive that greater amounts of support are available to them. The perception that a relevant online support community exists or knowing that thoughts and feelings can be posted to an SNS may make people perceive that online social support is accessible. Perceived social support may be more beneficial than enacted social support (Burleson and MacGeorge 2002). The reason for this is that people have a positive orientation toward feeling their network would provide support if needed. However, actually receiving support can involve host of complicated processes. Support seekers may feel uncomfortable requesting support, support givers may threaten the positive face by suggesting the receiver needs support, norms of reciprocity may be violated, and the communication surrounding a support exchange may be awkward and uncomfortable. On the other hand, although perceived social support may be viewed as better than the actual reception of support, perceptions of social support are still linked to past reception of actual social support (Hobfall 2009). If individuals post support-seeking messages and do not receive responses they may perceive less online social support to be available to them in the future.

Communication Processes

Supportive communication is the verbal and nonverbal behaviors intended to provide and seek help (Burleson and MacGeorge 2002). Supportive communication can help reduce uncertainty and increase perceptions of self-efficacy (Albrecht and Adelman 1987). Not all supportive communication is equal: "some forms of supportive communication are better than others—at least in some situations, with respect to certain goals, and as evaluated by certain criteria" (Burleson and MacGeorge 2002, 385). In some cases, the affordances and norms of different types of online communication can help facilitate better conditions for social support messages and yet in other cases online communication can make the provision of social support more difficult.

One message feature that has been shown to affect how successful or effective supportive messages are is person-centeredness. Person-centeredness refers to how much a message "reflects an awareness of an adaptation to the subjective, affective, and relational aspects of communication contexts" (Burleson 1987, 305). Low person-centered messages criticize or invalidate others' feelings (Applegate 1980; Burleson 2008). High person-centered messages acknowledge and validate the target's situation and feelings (Applegate, 1980; Burleson, 2008). The more person-centered a support message is, the more effective the support generally is (High and Dillard 2012; MacGeorge et al. 2011).

Another aspect of supportive communication is how responsive the support givers and their messages are to the individual to whom they are providing support. Supportive messages are most beneficial when communication is intentional and well-matched with the target's needs (MacGeorge et al., 2011). Responsiveness can communicate caring, provide validation, and help the support target cope with the stressor (Cutrona, 1996).

ONLINE SOCIAL SUPPORT GROUPS

Although the number of online support group users represents a small percentage of people, there are still hundreds of thousands of people that turn to online support groups for assistance and support through illnesses, transitions, difficult experiences and other stressors (Owen, Boxley, Goldstein, Lee, Breen, and Rowland 2010). Online support groups are electronic venues where people with similar concerns come together through communication technologies in order to discuss issues associated with their stressors (du Pre 2010; High and Solomon 2011; Preece 2000).

Online support communities are typically facilitated via message boards. However, online communities may also use other communication tools such as email lists or private chat functions. The different communication options allow people to post both public messages or have private dyadic interactions (Cummings et al. 2002). Online social support groups can be as simple as forums created as self-help groups. These groups can also be more structured experiences. For example, Comprehensive Health Enhancement Support Systems (CHESS) contain not only group communication but also educational components and sometimes expert leadership (Rains and Young 2009). Although these types of online spaces can be public or private and encompass different types of structure, these spaces share two common characteristics.

First, posters coming to these spaces are typically pseudonymous—that is, using a stable identity but not necessarily one that is connected directly to their fixed networks. The flexible network spaces of online support groups provide privacy for those who may not wish to either partially or fully disclose their stressor to their fixed network (Cummings et al. 2002). Received support may have the greatest benefit to the recipient when it does not create embarrassment or obligation (Bolger, Zuckerman, and Kessler 2000). When individuals disclose that they need support to their offline network they may feel embarrassed that these individuals now have this information about them. Support seekers may not want fixed network members to think differently or communicate differently with them based on the support issue. By choosing online sources of support, individuals can procure the support that they need without having to disclose potentially embarrassing information to people they interact with on a regular basis.

Two, people enter these spaces with the direct purpose of discussing some particular stressor. Support regarding this stressor from a support seeker's current network may be inadequate either because the support seeker's current network is not large enough to find the specific type of support they need or the network simply doesn't have the type of information or resources the support seeker needs (Cumming et al. 2002; Helgeson, Cohen, Schulz, and Yasko, 2000; Marsden 1987; McKenna and Bargh 1998; Turner, Grube, and Meyers 2001). Online support communities exponentially increase the probability of finding someone in a similar situation (Turner et al. 2001). Finding multiple others experiencing similar situations increases the diversity of perspectives and coping strategies available (Cummings et al. 2002).

Types of Support in Online Groups

Online support groups seem to be particularly useful for providing two kinds of support—informational and emotional support. Informational and emotional support are the most common reasons for using online support groups (Mikal et al.; Braithwaite et al. 2011; Ridings and Gefan 2004). Studies examining groups on a range of issues including Huntington's Disease, diabetes, pregnancy, and more have found that people join the groups primarily to gather information regarding their stressor and remain for the emotional support that is provided by others experiencing similar situations. (Coulson, Buchanan, and Aubeeluck 2007; Drentea and Moran-Cross, 2005; Newman et al. 2011). Online support may allow people to find greater diversity of information than is available to them offline while at the same time connecting with people who are experiencing similar situations and stressors. In addition, online support group members may have less emotional attachment to each other than strong tie networks. Consequently, both support seekers and givers may be able to be more objective. Support seekers may be able to describe their problems more objectively and fellow support group members may be more adept at providing an impartial view (Wright, Rains, and Banas 2012).

Informational Support in Online Groups

People report going to online communities for the purpose of information exchange (Ridings and Gefen 2004). Thus, online communication may be particularly well-suited for providing informational support (Mikal et al. 2013). Indeed, support seekers generally look for an online support group for the purposes of finding additional information regarding their stressor. For example, people newly diagnosed with diabetes might seek out a support community for additional information to help understand their new condition (Newman et al. 2011). People may seek out specialized support communities for informational support because the information that is provided by these communities is tailored for the specific stressor of the support seeker. For example, on a message board for Huntington's disease, a fifth of the messages included highly technical or factual information about the disease (Coulson et al. 2007). Informational support provided by online support communities can include helping people identify different coping strategies, find answers to questions, and get access and directions to additional sources of information (Coulson and Knibb 2010). The provision of informational support through the online group may help improve individual decision making because the online group allows participants to acquire more sophisticated ways of gathering information, learn from the experiences of others, and develop a better understanding of their condition or stressor (Barak, Boniel-Nissim, and Suler 2008). For example, Hoybye, Johansen, and Tjornhoj-Thomsen (2005) found that informational support provided by the online support community helped support seekers determine when they should seek out a second opinion from medical doctors.

Online support communities can provide diverse informational support (Mikal et al. 2013). Like other flexible networks, online support groups are primarily made up of weak ties, and weak tie networks tend to have greater diversity of information than strong tie networks (Walther and Boyd 2002). Thus, individuals may find a greater range of information from online support connections than they would if they did not have access to online support (Walther and Boyd 2002). The diverse experience of online group members and the access to a larger network are great advantages of online support groups (Wright 2000b). Not only can individuals receive a greater diversity of support, they can potentially receiver far more answers to their call for support than if they just queried one or even a few friends (Walther and Boyd 2002).

Emotional Support in Online Groups

Once an individual joins the group, that person may then find that the online support group is useful for also providing emotional support (Coulson et al. 2007). Emotional support from online communities can be beneficial as this type of support helps people feel better about themselves, provides validation of personal experiences, and may be associated with less perceived stress (Braithwaite et al. 1999; Coulson and Knibb 2010; Wright 2002b).

Online support groups can provide a place to meet someone who simply says, "yes . . . that happened to me too" or "I know what you are going through." Support seekers may turn to online support venues because there may not be others in their immediate community who have experienced the particular support issue (Walther and Boyd 2002). Women in the parenting boards often asked the question if *"they are alone"* (Drentea and Moren-Cross 2005), This question suggests that despite the ubiquity of the experience of parenting, new parents might feel isolated in regard to their specific parenting dilemma in their off-board networks and are seeking esteem support/validation from the online community. Vayreda and Antaki (2009) reported a similar phenomenon in their analysis of initial messages in bipolar support groups. One of the themes of initial messages in bipolar support groups was new members asking if there were others like them.

People who are in or who have faced similar situations or illnesses may be better able to provide empathy than offline network ties (Wright and Bell 2003). First, due to direct experience with a stressor, online support group members may have a deeper understanding of fears and feelings associated with that stressor (Turner et al. 2001). Second, online support groups may be perceived to provide even greater validation and empathy than offline support groups due to a process called solipsistic interjection. Solipisitic interjection is when online communicators read others' messages in the readers' own voice. This imprint of self onto the messages of others can make the reader feel even closer to the other group members. This process can lead to idealized perceptions and hyperpersonal connections (Walther 1996). Solipistic interjection and hyperpersonal perspectives can actually enhance perceptions of empathy and bonding with other group members which can help online support groups function (Barak et al. 2012).

Paradoxically, it appears that the benefit of an online support group is that it provides access to both network diversity and homophilous (similar) others. The key to this potential contradiction is that the members of the online community are different from the support seeker's pre-existing network but have similar experiences and stressors as the support seeker. The set-up that seems to help online groups facilitate social support best is when there is homogeneity within the community but heterogeneity in the types of information that members are able to provide (Coulson and Knibb 2010, Wright 2000b).

Other Support Types in Online Groups

Network support is provided in online support groups but rarely outside of initial interactions. Communities may focus on network support in initial interactions with newcomers to the group by letting newcomers know that the online space provides a network that they can reach out to that has experienced common stressors. However, Coulson et al. (2007) found that messages particularly focusing on network support were not common outside of messages welcoming newcomers.

Multiple studies of online support groups have found that tangible or instrumental support is the least common type of support provided online (Braithwaite et al. 1999; Coulson et al. 2007). This is not surprising given Wellman and Wortley's (1990) finding that physical presence was associated with providing services. However, although it is more difficult to provide instrumental support through an online forum, provision of such support does occasionally happen. One type of instrumental support on online forums is support providers facilitating connections to other offline support organizations (Coulson et al. 2007). Support group members may help put a support seeker in touch with an offline support group or a service provider who can provide additional care.

Affordances of Online Support Groups

The affordances of online support communities create spaces where individuals can seek support that is qualitatively different from offline support groups or relying on one's pre-existing network for support. Online support communities provide support seekers with anonymity, asynchronous communication, and decouple support requests and provision from the geographic location of the seeker and providers.

Anonymity

Online support communities are typically flexible network spaces where support seekers can be anonymous or pseudonymous. People consider the anonymous nature of online support groups the main advantage over offline forms of support (Wright 2000b). People may feel more comfortable disclosing information to a flexible network (Tidwell and Walther 2002; Rains and Young 2009). Furthermore, because anonymity facilitates emotional openness and self-disclosure, online support groups should be particularly good at providing emotional and esteem support in response to those disclosures (High and Solomon 2011). Often, issues that individuals are seeking support about may be stigmatized or embarrassing in the real world. Carriers of sexually transmitted diseases may fear being looked down upon. New mothers may wish to avoid a debate with their strong tie networks regarding the pros and cons of breastfeeding, sleep training, or babywearing. An individual with a disability may not want their network members to feel pity for them if they disclose some of the more difficult challenges of their disability. Online support groups allow individuals to remain anonymous while discussing stigmatized issues (Walther and Boyd 2002).

Thus online support groups provide an important avenue for individuals to be able to seek out social support. For example, experiencing an illness that is "embarrassing, socially stigmatizing, or disfiguring" leads people to seek the support of similar others (Davison et al. 2000), but these people may feel socially isolated from offline support. Having access to an online support group can ease those feelings of isolation (Coulson and Knibb 2010). At the same time, embarrassment over awkwardness or portraying oneself inappropriately often leads to avoidance by the embarrassed one and others around them (Sharkey and Stafford 1990). The anonymous nature of online support groups can lessen the effects of embarrassment or communication apprehension and help people feel more comfortable with seeking online help for embarrassing conditions (Braithwaite et al. 1999; Mikal et al. 2013).

Another advantageous aspect of online support groups is that the online group does not provide feedback to the individual's fixed network connections (Walther and Boyd 2002). Online anonymity may allow people an outlet for disclosures that represent facets of themselves they do not wish to disclose within fixed networks (Shaw and Gant 2012). Requests for emotional support often require the disclosure of negatively valenced information. People may prefer talking with people they meet through online support groups due to reduced risk of experiencing the possible negative social consequences from disclosures regarding socially stigmatized conditions or opinions (Wright et al. 2012). Going to an online support group can mean that people can avoid negative self-presentations to their fixed network (Newman et al. 2011).

Support seekers may also be concerned about disrupting the privacy or betraying the confidences of close network members. Coulson et al. (2007) found that individuals with rare genetic diseases may feel they are betraying their close family members if they disclose their experiences to co-members of their family member's fixed network. The anonymity of an online group may give those individuals an outlet to disclose without having their disclosure impact other members of their network (Coulson et al. 2007). Wright (2000b) also found that members of online support groups felt it was easier to be open in the online forums than with offline network members.

The low cost of exiting flexible networks is also an important feature of online support groups. The ability to leave an interaction at any time appears to be an important advantage of online support (Walther and Boyd 2002). If support seekers find that a particular group is not as supportive as they would like or if they do not want to be associated with an embarrassing issue, they can easily exit the group. People can ask a question, receive support, and then remove themselves from the group or return to lurking.

The anonymous, reduced cue environment also helps support seekers avoid negative reactions. Barak et al. (2008) argued that not only are members anonymous, they also are "invisible." Group members do not have to worry about appearance, any problems affecting physical appearance or speech, or any other gatekeeping features of the self that might keep others from reaching out with support or responding to requests for support (McKenna and Bargh 1999). The reduced cues in online support groups also means that support seekers cannot view nonverbal signs of disaffection or disgust. Thus, even if a support seeker's post is received negatively by other group members, the poster may never know.

Asynchronous

Another affordance of online support groups that helps facilitate the transmission of social support is the asynchronous nature of the message board communication that hosts many support groups (Preece 2000). The asynchronicity of this form of CMC can increase the availability of support, help communicators form more carefully crafted requests and support messages, and facilitate a message reception process that can improve the quality of the received support.

Online support groups are convenient for support seekers because they are available almost any time (Wright 2000b; Wright and Bell 2003). This availability allows members to participate according to their wants and needs (Newman et al. 2011; Rains and Young 2009). Queries for support can be posed at any time and support seekers can check back for responses at their convenience (Walther and Boyd 2002; Mikal et al. 2013). Individuals can work in support-seeking around their other daily commitments which may not be possible with an offline support group (Coulson and Knibb 2010).

Asynchronous communication gives both support givers and seekers time to manage their emotional reactions and think carefully about how to package the emotions into messages soliciting, providing, or responding to support (Mikal et al. 2013). The ability to carefully edit both requests and responses may help support seekers and givers present more tailored support messages than might be presented in offline settings. Thus, online support has the potential to more thoughtful (Walther and Boyd 2002). In addition, support receivers can receive the support without needing to manage their nonverbal expressions. Support receivers can also take more time to process online support messages (Walther and Boyd 2002).

The asynchronous and written nature of the communication allows individuals to return to support messages over and over again. Burleson (2010) has argued that message recipients may find messages more supportive when they take more time to process the message. Online social support affords the recipient the opportunity to mull over messages, return to them, and perhaps consider a message more fully than the recipient might have been able to in a face-to-face situation. Thus, if Burleson's theory regarding social support and message processing is correct, online support messages could potentially be more supportive than those delivered face-to-face. However, the research in this area is limited, so there is also a possibility that this effect is merely amplification. If this is the case, then good online support messages would still have a greater positive impact than offline support messages, but ruminating over negative responses to support requests could also have a greater negative impact than face-to-face messages.

Transcend Geography

Online support allows individuals to connect with others who are in a position to provide support regardless of the physical location of those others (Mikal et al. 2013). The ability of the online support group to transcend physical space can be particularly useful for people with limited mobility or who have difficulty attending an offline support group (Braithwaite et al. 1999; Davison et al. 2000, Mikal et al. 2013) For example, Mo and Coulson (2009) found that members of an HIV/AIDS support board that had more limited physical functioning were likely to be more frequent users of online support groups. Drentea and Moran-Cross provided another example by noting that new mothers can access online support without having to pack up and transport the baby (Drentea and Moren-Cross 2005).

Online support groups may also be beneficial for people who suffer from rare conditions. The online nature of the group means that the people with the condition can meet regardless of where they are geographically (Davison et al. 2000). A given community may only have a few individuals with a specific ailment, but individuals from multiple areas can come together for support online. This feature of online social support may be particularly important for rural or less populated areas as these communities may be less likely to have enough density of individuals with any particular condition for a support group to exist. The ability to call on a non-local group for support can also mean that support seekers are less likely to exhaust their local social support network. Norris and Kaniasty (1996) found that people who repeatedly call on support or require large amounts of support (in the wake of a disaster for example) may find that their available social support decreases over time. Those who have the type of larger and more diverse social support networks that online support can facilitate can call on those contacts for greater support for a longer period of time.

In addition, the online social support group has the ability to remain constant while an individual is experiencing stress or transition. The online group can remain available even if the support seeker must move from one physical location to another. Thus, the online group may provide a sense of consistency for the support seeker even if other parts of their life are in flux (Mikal et al. 2013).

Are Online Support Groups Beneficial?

The above affordances mean that a wide variety of benefits are *potentially* available from online support communities. However, the question remains if people are able to take advantage of the potential benefits of online support groups. Researchers have found evidence for some benefits. Users of online support groups reported greater use of coping strategies than non-users (Mo and Coulson 2009). Perceived effectiveness at dealing with a physical condition was associated with greater participation in an online support group (Cummings et al. 2002). Also, the longer people stay in a social support group the more benefits they perceive (Rains and Young 2009).

The type of support group may affect how beneficial the group is for a support seeker. Rains and Young (2009) conducted a meta-analysis of groups that focused on health conditions, involved computer-mediated interaction between members, had an education-related component, closed membership, and fixed start and completion points. Individuals who participated in these more comprehensive type support groups perceived a significant increase in social support, quality of life and self-efficacy, and significant decreases in depression.

The size of the support group may also affect the potential benefits available. Group size was positively associated with improved perceptions of quality of life but very large groups resulted in less perceived social support. Individuals may perceive the availability of more resources when in a larger group but in a very large group people may feel lost in the crowd and less supported if they have difficulty making dyadic connections (Rains and Young 2009).

The simple act of writing about one's problems on an online forum may provide positive benefits to support seekers (Barak et al. 2008). Writing about feelings and experiences associated with difficulties has been shown to decrease negative emotions and increase positive emotions (Esterling, L'Abate, Murray, and Pennebaker 1999), and increase feelings of control and empowerment (Hoybye et al. 2005). Pennebaker (1997) argued that emotional writing can affect physical health in positive ways. Guastella and Dadds (2006) found that writing about an upsetting experience can help individuals make more sense of their experience and may leave them feeling like they are willing to discuss the event with others. Individuals who post messages about their experiences in online support groups may benefit both from the posting as well as the practice they gain in framing their messages. This practice can help support seekers improve their ability to share those experiences and seek support from offline network members.

Another factor that may affect the usefulness of online support groups is how support seekers integrate the online support with other components of their overall support system. People may benefit from online groups more if their friends and family also engage with the online support group (Cummings et al. 2002). However, this cumulative effect only works if the individual perceives their family and friends as being generally supportive. In cases where individuals are able to integrate online and offline support, online support group members who had more support from their offline social networks were more likely to help others in the online group (Cummings et al., 2002)

The level of participation in an online support group may also affect how beneficial the group can be to the support seeker. People can actively participate on a board, but the majority of people in any given online community tend to lurk or simply passively read messages without responding. Group membership in online communities, is generally pretty fluid. For example Cummings et al. (2002) found that 72% of the members of an online hearing loss support group were still in the group three months later, and 75% had dropped out nine months later. This suggests that groups might have a smaller core of members committed to the group and a larger number of people simply passing through.

In general, research suggests that more active participation may lead to greater feelings of social support. For example, active participants on a suicide prevention board gained more emotional relief than passive participants (Barak and Dolev-Cohen 2006). Active participants on an HIV/AIDS support group reported receiving more social support and having more satisfaction with the online support community than lurkers. Individuals who participate in online support groups may also be more willing to seek out professional help and other forms of social support (Cummings et al. 2002).

In addition, taking on the role of providing support messages can help bolster the support provider. Support and information providers on online forums may feel empowered by taking on the role of guide or helper (Barak et al. 2008). Such communicators go from being dependent, passive support receivers to active participants who display strength and empowerment. This type of participation may help stabilize and grow online support communities. Getting people to stay in the group is likely an important part of creating the community aspect of an online support group. Participants who are willing to reach out to similar others may engender a feeling of belonging that induces people to stay in the group. Those people can then provide support to newcomers in their turn (Barak et al. 2008).

Although active participation does seem to be more beneficial that lurking, lurkers can still gain certain types of support such as information or validation (Cummings et al. 2002). Lurkers may be able to have greater perceptions of available support because they know that the support community exists. Lurkers may also be able to realize particular types of support through receiving messages from the online communities despite a lack of active participation. For example, lurkers can easily garner informational support through reading the posts of others or validation when they read the reports of others in similar situations. Mo and Coulson (2010) found no difference between self-efficacy, loneliness, depression, or optimism between posters and lurkers. Wright (2000b) found only a limited relationship between the total number of messages exchanged and satisfaction with the online group.

Disadvantages of Online Support Groups

Online support groups are not without their disadvantages. As noted above, online support groups are useful because they are anonymous and one of their primary utilities is for informational support. However, these features may make it difficult for support seekers to determine the credibility of information provided by online group members (Wright 2000b). Although support groups may be useful for finding and transferring information, individuals should be cautious about the information they receive. The anonymity that allows individuals to feel comfortable with self-disclosure may also work against being able to perceive the fellow community members as trustworthy sources of information (Coulson and Knibb 2007, Drentea and Moran-Cross 2005). Faulty information may be particularly problematic in health related boards where the information could easily contain misperceptions or misunderstandings of technical information (Coulson et al. 2007).

Another potential disadvantage is that it can take more time to feel comfortable in an online group than in an offline setting (Barak et al. 2008, see also Walther 1992). Yet, over time, group members may form emotional bonds and a sense of community that allows them to trust information that is shared within the community. There is also some evidence that homogeneity in a community may lead to increased trust. Thus, participation over time may help alleviate the trust issues. However, trusting others does not ensure information is credible. Groups can develop blind spots or promote misinformation. Online support group members should probably take some care to validate the veracity of information shared on the board with expert sources or professional opinions. Taking part in an online support group can be helpful but it may be deleterious if members try to substitute the support group for needed treatment. This may be obvious in the case of groups devoted to cancer support, but more confusing in the case of groups devoted to conditions such as depression (Barak et al. 2008).

Another potential issue is that being able to find detailed descriptions of behaviors you might be trying to avoid might be counterproductive. One of Barak et al's participants self-identified as a "cutter," someone who self-harms by cutting into their skin. This woman was concerned that detailed descriptions of cutting might make those prone to self-harm more likely to pursue the behavior. Groups dedicated to support on issues such as eating disorders may unwittingly encourage negative behaviors by providing new-comers with disordered eating descriptions of strategies they hadn't yet considered. Also, support "style" groups exist, such as "pro-ana" groups, that provide social support for negative behaviors such as anorexia.

Some people simply prefer face-to-face interaction to the reduced cues environment of online support groups (Coulson and Knibb 2007). Online support group participants in multiple studies noted that online groups simply can't provide the haptic affection that is often an essential part of face-to-face social support provision (Newman et al. 2011; Wright 2000b). Wright's (2000b) participants also noted that not being able to hear someone's tone of voice was sometimes a disadvantage due to the delay between the initial post and when the feedback would be received.

The reduced cue environment can also lead to negative communication behaviors that detract from the ability of the online support group to provide a supportive environment. Due to the online disinhibition effect (Suler 2004), some individuals may feel comfortable flaming others or trolling the community. Communities can also experience turmoil and conflict (Drentea and Moran-Cross 2005). Due to the limited nonverbal cues available in text-based group message boards, misunderstandings or confusion that can lead to hurt feelings that may be difficult to rectify (Drentea and Moran-Cross 2005).

Finally, individuals may also prefer proactive rather than reactive support. Wright (2000) found that older adults were more likely to form companionship connections than support connections online. People may build their online networks which can help provide support when necessary rather than seeking out support groups as a reaction to a specific stressor. On the other hand, Wright (2002) argued that "it may be that on-line support group participants seek supportive relationships during times of acute stress as opposed to desiring to maintain relationships with others in the group consistently" (95). This pattern would also account for findings that people tend to just pass through support communities. Some individuals may prefer seeking out emotional support only from people they know personally (Newman et al. 2011). However, communication technologies can also help connect individuals with support from their network that they communicate with both on- and offline.

MEDIATED SOCIAL SUPPORT FROM NETWORKED
INDIVIDUALS

As discussed earlier, most online communication occurs with individuals whom we know from offline communication as well (Ellison et al. 2007). Most online social support comes from others whom we know offline too (Fox 2011). We can use CMC to send and receive social support from these individuals. Using CMC for relational purposes such as relational maintenance positively affects the amount of perceived social support that is available. One way to pursue relational communication with network connections is through SNS, of which Facebook is currently the most popular (Duggan and Smith 2013). A larger number of connections, or friends, on Facebook may lead to greater amounts of perceived social support (Akbulut and Günüç 2012).

SOCIAL NETWORK SITES AND SOCIAL SUPPORT

Increased Network Connections

SNS allow individuals to maintain both close and weak tie network connections. SNS have long been considered places where individuals could build networks of social capital (Ellison et al. 2007). However, the type of network SNS users choose to maintain via an SNS may have a large effect on what social support can actually be procured from the network.

SNS such as Facebook create an easier way to signal support needs to a wide variety of network members (Vitak and Ellison 2012). However, Facebook has been shown to be particularly helpful for accessing support from weak tie network members (Vitak and Ellison 2012). The weak ties may be available locally or they could be network ties from older support networks that the support seeker has physically moved away from (Mikal et al., 2013). Maintaining larger networks of SNS connections may not only help increase perceived available support but can also keep individuals from exhausting their support network by diffusing support requests over a larger group.

However, these positive effects of a larger Facebook network will only work if the individual believes they have created a Facebook network that cares about the individual. Although Facebook helps users connect to weak tie support, support from weak tie networks may seem less sincere (Vitak and Ellison 2012). Emotional support is typically only sought from weak ties when there is some deficiency in the strong tie network rendering strong tie network members unable to provide support (Adelman, Parks, and Albrecht 1987). Individuals are more likely to perceive emotional support from their Facebook network if they perceive they have higher levels of attitude and background similarity (Wright 2012a). Thus, only adding quality connections on an SNS will improve perceived social support (Nabi, Prestin, and So 2013).

It may be difficult to mobilize weak ties for social support. Jung, Gray, Lampe, and Ellison (2013) found that the sheer number of Facebook friends was not associated with being able to have a request filled via Facebook. Rather, the *types* of social capital people reported were the better predictors of the fulfillment of favor requests. Thinking that interactions with current Facebook friends will help the Facebook user find new friends (a form a bridging social capital) was negatively related to the fulfillment of favor requests. On the other hand, forms of bonding social capital such as having people who can help solve problems, discuss personal problems, or borrow money from was a positive predictor of favor request fulfillment.

Increased Perceived Social Support

While it may be difficult to extract actual social support from weak tie networks, maintaining network connections via Facebook might still allow individuals to perceive greater amounts of available social support. Perceiving social support to be available through an SNS can have a positive effect on the SNS users. For example, perceived emotional support from Facebook has been shown to lower perceived stress (Wright 2012a).

In general maintaining larger network sizes has been associated with greater levels of social support (Israel and Antonucci 1987, Wellman and Gulia 1999), thus is not surprising that studies of Facebook have found that greater numbers of Facebook friends are associated with having more perceived social support (Akbulut and Gunuc 2012; Nabi et al. 2013). These findings may be because the number Facebook friends can be related to overall network size. The more network connections one has in general, the more Facebook friends they are likely to have. However, Nabi et al. (2013) did find that for people who have experienced a life stressor, having more FB friends helped with perceptions of social support above and beyond the effect of general network size.

Ease of Requests

The status update and comment features of Facebook allow support seekers and providers to easily communicate requests for support as well as supportive messages. Ellison, Gray, Vitak, Lampe, and Fiore (2013) argued that Facebook can be used to convert social capital by asking questions and making requests from Facebook friends. Participants talked about it being easier to put out requests for information to Facebook rather than emailing every network member that might know the answer (Vitak and Ellison 2012).

However, some of the communication norms associated with SNS may make supportive communication difficult to procure through SNS.

Ellison et al. (2013) defined Facebook requests for support as *mobilization requests*. Mobilization requests were status updates that included a request for some type of support or assistance. Most requests for support in Ellison's study were either favor requests or opinion polls. A smaller number of requests were for facts, social coordination, or recommendations. Facebook seems particularly useful for information seeking (Ellison et al. 2013; Jung et al. 2013; Vitak and Ellison 2012). Facebook is convenient for informational support because a wide range of responses come quickly (Vitak and Ellison 2012). Requests that require low amounts of effort from the responder such as providing an opinion or some piece of information may be the most common type of Facebook support requests and the most likely to garner supportive messages.

How Facebook Support Requests are Perceived

Although the affordances of Facebook make it easier to post requests for support, such requests may not always be viewed positively. For example, Vitak and Ellison (2012) found that some people avoided posting support requests on Facebook because they did not want to appear needy or inspire pity (Vitak and Ellison 2012). This finding suggests that these individuals may find others' requests for support on Facebook as inappropriate (needy). The norm for Facebook is to post positive disclosures (see Day 2013) so posting disclosure-seeking support on Facebook might lead to negative interpersonal outcomes. Posting broadcast response-seeking messages on Facebook has been shown to be correlated with lower friendship quality (McEwan 2013a) and messages with low positivity and high negativity receive undesirable responses (Forest and Wood 2012).

Facebook also allows individuals to not just post support messages but to construct their overall communication and profile as being in need of social support. If individuals resist direct support requests in order to not appear needy, they may still communicate a need for support in a more passive manner. High et al. (2014) argued that the use of more of Facebook's affordances to convey a need for support increases the amount of emotional bandwidth of the support request. Emotional bandwidth is "both a direct and indirect means of information revelation that is communicated through technological affordances" (High et al. 80).

Emotional bandwidth is more than just self-disclosure: it is both the emotional level of a disclosure and the number of affordances of a platform used to convey the disclosure. It is both how something is disclosed as well as the content. For example, on Facebook an individual conveying a breakup in a high emotional bandwidth way could post a status update with an sad tone, change their relationship status to Single, change their profile picture to them looking sad, and add "Cold November Rain" to their list of Favorite songs. Conversely an individual conveying a breakup with low emotional bandwidth might simply move their relationship status from "In a Relationship" to "Single."

Differences in the level of emotional bandwidth used for a variety of disclosures could be imagined. An individual with a family member with cancer could go low bandwidth and maybe just join a group against cancer or they could go high bandwidth and join a group, post multiple pictures from attending fundraising races and events, change their profile picture to that family member, and post multiple status updates with disclosing their feelings regarding their family member and the disease. When individuals communicate support needs using low bandwidth it may be hard to have enough information to know to offer support, but when individuals use high emotional bandwidth for support needs the repeated disclosures may cause fatigue in the potential support givers.

Requests for different types of support may facilitate different outcomes. High et al. found that using more of Facebook's affordances to communicate a need for support following a breakup led to undesirable responses from the message receivers. People were less willing to provide emotional or network support in the high emotional bandwidth condition (High et al. 2014). However, in response to instrumental requests, Jung et al. (2013) found that the more often an individual requested instrumental support the greater number of responses they were likely to get from their network connections. Individuals might be more likely to respond to low cost requests such as a quick informational question than get involved in the potentially higher cost interaction of attempting to cheer a friend who is very despondent over an emotional issue.

The nature of network may also affect the different responses found by High (2014) and Jung et al. (2014). Jung et al. (2013) argued that this could be because frequent askers interact on the site more (and thus may have more reciprocal interactions banked) or that they could be more skillful at framing their requests. However, it may also be that those who have networks that are responsive are more likely to actually post requests. The experimental design used by High et al. meant that the viewers of the support seeking profiles were strangers to the individual requesting support. People might be more likely to provide support to an individual that they know. Again, although Facebook's utility is in providing the communication technology needed to maintain a weak tie network, weak tie networks may not be the most appropriate for providing some types of social support (particularly emotional). Having strong tie network members available to interact with online may improve the chances of social support requests succeeding (Lin and Bhattacherjee 2009).

People with the most need for online social support may find it the most difficult to actually receive support from the network. People with low self-esteem had a tendency to post low positivity/high negativity messages (Forest and Wood 2012). These are exactly the type of messages that are seen as most inappropriate on Facebook (Day 2013). People who could use Facebook support the most may be unable to craft messages that allow them to tap into the network support.

In addition, because the norm for Facebook is to post positive information, people may be likely to post achievements (which could garner support through congratulations on the achievements), but not want to post about negative things that they need support for. Participants in Newman et al.'s (2011) study reported posting about positive things they had accomplished but not the struggles they had during or on the way to those accomplishments. In particular, posters did not want to share health information with their weak tie connections. Thus, Newman (2011) found that Facebook was "not an effective venue for interacting around health." The very issues that people may need the most support for may also be those that are the least appropriate for discussing via Facebook.

Those who are the most steeped in social media use may be the most likely to both seek and supply social support on SNS. Self-efficacy regarding internet use is related to receiving online social support (Lin and Battacherjee 2009). People with a strong preference for online social interaction are more willing to provide social support through Facebook (High et al., 2014). People who perceive high levels of community on Facebook were generally more willing to try to provide high-quality support via the SNS (High et al. 2014).

CONCLUSION

Individuals perceive social support provided by CMC to be less useful than face-to-face communication (Schifferin et al. 2010). However, online social support can fill in gaps from the online support network and provide valuable informational support and validation that similar others exist in the world. CMC allows for the expansion of the network through connecting with individuals on SNS or finding people going through similar stressors in online communities. Large social networks can provide support but still create difficulties in finding the right member of the network to provide the right type of support. CMC can help people shortcut that process by posting issues and concerns in hopes that the right network member will respond or by allowing individuals to go directly to an online group that should have the requested resources.

The flexible networks of anonymous, online support communities may actually be a more appealing choice for seeking online support than the fixed networks catalogued by social network sites. "The need to express a need for support can run at odds with the need to present oneself as a positive appealing member of the community" (Newman et al. 2011). People want support from others, but they want their health statuses to be viewed favorably and do not want to bore others with inappropriate communication (Newman et al. 2011). People may choose online support communities instead of Facebook because those communities are designed for support, it is easier to find similar others, and support is available around the clock (Newman et al. 2011). However, the ability to gain support from both flexible and fixed networks represents one of the important advantages of using communication technology to join and maintain networks.

Chapter Nine

Virtual Cosmopolitanism in a Networked Society

Miriam Sobre-Denten

As argued throughout this text, communication technologies allow people to expand their communication networks beyond their physical locations. This compression of space allows for the greater potential of intercultural contact and interaction. Online intercultural interaction can be potentially beneficial to both individuals and societies, but there is also the concern that intercultural interactants can misunderstand each other, reify inequitable social structures, or bolster harmful stereotypes. In order to fully engage in the potential offered by networked technologies, people need to approach mediated intercultural communication mindfully, ethically, and with empathy. This approach is virtual cosmopolitanism (McEwan & Sobre-Denton, 2011; Sobre-Denton, in press).

COSMOPOLITANISM

Cosmopolitanism is defined by Sobré-Denton and Bardhan (2013) as "an ethical and philosophical framework through which we may envision human and mediated intercultural communication in a more humane world" (174). Cosmopolitan communication has several characteristics. First, it is simultaneously concerned with how local actions are affected by and affect the global sphere, and vice versa. Second, it involves an ethical orientation to the world and its people through day-to-day actions. Third, it entails a curiosity and respect for Others who are different from us (rather than attempting to minimize or correct for difference). Finally, virtual cosmopolitanism requires understanding that while our values may be very different from those of members of other cultures, those cultural Others hold their values just as dear to them as we do to us; therefore we can build empathy with them despite differing belief systems (Sobré-Denton and Bardhan 2013, Hansen 2011). In today's age of globalization, cosmopolitanism provides people with an ethical stance toward themselves, the world, and difference that must be understood as they increasingly interact with those who seem very dissimilar. Virtual cosmopolitanism allows for this ethical stance to inform communication that occurs within online spaces of intercultural contact.

History of Cosmopolitanism

The origin of the word cosmopolitan is believed to come from Diogenes. The literal translation comes from the Greek word κόσμος (*cosmos*) meaning "world" combined with the word πολίτης (*politēs*) meaning citizen. Thus, the literal translation of cosmopolitanism is citizen of the world (Kleingold 2006). The Stoics of Rome adopted the term to further the belief that human beings dwell simultaneously in two spheres: the global and the local (Nussbaum 1997). In the late eighteenth century, the theory was taken up by Kant and other Enlightenment philosophers, who advocated the distancing of the self from all "parochialisms emanating from allegiances to nation, race, and ethnos" (Anderson 1991, 267).

More modern versions of the term focus on the idea of "global citizen identity" that blurs transnational boundaries and calls for responsibility to and toward all humankind (Beck 2006; Hannerez 1990, 1996, 2006). Although nation-state boundaries are blurred and critiqued within the framework of cosmopolitanism, locality is still recognized. Appiah (2006) argued that global citizens are simultaneously loyal to both local and global spheres. This ethical stance has guided work in sociology, political science, ethnology, international relations, and communication (Beck and Sznaider 2006).

Critical and Postcolonial Cosmopolitanism

Today, in the realm of intercultural communication, cosmopolitanism is often treated as a critical or post-colonialist theory (Sobré-Denton and Bardhan 2013). Cosmopolitan communication is defined as a "world- and Other-oriented practice of engaging in deliberate, dialogic, critical, non-coercive, and ethical communication" (Sobré-Denton and Badhan 2013, 173). In other words, cosmopolitanism involves all of us, whenever we cross borders (physical ones, virtual ones, imagined ones). Cosmopolitanism impacts both our relationship with those who are different from us, as well as our understanding of and impression on both our local communities, where we live now, and the global community as a whole. This is a very useful theory, particularly from the critical perspective, as it can be applied at several levels. Cosmopolitanism can be viewed simultaneously as an orientation to the world and difference, as an identity or behavioral stance that keeps us focused on ethical obligations to others (globally and in our own backyards), as a way of understanding and navigating communication channels, and as a way of teaching and learning that embraces difference (and the ways we deal with it).

This critical and postcolonial cosmopolitanism brings us to the questions of social media, the shrinking world through greater technological as well as physical mobility, and the impacts these have on cosmopolitanism. With that in mind, the concept of *virtual cosmopolitanism* has been proposed by McEwan and Sobré-Denton (2011) and Sobré-Denton (in press) as a new channel for realizing the practices of engaging in ethical communication with culturally different others in today's age of globalization.

VIRTUAL COSMOPOLITANISM

The first characterization of virtual cosmopolitanism is provided by McEwan and Sobré-Denton (2011), who defined it as cosmopolitanism which is "facilitated by mediated social spaces . . . in which cultural and social capital may be transmitted through social media networks, that allows for a greater transnational spread of ideas than corporeal cosmopolitanism" (253). Individuals in the current age of globalization must focus on the impact of new media in networked societies. Intercultural communication, in particular, is poised to be greatly influenced by the blurring of borders and the shrinking of space and increasing of networked individualism through social media. Kathryn Sorrells (2012) stated, "clearly, advances in communication technology in the global context facilitate intercultural communication among friends and intimate partners to meet, develop friendships, and maintain contact particularly at great geographic distance" (166). Gajjala (2012) also noted that "cyberspaces have become the nodes at which various locals connect and disconnect in the production of the global" (2).

A big issue in terms of technological mobility has generally been one of access to the gigantic web of social connections and information. Today, that access is becoming more widespread. As such, it seems to differentiate more based on age and education level rather than on geographic location. In other words, today (and increasingly as we move into a more digitized world), the question becomes less one of internet access and more one of technological skill and mobility (Gajjala 2012). Virtual cosmopolitanism stands within the tension of this debate, as it involves not only the skill to create and negotiate virtual identities, but also to expand the imagination beyond the local, and to gain and share cultural capital.

Virtual cosmopolitanism, given the shift of the digital divide from geographic to age- and education-based, can be seen as using internet-based technologies as a channel through which to provide cosmopolitan experiences for those who might not otherwise have access to them. Border and boundary crossings in a networked society are not as regulated by citizenship rights, visas, and financial privileges. An SNS account, for example, is much easier and cheaper to access than say, a plane ticket from Baltimore to Brazil. It should certainly be noted that socioeconomic status does impact technological mobility, and that western imperialism can be manifested through media imperialism (e.g. the use of English as the primary language of technology). However, increased internet access and the widening net of technological reach can certainly be harnessed to create greater cosmopolitan spaces than was possible ten, twenty, fifty, or a hundred years ago.

Examples

An example of virtual cosmopolitanism can be seen through Sobré-Denton's (2011) study of INTASU (an organization of international students at Arizona State University), a multinational, multicultural student group active at Arizona State University from 2003-2012. This group was housed in a Yahoo groups page, and at its peak proliferated to over 400 members in 25 countries, some physically located in Arizona, and others spread out all over the world. The virtual community created through Yahoo groups listserv (and a later Facebook page) provided opportunities for members to arrange visits to each other in other countries, to create their own idioms and norms, and to become empathetic to communities far from their theirs. This empathy develops from the increased imagined communities, mindful exposure, and ability to share and communicate with people from distant cultures that online communication engenders. In this manner, then, virtual cosmopolitanism provides spaces of networked individualism (Rainie and Wellman 2012). Participants in virtual groups can choose to connect across cultural boundaries through social media and digital communication without the requirement of transnational travel. Communication technology gives individuals who may not get to travel voluntarily or frequently access to faraway parts of the global world, as well as ways to learn about others' localities and share information about their own.

Another example of virtual cosmopolitanism processes can be found in Christiansen's (2012) work on Turkish diasporic communities living in Sweden. Sweden is home to an estimated 67,700 Turkish expatriates, 45,000 of whom were born in Sweden, some of whom migrated voluntarily and some involuntarily. Christensen (2012) described how the use of digital communication in migrant communities allows the creation of virtual space that stands in for offline, corporeal space of a nation or culture. Networked individualism, in which (according to Wellman 2002) people are becoming increasingly connected to one another through networks that move beyond their tradi-

tional spaces of work and "home," decreases the need for place-based localities. Virtual communities formed through digital media (such as the Facebook page "Isvec'teyiz ('We are In Sweden) allow for the substitution of
corporeal space of acceptance (or the physical nation-state homeland) with a
more integrated, cybernetic space (Christensen 2012). The Stockholm en-
clave where most of the migrants reside, Rinkeby, has largely become a
space of the "foreign" or "alien," which leads to further feelings of estrange-
ment, and a stronger need for ties to other diasporic groups. Virtual cosmopolitanism exists here as a space that allows members of such social networks to find spaces of home and belonging, as well as solidarity with
similar others they might not otherwise have access to. This example illus-
trates how the kinds of kinship systems previously relegated to corporeal
places can now be said to exist in virtual spaces. These spaces allow for
borders and boundaries to be crossed with greater ease and provide senses of
home and belonging that previously would not have been as possible. In such
groups, displaced migrants can find spaces of belonging and identification
with others in similar positions.

An example of virtual cosmopolitanism within the context of education is
through the work of the group Space2cre8. Space2cre8 was an adolescent
literacy program that brought together teens from several countries around
the world (including the US, Australia, Norway, Taiwan, India, and South
Africa) who "collaborate across sites to create and exchange digital artifacts
using an online multinational and multilingual network" (Harper et al., 2010,
10). This program works with the teens to set up profile pages similar to
Facebook, through which they can begin dialogues and the exchange of
artifacts (such as poems, photos, games, videos and music) with participants
in other parts of the world. This collaboration eventually leads to the formation of intercultural relationships. Networked individualism can also be explored here as the participants connect with one another outside of their local
home spaces, transferring ideas and artifacts beyond traditional borders and
finding "spaces to create" new identities and communities.

THE BENEFITS OF VIRTUAL COSMOPOLITANISM

Virtual cosmopolitanism can be a beneficial approach for several reasons. It
provides a framework through which to utilize new media as a means for
learning about and understanding cultural difference without the financial
capital required of most voluntary travel. Pedagogically, virtual cosmopolitanism can be used to facilitate mindful interaction with students and scenarios that would have been much more difficult to access in the era predating
the internet. Additionally, virtual cosmopolitanism can broaden the imagination to encompass communities and ways of life that are culturally and cor-

poreally distant. Virtual cosmopolitanism provides a framework for using new media to facilitate intercultural contact and learning, which brings mindfulness into a process that might otherwise be experienced as minimization of differences, stereotyping, and culture shock.

In terms of engaging intercultural communication, virtual cosmopolitanism provides useful pedagogical tools that give students opportunities to learn about and interact with physically and culturally distant Others, in a manner that may be less intrusive or threatening than in face-to-face interaction. The Space2cre8 provides a hybrid space through social media for identity development and intercultural learning that allows for students to learn how to respectfully and effectively learn about other cultures, while not having to leave the relative safety and pedagogical monitoring of their home environments (Hull and Sturnaiuolo 2014). In this case, the students are coached to take care in creating their virtual identities as they will be communicating with culturally different Others, and have the opportunity to engage in facilitated and reflexive interactions with those of similar age groups and interests who physically reside in geographically distant cultures.

Virtual cosmopolitanism also allows for the expansion of the imagination from local to global settings, which can increase empathy, cultural curiosity, and cultural self-awareness (Sobré-Denton, Carlsen and Greuel 2014). Kanno and Norton described imagined communities as "groups of people, not immediately tangible and accessible, with whom we connect through the power of imagination" (2003, 241). The extension of the imaginary to include those who are socially close to individuals while being physically far from them leads to the sense of reflexive loyalty to those whose customs and practices are new to them: Hansen (2011) noted that "cosmopolitanism constitutes an orientation in which people learn to balance reflective openness to the new with reflective loyalty to the known" (1). As can be seen in both the INTASU and Space2cre8 examples provided above, virtual cosmopolitanism gives space for the creation of social networks that include members of local/home cultures as well as members in far-off locations across the globe. Knowledge and interaction with folks who are physically distant through real time in social media expands the critical imagination of the individuals engaged in such interactions. This expanded critical imagination can also create a sense of reflective openness and loyalty (Hansen 2011) to those who are physically far from them as they create and sustain friendships based on virtual cosmopolitan communication. On INTASU, Sobré-Denton (2011) noted that "specifically, members of the group cite the tendency to attend to cultural news stories and conflicts with a more open mind—especially if these stories include information on groups they formerly stereotyped—now that they have met people of that culture group and been able to learn from them" (87). Space2cre8 also allowed students to engage their imaginations to become more empathetic to those culturally different Others with whom they communicate. In short, once people expand their imaginations to encompass distant locales, and their empathy to become aware and to care for individuals who live in those locales, they are more likely to feel a sense of reflective loyalty and openness to those individuals, and by extension, other members of that culture.

However, it must be noted here that virtual cosmopolitanism does not simply delineate the experience of communicating with culturally different Others through social media. The mere facilitation of contact doesn't guarantee virtual cosmopolitanism any more than the mere presence of two people from different cultures conversing indicates intercultural communication competence. In order to engage in virtual cosmopolitanism's benefits, several criteria must be followed, including an ethical orientation to the world beyond one's locality, an embodiment of empathy with those who may be quite different from one's typical social circle (in terms of nationality and geographic location, maybe, but it can also apply to race, ethnicity, religious identity, sexual and gender identities, etc.), an understanding of the global repercussions of such interactions, and a desire to engage with those who are different without minimizing or negating those differences. What follows is a discussion of some of the challenges to approaching intercultural communication through virtual cosmopolitanism.

CHALLENGES TO VIRTUAL COSMOPOLITANISM

Virtual cosmopolitanism cannot be described as the cure-all for intercultural communication and social media in a networked society. Without careful facilitation, the increased spread of context-free contact through unfettered technological access to world events and ability to communicate across cultural boundaries can have some serious shortcomings, and, if used for negative ends, can lead to disastrous outcomes. Several studies have shown that increased use of social media may lead to increased cultural isolation instead of greater global networks (e.g., Hur and Gupta 2013; Seligman 2011). Students studying abroad with access to smart phones and social media may be more likely to experience other cultures through that media rather than in the immersive sense that traditional study abroad embraces. Research on Hostelling International has shown that often times, due to the internet access throughout the hostels (in common areas as well as in dorm rooms), travelers tend to spend most of their time on Facebook or engaging in other socially mediated interaction, rather than getting to know other travelers. This goes against the general intent of youth hostels as spaces for increased social interaction among guests from several different national and cultural origins (hence, the inclusion of common areas and dorm rooms, rather than traditional hotel lobbies and private guestrooms) (Sobré-Denton et al. 2011). So, while virtual cosmopolitanism can provide individuals with the *possibility* of greater opportunities to engage with culturally different Others, it can paradoxically divide them from those experiences. Sojourners may choose to share photographs of historical monuments, chat with friends at home, live tweet or send status updates rather than engaging with their host culture *in situ* (Wooley 2013). A further example of this can be seen in Sobré-Denton's (2011) work on INTASU; one of the findings was that membership in the socially mediated organization can actually hinder adaptation. That is,

> in circumstances where the group is the ONLY form of salient interaction within the host culture, such interaction may cause its members to avoid the kinds of interactions that are necessitated by adaptation—the kinds of trial and error interaction with the host culture that, while it may cause growing pains at the time, eventually leads to better understanding of the host culture. (Sobré-Denton 2011, 89)

While Sorrells (2012) noted that "clearly, the circulation of media regionally and globally escalates the flow of information and images interculturally, which exposes people to different cultures," this exposure to multiple conflicting and often context-free (or misinterpreted) messages "can fragment and disrupt local and national cultural identities" (134). Socially mediated images, texts, and videos can be shared without context, which can lead to misrepresentation of cultural ideas and scenarios. Worse, such messages can be framed according to the sender (which is a particularly important issue due to the lack of peer review in the new media environments). For instance, after Hurricane Sandy hit New York and New Jersey in 2012, Gupta, Lamba, Kumaraguru and Joshi (2013) note that malicious social media use involved the dissemination of fake pictures on Twitter to create rumors and even to reallocate resources and funds from relief efforts. To complicate matters further, social media is also not always consumed in the manner intended by the producer. Messages can easily be misconstrued without face-to-face context, or through lags in response time, or in the absence of familiar cultural markers in the form of nonverbal communication. In the context of the misrepresentation of Uganda's *Invisible Children* documentary leading to the Twitter hashtag #Kony2012, Daley (2013) noted that

> fabricated perceptions of truth can create a trend but falsity ultimately leads to failure. The lessons: social networking is a start but cannot be the heart of information; slogans, manipulation, and persuasion make a difference; and truth and trust create the ultimate route to success. (151)

Because this particular movement was sensationalized and went viral so quickly and without any form of peer review, many consumers of social media across cultural groups experienced the controversies that exist when information isn't checked before being disseminated.

Indeed, virtual cosmopolitanism may actually facilitate spaces for more nefarious activities. As has been noted previously in this chapter, mere intercultural contact alone has been proven to not be enough to further intercultural communication and the construction of positive intercultural relationships—in fact, such untrained contact can be detrimental to intercultural dialogue. In other words, contact with different cultures is not enough to promote understanding. Important concerns must be met *before* contact can potentially improve circumstances on both sides, which groups facilitating intercultural contact (such as international exchanges) must take into account. Some of these preconditions include equal status of contact group members, strong institutional support for the contact circumstances, potential for further contact beyond the immediate situation, maximizing cooperation and minimizing competition between contact groups, equalizing numbers of group members, and focusing on the individual rather than the cultural (Martin and Nakayama 2007). Clearly, virtual cosmopolitanism may not provide these important antecedents of contact, and further, may give the impression (due to ease of social networking) that such equality of stature and institutional support might exist when really it doesn't. Identity vulnerability resulting from cultural isolationism may lead displaced individuals to turn to virtual cosmopolitanism as a safe space alternative for finding and making connections in new cultural situations. Unfortunately, if such spaces are not monitored, or don't focus on the important criteria described above, such virtual intercultural communication can provide breeding ground for dangerous cross-cultural alliances, extending to the recruitment of potential terrorists or freedom fighters for various social and cultural causes.

The final challenge to virtual cosmopolitanism comes in terms of issues of access to and understanding of how to utilize social media for the purposes of broadening one's social circle across physical corporeal divides. Not everyone has equal access to computer technology, smart phone platforms, and social network sites. Additionally, not all social media users mobilize their technological access to engage in mindful intercultural interactions with culturally different (and distant) Others. While most places in the world now have internet access, it can be spotty and difficult to work with in poor and rural areas. Even within the last couple of years in the United States, there are many Americans who have no option to gain broadband access due to living in rural areas (Brodken 2012). As social media is highly driven by the immediacy of access to and ability to communicate with multiple people at varying distances in a moment, the very opportunity to engage in communication building toward virtual cosmopolitanism is still an issue. It is imperative to note that not everyone has equal access to a networked society.

Notably, most of the challenges to virtual cosmopolitanism described above only pertain to circumstances where the criteria for cosmopolitanism described at the beginning of this chapter—an ethical orientation to the global beyond the local, empathy for those who embody cultural difference, awareness of the global repercussions of intercultural interactions, and desire to engage across without minimizing such differences—are not adhered to. Virtual spaces facilitate such intercultural interactions; however, without mindfulness such easy access to difference can cause more problems in intercultural communication than it solves. The biggest issues to be tackled in terms of utilizing virtual cosmopolitanism in a networked society lie in shifting the focus of networked individuals to an empathetic, mindful stance. As discussed by McEwan in the introduction to this text, this is hardly a straightforward process: new competencies are imperative and new literacies must be learned. For this reason, virtual cosmopolitanism must not be seen as an inevitable outcome to increased intercultural communication opportunities through social media. Rather, it must be seen as a privilege that must engage knowledge, skills, and motivations to communicate appropriately and effectively across cultural and digital divides.

CONCLUSION

Future research in virtual cosmopolitanism seems to be proliferating as the internet and social media continue to grow and spread their influence. This is fortunate, as networked individualism does not preclude mindfulness. As can be seen in the use of social media to foment political and social movements, the simple dissemination of intercultural information without context can be at best misleading and at worst quite dangerous. Future work in virtual cosmopolitanism should include the study of how social activism and cosmopolitan solidarity (Kyriakidou 2008) can be used to create social justice without the spread of false or misleading information. The presence of mass national and global protests, such as the Occupy movements or the events (and aftermath) of the Arab Spring, can be harnessed with more responsibility, and more effectiveness, though an understanding of virtual cosmopolitanism. As the networked society spans traditional corporeal boundaries, so does the opportunity to create and respond to responsible social justice movements, such as those reacting to climate change or human rights abuses, in a manner that is more immediate and should, as such, be more critical and socially responsible.

Virtual cosmopolitanism can also be explored in the future as a means through which to participate in pedagogical experiences that are comparable to studying abroad or hosting an exchange student without the financial privilege and expenditure previously required. Facilitated programs such as

Space2cre8 and carefully monitored social groups such as INTASU can provide experiential learning for ethical communication, respect for and acceptance of difference, empathy, and the growth of cultural self-awareness. But, this can only occur as long as the socially mediated interactions remain a window through which to engage with difference, rather than a door to keep it out. Future research can and should focus on ways that virtual cosmopolitanism can be harnessed to teach students about global events and their consequences in local space.

The most important implication of virtual cosmopolitanism in a networked society lies in the understanding that while technologies and mobilities are shrinking the world, these social media skills are a privilege that should be engaged with through mindfulness. Intercultural communication becomes more and more imperative as the world grows smaller and we bump up against culturally different Others on a more and more regular basis. This involves a much greater sense of responsibility, both for the impacts of the individual at a local level and the ways that those are reflected in the global sphere, and for the notion that everyday actions and interactions are equally as important on the world stage as they are in the mundane environment we move through every day.

Chapter Ten

Always On, Always Present in the Network: The Influence of Mobile

The previous chapters of this book have focused on the processes and functions of communication via networked technologies rather than the specific devices people use to access various online social network opportunities. This focus is strategic in that engaging in online communication processes such as relational formation or maintenance is similar whether online communication sites are accessed through a desktop computer, laptop, or mobile device. With some exceptions for processor speeds or router issues, the hardware that makes the communication possible has generally not played a large role in the independent and dependent variables involved in mediated social communication. However, the introduction of lightweight, personal communication devices, which allow for voice and text calls, and can be connected to online social platforms, may indeed influence the structure and function of interpersonal communication and social organization processes. The introduction of mobile devices mark a shift to a "personal communication society" (Campbell and Park 2008, 371) and may change the way we communicate with our networks, furthering the shift to networked individualism.

Mobile has changed both interpersonal and mass communication. In terms of the latter, smart technologies allow people to tailor the streams of information they access through aggregation by technology (e.g., using an RSS feed) or through curation from our social networks (e.g., following our particular Twitter feed). In terms of the former, with the widespread adoption of mobile communication technology, communication is now sent from person to person rather than place to place. No longer do people need to send a mailed missive in hopes that it will reach a party in a reasonable length of time or call a place that they think their intended co-communicator might be in order to bring them to the phone. Now messages can be sent directly to fellow network members without any intermediary. Not only can people reach out directly to others, they can reach them almost anytime, anywhere (Campbell and Park 2008;Wellman 2001).

Mobile communication has only been a part of our repertoire of social communication options for a brief time (Ling 2008). Although the first public discussion of the type of cellular radio network that would eventually support our modern mobile communication occurred in the pages of the *Saturday Evening Post* almost 70 years ago, designs for mobile telephone devices didn't appear until the 1970s (see Farley 2005 for an excellent review of the early history of mobile communication systems). Motorola filed for a patent of their cellular radio system October 17, 1983, leading to mobile devices coming into widespread use by the 1990s (Ling 2008, Farley 2005). By January 2006, 2.17 billion mobile phones were in circulation, more than one for everyone on the planet (Srivastava 2008). Today, 90% of American adults have a cell phone. Phone ownership is fairly evenly distributed across gender, racial, education, and income strata. There are some slight age differences with nearly everyone from 18-49 having a cell phone (98% of 18-29-year-olds, 97% of 30-49-year-olds), 88% of 50-64-year-olds having one, but only three quarters of individuals over 65 have a cell phone. (Pew, 2014). In addition, the spread of mobile communication is a global phenomenon; 81% of Indians over 16% have a mobile phone. Ninety-eight percent of Russians, 84% of Brazilians, and 99% of South Koreans use a mobile device (Nielson 2013).

The first mobile phones were clunky devices that allowed users to place only voice calls. In 1993, Nokia became the first cell phone manufacturer to sell a model that supported short message service (SMS) known today as texting (Erickson 2012). By 2007, Americans were sending and receiving more text messages per month than phone calls (Erickson 2012). Today 81% of American mobile phone users text (Nielsen 2011). Teens send thousands of messages per month (Neilson 2011; Lenhart, Ling, Campbell, and Purcell 2010), but even messages sent by individuals over 55 has increased exponentially in the last few years (Neilson 2011). The heavy saturation of mobile devices has important social implications—not only is the mobile user available at almost any time, she or he can generally assume that the majority of their network contacts are also be perpetually available to them (Campbell, Ling, and Bayer 2014).

Although mobile users primarily use their phones for voice calls and text messages (Ling 2008; Katz 2008; Nielson 2013), the introduction of mobile devices capable of accessing the internet has opened up a wide range of application-based communication options. The iphone was introduced in 2007 (Erickson, 2012). Although devices that could connect to the internet and email applications such as Blackberry had existed prior to the iPhone, the introduction of the iPhone resulted in the mobile computing explosion. Now with iPhones or the later competing Android models, people can use their phones for voice calls, SMS, to send email, check SNS such as Facebook, keep tabs on their Twitter stream, play games (including games with other members of their social network), listen to music, watch videos, take pictures, and much, much more (Neilson 2011). Sixty-four percent of American adults now own a smartphone that can run mobile internet-based applications (Smith 2015). Although people primarily use their smartphones for text messaging (Neilson 2013b; Smith 2015), using a smartphone for internet applications is actually more popular than using the phone for voice calls (Smith 2015). Blends of text messaging functions and online applications are also available. For example, nine percent of smartphone users use the picture-based messaging service Snapchat (Duggan 2013).

Mobile devices have changed both how we use the phone as well as how we use computers and engage in computer-mediated networks (Ling and Donner 2014). Rather than reliance on a fairly stationary "desktop" computer to check in with our various network connections, we have the potential to interact with others synchronously, throughout our day (Campbell and Park 2008). In addition, smartphones can help reduce the digital divide by providing cheaper internet access to low income Americans. Although smartphones are more expensive than a regular cell phone, they are a cheaper way to get online than purchasing a home computer and broadband service. In addition, smartphones are person-based rather than place-based and thus are less likely to be affected by housing insecurities. Low-income Americans are more likely to be smartphone dependent, meaning that they own a smartphone but do not have home internet access (Smith 2015). Smartphones allow low-income Americans to enter communication networks that they may have previously been physically restricted from due to low broadband adoption.

The ubiquity of mobile phones has changed how people interact with network ties and others around them. Society is developing new social norms to regulate our use of mobile devices as well as how these devices blur the boundaries between public and private communication (Ishii 2006). Mobile devices may encourage people to turn away from interactions with physically co-present others in order engage in social presence with network connections through their phone. The heavier communication work demanded by maintaining the networks necessary to thrive in networked individualism may be tucked into the interstices of the day.

DEVELOPMENT OF MOBILE-RELATED NORMS

People, Not Places

As noted, the mobile phone is a fairly recent development in the history of mediated communication, but a development that has quickly become integrated into our daily lives (Ling 2008). It is no longer a novelty but rather an expected component of communication within our networks (Campbell et al. 2014). One of the most dramatic modifications the adaptation of mobile devices has on communication and networks is that mobile technology allows communicators to reach directly out to other network members instead of calling to a particular location hoping our desired co-communicator is there. (Campbell and Park 2007; Ling 2008; Ling and Donner 2014; Wellman 2001, 2002). Mobile "shifts the dynamics of connectivity from places to individuals" (Wellman 2001, 238).

The shift to place-to-place communication to person-to-person allows for more perceived privacy between the communicators. Communication does not have to be routed through phone lines that serve multiple individuals. Text messaging can be even more private (Pettigrew 2009; Srivastava 2009). Text messaging can occur surreptitiously. Others in the vicinity may not know texting is occurring and even if they are aware of text interactions around them, they can't eavesdrop on the conversation. Youth across the world take advantage of this privacy in order to communicate with their peer networks outside of the range of parental supervision (Ishii 2006; Kaseniemi and Rautianen 2002).

Politeness Norms in Public Places

The shift from person-to-person communication also means that as people move through public spaces their mobile devices are also present. In the past in order to physically make a phone call a person would likely need to be in the privacy of their home or office or using a phone like a pay phone that had a physical shield between the caller and co-present others. The introduction of mobile devices means that communicators can and do take phone calls or engage in text messaging almost anywhere. Phones now exist in places where they never were before and can be used at times that would be abnormal in the past (Ishii 2006; Palen, Salzman, and Youngs 2000). As mobile devices become more common social norms emerge to guide the appropriate use of mobile communication devices in public spaces.

Some spaces may be seen as more appropriate to engage in mobile communication than others. People may overlook a quick check-in in a hall or a longer conversation in a crowded, already noisy location. Other spaces such as a meeting, a class, or a cultural location, may be viewed as inappropriate spaces to subject others to half of a phone conversation (Wellman 2001). Different types of mobile communications may work better in public spaces as well. For example, one of Ling and Yttri's (2008) participants reported asking his wife to only send text messages to him during his commute because he did not wish to disturb other passengers with a phone call. Multiple studies have reported that students may choose to text in class *because* they see it as a polite alternative to taking a phone call (Ito and Okabe 2005; Ling and Yritti 2006; Kasesniemi and Rautianen 2006). However, these context norms are clearly not universal. People do in fact take calls at cultural events, meetings, and classes. Instructors may disagree with students about the perceived politeness of texting in class.

Clearly, norms for the use of mobile devices in public places are still being developed (Campbell and Park 2007). Early views on public cell phone usage held that public usage of a cell phone was rude or boorish. However, there is evidence that this view is changing (University of Michigan 2006). Older individuals (60-68) were far more likely to hold the attitude that "using a cell phone in public is a major irritation for other people" (74%) than younger people (32%) (University of Michigan 2006).

Norms will continue to adjust as even more members of society adopt mobile devices. Palen et al. (2000) found that people who did not have a mobile phone held strong negative opinions about mobile phone use in public. However, just two weeks after acquiring their own mobile phone, participants began to loosen up on their negative perceptions of public mobile phone use. For example, one participant who held very strong opinions about public mobile phone use, after acquiring a phone began to see the value of public phone calls and admitted to being less judgmental about how others used their phones in public. After 4-6 weeks most participants no longer cared what others thought of their mobile phone use despite their strong negative opinions prior to owning a phone (Palen et al. 2000).

As mobile communication becomes more common society will likely adapt to consider the use of mobile devices in public spaces a normative behavior. People will make choices regarding how they handle both their own mobile interruptions and the intrusions by others' devices. Those receiving mobile communication while in the physical presence of others can ignore the interruption, sincerely or half-heartedly apologize as they answer, or simply stop and take the call without explanation. Co-present others could choose to take offense at the interaction, nod and permit it, or try to continue the co-present interaction despite the phone call. (Ishii 2006).

A likely development is that people will engage in civil inattention in the presence of others who are using mobile devices. Civil inattention refers to actively not paying attention to a co-present individual (Goffman 1971). Goffman posed that individuals may engage in civil inattention when people either come into closer proximity than is socially normative (typically due to some structural issue, such as stools at a lunch counter or bar or riding an elevator with someone) or when people are involved in a communication event that does not concern others who are present (such as dining in a restaurant within hearing range of other patrons' conversations). Engaging in civil inattention may become a go-to strategy for audiences of mobile communication (Ling 2008). Those hearing the conversation may politely quasi-ignore it and expect that others will return the favor at some later time. We can see evidence of civil inattention when we consider encountering someone who is speaking into a hidden earpiece. At first we might give that individual direct attention as we try to determine what they are telling us. As we realize they are engaged in mobile communication we turn our gaze and attention elsewhere. At times people even apologize for giving attention in a scenario where civil inattention would be more appropriate.

TIGHTENING TIME AND NETWORKS

The ubiquity of mobile communication allows people to move throughout their day while weaving in communication activities with network members (Ito and Okabe 2005; Ling and Donner 2010). Mobile allows us to communicate with whom we specifically choose to communicate rather than others who just happen to be around. People can use their mobile devices to make very fine adjustments to their movements and timing in order to meet up with their chosen network members without sacrificing much time to waiting on others. In addition, for times when individuals are waiting or in between activities, mobile allows for us to quickly check in with chosen co-communicators.

Time

Micro-coordination

Mobile phones allow us to engage in micro-coordination with our network members (Ling 2008; Ling and Donner 2010). People can use their mobile devices to coordinate future interaction while moving through different spaces. As people with mobile devices are no longer dependent upon remaining in some physical location to receive communication, they can quickly adjust the timing and location of plans as needed (Campbell and Park 2008; Ling and Yttri 2002). Network members can coordinate as needed while moving toward a simultaneous location (Palen et al. 2000). Using mobile devices, network members can let other members know if they will be late or early. These notifications free others from having to spend time staying in one spot waiting for their connection (Ito and Okabe 2005).

Micro-coordination can also apply to the completion of everyday tasks. For example, the ability to ask a housemate to stop at the store during their commute can save the time it would take to make a second trip if the message only reached them upon arriving home (Ling and Donner 2010). In these ways communication through mobile devices allows time that would previously have been spent waiting on others or making additional trips for errands to be used for other activities.

Filling the Interstices

Mobile communication devices allow people to fill potentially idle moments with interactions through their device (Castells, Fernandez-Ardevol, and Sev 2004; Ling 2008). Dimmick, Feaster, and Hoplamazian (2011) called these small snippets of time that people can now fill with quick mobile communication, *interstices*. They argued that people use mobile to convert the *interstices* into communication time. Downtime while waiting for a bus or flight or attending a less than exciting meeting can be filled with checking email, sending texts, or scrolling through an SNS such as Facebook or Twitter. Texting can occur during situations where a phone call would be inappropriate (Ito and Okabe 2005). Couples are able to text each other during gaps in their day where other media (such as a voice call) would be inappropriate (Jiang and Hancock 2013). Through filling the interstices people may be able to make more productive use of their time in regard to pursuing relational and interactional goals.

Expanding Interactions

Mobile communication also allows us to extend our communication about co-present communication events (boyd, 2014). Easy access to our network allows for the coordination of plans and activities before communication events (Ling 2008). People can stay in contact between face-to-face meetings as well as organize and prepare for face-to-face interactions. Communication events can also expand beyond the co-present event as people use mobile communication to rehash their experiences and share stories and interpretations of the events they experienced together (boyd 2014).

People can also use mobile communication to expand interpersonal communication events to others who could not be present. Ito and Okabe called this the "augmented flesh meet" and described teenagers calling or texting other friends who were not present in order to share gossip or get opinions on some topic. Adults may do similar things by texting a question to a family member who is not present at a reunion or sending a query to a colleague who is unable to attend a meeting in person.

Network Choices

Mobile users are accessible at a personal rather than physical address—their mobile telephone number. People can become quite attached to their particular phone number and show a preference for taking their number with them when they change mobile carriers (Castells et al. 2004; Ling and Donner 2010). While it has been theorized that a person's identity becomes attached to his or her number, it is more likely that the preference for keeping one's number stable is tied to network rather than identity needs. People don't wish to change their number because changing it changes their "location" within the mobile network and requires their entire network to update their phones. People do "become" their number but do so in the background of the system—most phones have caller id so the number isn't particularly evident. However, when a person changes their number other network members' ability to reach that individual is lost.

Through the implementation of stable "locations" of network members within our mobile system, mobile communication reduces the impediments to finding and communicating with them. Although, on one hand, mobile communication allows for potential communication with a broad range of network ties, the stability provided by mobile devices also allows people to be selective regarding co-communicators. When everyone is perpetually accessible via mobile, communication choices are less tied to happenstances of time and place. Thus, we see that mobile communication is typically used to communicate with close friends and other strong tie relational members rather than weak tie network members (Ishii 2006).

The Presence of Strong Ties

Although mobile phones allow us to keep hundreds of contacts at our fingertips, most mobile users communicate on a regular basis with only a few individuals (Onnela, Saramäki, Hyvönen, Szabó, Lazer, Kaski, Kértesz, and Barabási 2007). Although mobile communication frees our communication from being locally bound, the people we communicate with most often on our mobiles are geographically close (Ling 2008). Mobile phones can reinforce strong ties by allowing network members to weave together co-present interaction and mediated distant exchanges into a coherent fabric of networked interaction (Kim, Kim, Park, and Rice 2007; Licoppe, 2004). Evidence suggests that mobile phones are indeed used primarily to communicate with strong ties such as family and friends more than weak ties (Castells et al. 2004; Ling 2008; Matsuda 2005; Miyata, Boase, Wellman, and Ikeda 2005).

The types of messages shared through mobile communication, particularly text messaging, are also particularly well suited for communication between strong ties. Communication via mobile phone is typically one-to-one communication (Onnela et al. 2007). Texting and calling via mobile phone is correlated with higher levels of integration into a close social network and greater amounts of social capital (Campbell and Kwak 2010). On the sender side, mobile systems allow us to access our support systems whenever and wherever they are needed (Wellman 2001; Ling and Donner 2010). People can use interstices to share little thoughts with close others throughout the day via text messaging (Licoppe 2004). These messages may signal an important relational message–social presence.

Mobile communication allows close friends, family, and romantic partners to feel a sense of each other's presence throughout their day. People may experience a sense of "persistent social space" between them that is created through the availability of constant communication (Ito and Okabe 2005). This feeling of presence through mobile communication has been noted by several scholars. Wei and Lo (2006) called it symbolic proximity. Ito and Okabe called it ambient accessibility. Through calls and text messages close ties can feel present to each other even when they are physically at a distance. Presence is facilitated by network members keeping each other up to date with plans, daily events, and messages that reaffirm strong bonds (Christensen, 2009). New applications such as Snapchat can help increase presence as co-communicators and/or their surrounding physical space become part of the message. Throughout the day, whenever we wish to reach out to a member of our network, we can use our mobile devices to initiate the connection immediately (Ling, 2008).

On the receiver side, there is a sense that calls and messages coming into one's mobile phone are more likely to be calls we want to receive. Because there is no directory of mobile phone numbers, with the exception of robocalls, most of the calls and texts we receive are from people and entities to whom we have personally revealed our mobile number (Licoppe and Heurtin 2001). However, it is possible for message senders to go too far in attempting to establish continuous social presence. Frequent texting in dating relationships is associated with both greater control over the romantic partner and the perception that one's partner is restricting their own freedom (Duran, Kelly, and Rotaru 2011). Social presence allows a romantic partner to feel that they are constantly engaged in their romantic partner's day but people may not necessarily want their partner to constantly check in on them (Hall and Baym 2011). Generally, couples are more successful when they coordinate their need to feel connected yet operate as individuals (Baxter and Montgomery 1998). Furthermore, if in the moment the mobile user would prefer not to communicate with that particular network member, mobile devices are designed to easily screen incoming communications.

Many text messages contain fairly mundane content (Ling and Donner 2010). Texting is considered fine for small check-ins, requests to pick something up, or sending cheerful messages. On the other hand, using mobile for "serious conversations" is generally frowned upon. For example, many people see using text messaging for break-ups as a terrible communication choice (McEwan 2013a; Taylor and Harper 2003). Text messaging is also seen as an inappropriate choice for conflict communication (McEwan 2013a).

Friends

Mobile users make most of their phone calls to a small number of close friends (Onnela et al. 2007). Mobile communication provides easily accessed opportunities for instrumental and expressive communication among peer group members (Campbell and Kwak 2010; Ling and Donner 2010). Close friends tend to integrate multiple media into their communication. Igarashi, Takai and Yoshida (2005) found that friends who communicated using both face-to-face and mobile channels were closer friends. Their finding is in line with Haythornthwaite's (2001) work on multiplexity which suggests the closer people are the more channels they use to communicate with each other.

Teenagers and young adults may be the most likely to use mobile communication specifically for friends. Japanese youth were more likely to use mobile media with friends than family (Ishii 2006). Furthermore, mobile communication helped young communicators stay in touch with individuals that they might otherwise have lost contact with such as friends from previous schools (Matsuda 2005). Without mobile devices, young people are fairly reliant on school structures and parental transportation to help them maintain social relationships. Mobile devices allow youth more choice in the relationships they are able to maintain.

Family

Cell phones can help people stay in greater contact with their family members (Wei and Lo 2006). Mobile communication can facilitate feelings of closeness between family members even when they are physically separated (Christensen 2009). Although mobile communication can connect people to a wide variety of family members, mobile communication is used particularly often between parents and children (Christensen 2009; Lenhart et al. 2010; Ling and Donner 2010).

About half of U.S. teenagers who have cell phones received their first phone at age 12 or 13 (Lenhart 2010). An overwhelming majority (98%) of parents of teens who had cell phones said that their child has the phone so that the parents can be in touch regardless of the teen's whereabouts. Ling (2008) argued that this hyperconnection between preteens or teens and their parents serves as a "vicarious umbilical cord" (14). However, both teens and parents perceived that the cell phone gives the teens *more* physical freedom because parents are willing to let their teenage children roam farther if they can quickly be in contact. (Lenhart et al. 2011). Teenagers do in fact use their phones to update their parents. Teens may call or text their parents several times during the day while their parents are at work (Christensen 2009). Mobile allows families to stay in contact throughout the day even in environments where the family unit is not physically together throughout the day due to school and work (Christensen 2009).

Children of divorced parents may get phones earlier than children in non-divorced families. Most likely this helps the children keep track of blended family arrangements as well as connect back to the non-resident parent. Using mobile phones also allows the ex-romantic partners to bypass each other and reach out directly to the child (Ling and Donner 2010)

Adult children also use mobile devices to stay in communication with their parents (Ling and Donner 2010). Young adult children today may have more regular contact with their parents than any other generation and this contact may be increasing. In 2002, Ling and Yttri found that the rate of contact between adult children and parents declined over time but in a 2014 study by Platt, Bourdeaux, and DiTunnariello (2014) most college students said they were still in daily contact with their parents via their mobile devices College students use mobile phones not only to stay in contact with their parents but also to access parental emotional and instrumental support (Chen and Katz 2009). Most of the contact between college-aged children and their parents occurs via text messaging rather than voice calls (Platt et al. 2014) which may mean young adults and their parents keep up a sense of presence in each other's daily lives that was unavailable to previous generations.

Romantic Partners

Finally, many mobile device users use the capabilities of their mobile phones to stay in contact with their romantic partner throughout the day. Mobile device users may be particularly likely to use texting rather than voice calls to stay in touch with romantic partners (Brody et al. 2009; Brody and Pena 2015; Houser et al. 2012; Jin and Pena 2010; Matsuda 2005). People can generally send more texts throughout the day than they can engage in voice calls. The increased frequency of communication between texting romantic partners may provide a greater sense of presence throughout the day (Petti-grew 2009). Romantic partners may engage in rituals such as texting each other when they go to bed or wake up in the morning (Taylor and Harper 2003). Texting may be perceived as useful early on in romantic relationships because the asynchronous nature of the medium may remove some of the awkwardness that occurs in face-to-face situations with early daters. Regard-less of the stage of the relationship mobile communication is used to help couples plan face-to-face meetings, exchange romantic messages when they are not physically together, and maintain a sense of presence in each other's lives (Ling 2008).

What partners text each other about may have an effect on the quality of their relationship. Texted relational maintenance messages have a positive effect on romantic relationships (Brody et al. 2009; Brody and Pena 2015;

McEwan and Horn 2015). Romantic partners are particularly likely to use texting for relational maintenance if they perceive texting as a synchronous communication channel (Brody et al. 2009). People who view texting as synchronous may see texting as an appropriate way to maintain presence in their romantic partner's day.

However, not all messages maintain relationships. Engaging in conflict and serious discussion has a small negative relationship with relational satisfaction as does sending multiple texts if one's romantic partner doesn't respond right away (Miller-Ott, Kelly, and Duran 2012). The frequency of texted messages that are not related to relational maintenance strategies may be negatively correlated with relational satisfaction (McEwan and Horn 2015). When partners are satisfied with how mobile phones are used in a relationship they experience greater overall relational satisfaction (Miller-Ott et al. 2012).

For long-distance romantic partners, interaction via text messaging may have mixed effects on the relationship. Long-distance couples can use text messaging to maintain their relationships. Partners might save and revisit texts as a symbol of their partner's love. However, this type of reminiscing may also lead to idealized views of their long-distance partner (Jiang and Hancock 2014). Mediated communication including text-based, asynchronous mobile messages can produce large idealizations, or unrealistic positive impressions, in romantic couples (Jiang and Hancock 2014; Stafford and Merolla 2007). Idealization can have a negative effect on long-distance relationships (Stafford and Merolla 2007). Partners who over-idealize their long-distance love may create hyperpersonal impressions of their romantic partner that cannot survive when partners transition to geographic proximity (Stafford and Merolla 2007).

CHALLENGES

Although mobile communication can provide benefits for close relationships, there are multiple societal and personal challenges related to the use of mobile devices. Mobile communication might allow people to be overly selective in their choice of interaction partners. Mobile devices may also make it more difficult to create communication boundaries which may lead to spillover between work and home life and exacerbate bullying situations.

Telecocooning and Absent Present

Mobile technology allows communicators to be increasingly selective regarding which network connections they wish to privilege (Campbell and Park 2007; Igarashi et al. 2005). People may use technology to maintain carefully selected homogeneous networks and avoid diverse ties. (Campbell and Kwak 2012; Ling 2008; Matsuda 2005). This process is called *telecocooning* (Kobayashi and Boase 2014). Heavy users of mobile media may interact with increasingly homogeneous network ties. A heavy focus on homogeneous ties has been associated with greater social cautiousness and less tolerance of differences in opinions in Japanese adolescents (Kobayashi and Boase 2014).

Telecocooning could also lead to people becoming absent in their co-present interactions. If people are filling the interstices with a focus on their phone and close others, they may miss out on chance meetings with more diverse connections. If mobile users choose to focus on connections via mobile phone rather than proximally close others, they may experience a phenomenon Gergen (2002) termed "absent present."

Being "absent present" is a situation where people are physically present but communicatively absent or "absent present" (Gergen 2002). People can shift in and out of their present reality by checking their phone (Turkle 2008). Co-present others may not even fully realize when people are "gone" into their phone. This type of multi-tasking may create communication problems both in the mediated and co-present interaction. In a study by Bowman and Pace (2014) individuals who were attempting to play a matching game while holding a conversation via a mobile voice call or texting did worse on both the cognitive task at hand (the game) and scored lower on variables related to the conversation such as communication satisfaction, comfort, and conversational recall than individuals who were only having a conversation. Being "absent present" can also take us away from connections that we might have formed through public interactions if we were not engrossed in messages from our mobile device (Gergen 2002).

Work-Life Spillover

Mobile communication allows us a greater amount of flexibility in being available for and responding to work-related communication. We can receive phone calls, texts, and even emails when we are away from our desk and even out of the office (Ling and Donner 2010). As mobile communication blurs the boundaries of space—allowing an individual to be contacted by work at home and by family at work—people may move between work and home communication at any time. However, this perpetual accessibility may be connected to work-family spillover (Chesley 2005). Spillover occurs when work intrudes into time set aside for family time and family concerns spill into work time. Mobile phone use is associated with negative forms of work spillover which lowers family satisfaction in a way that regular computer use does not (Chesley 2005). Turkle (2008) argued,

Adults are stressed by new responsibilities to keep up with email, the nagging sense of always being behind, the inability to take a vacation without bringing the office with them, and the feeling that they are being asked to respond immediately to situations at work, even when a wise response requires taking time for reflection, a time that is no longer available." (Turkle 2008, 127)

Spillover can also occur from home to work. For example, Ling (2008) recounted a story of a woman answering a phone call from her daughter in a meeting. Turkle (2008) noted that when phone calls come in from family members it recalls to our coworkers that we have roles outside of our professional identity. These reminders of family status and intrusions from home life may have a disproportionate impact on women who must work harder in general to maintain a professional identity (Cheney and Ashcraft 2007; Davies 1996).

Spillover may also be an issue for children and teens experiencing bullying at school. Access to mobile communication means that bullying communication can be delivered to the victim at any time. Prior to mobile communication, the home might have served as a refuge from upsetting interactions at school. However, given the amount that teens are connected to their mobile devices (Lenhart et al. 2010), mobile allows bullying communication to be delivered to the victim at anytime, anywhere (Ling and Donner 2010).

CONCLUSION

Mobile communication allows people the ability to more deftly manage their network communication by allowing people to use the interstices of their days to complete the communication work that is needed to handle maintaining varied network ties. Communication through mobile devices may be particularly useful for engaging with strong ties and maintaining a sense of presence with friends and loved ones even when physically removed. Yet, while mobile communication can bring us closer to strong ties it may also pull people away from possible weak tie connections or new connections people might make through happenstance. In addition, the always-available nature of mobile communication can make it difficult to remove the self from connections that we would prefer not to be in contact with all of the time such as work or bullies.

Chapter Eleven

Waypoints

Communication technology holds much promise for facilitating greater transparency, greater access to diversity and increased connectivity with networks and network ties. Early adopters of communication technology often trumpeted how technology might facilitate positive social change by flattening hierarchies (Sproull and Kiesler 1992), disseminating information (Castells 2001), providing new avenues for social support (Ridings and Gefen 2004), and offering new ways of creating network ties (Rainie and Wellman 2012). Promoters of the transformative possibilities of communication technology argued technology would be no less than disruptive (Klosowski 2014). Flashy advertisements promise seamless integration of mediated communication into our daily activities. The advent of communication technology was posited as having the potential to shake up many of the communication processes related to interpersonal and societal communication.

Although new technologies are exciting, the potential for disruption by communication technology also inspires anxiety among citizens and pundit alike. Concern has been expressed that technology might be ruining romance (Gray 2012; Davis 2013), sex (Adams 2014), our morals (The Telegraph 2009), our cognitive abilities (Carr 2010), our mental health (Greenfield 2012), our lives (Newman 2013) and the world (Confino 2013). These technology-elated anxieties are not new. McLuhan (1964) argued that each previous incarnation of advancement in communication technology ushered in a new age of anxiety. For example, McLuhan noted that "with the telegraph, man had initiated that outering or extension of his central nervous system that is now approaching an extension of consciousness with satellite broadcasting" (252).

The anxiety related to extending our consciousness and social awareness far beyond our tactile self through the introduction of internet-based communication technology is evident in multiple books both for academic and general audiences (Bauerlein 2009; Carr 2011; Turkle 2011; Perlow 2012). Article after article beseeches the readers to "put down the smartphone," "unplug" and "really" connect with others (Bratskeir 2013; Neighmond 2014; Stern 2012). The assumption made in these treatises is that to communicate in the same physical space is to engage in "real" life and is more valuable than mediated communication.

Our collective experience of technology is most likely somewhere between the euphoria and the anxiety. Communication technology does connect us in new ways, but as noted throughout this book these paths may be challenging to navigate. Our adoption of and adaptation to new technologies represents a nuanced dance between rigidity and flexibility, managing close and weak ties, reaching out to others, engaging in reflections of ourselves, and understanding our new reality. A text such as this one can only represent an intermediate location between extant research and future development—a waypoint in our navigation of technologically networked societies. Although technology changes our communication world rapidly the synthesis of previous research can help provide an understanding of where we have been and guidance on the path to the future. This chapter outlines a series of waypoints, coordinates scholars have developed understanding about, along our societal journey into technologically networked individualism.

VIRTUAL IS REAL

From the inception of widespread online communication, there has been a tendency to label interaction that occurs online as "fake" and interaction that occurs offline as "real" (Jurgenson 2012). Even today people will query why others will want to engage in dating or friendships or conversations that are "fake." However, the separation between real and online is a spurious division (Ellison 2013; Jurgenson 2012). Although the term virtual is often used (indeed it is used in this very text) as a synonym for online, the term is not synonymous with a lack of truth or reality. Rather, to be virtual can speak to a lack of physicality, or something carried out via the means of computing (New Oxford Dictionary 2010). Neither a lack of physical presence nor the use of a computer makes a particular communication less real. Online communication is just as real as any communication can be considered real in that it involves human senders and receivers, engenders feelings and reactions, and leads to relationship development, maintenance, and deterioration (Baym 2010; Ellison et al. 2011; Ledbetter 2009; McEwan et al. 2014; McKenna et al. 2002; Parks and Floyd 1996; Parks and Roberts 1998; Tufekci 2012; Walther 1992). Networks articulated by online social network sites are real connections; in fact these connections might even be less ephemeral than weak tie connections that are maintained only through offline channels. Relationships formed by online daters are real relationships that sometimes lead to real marriages and real children (Smith 2013). Support offered through online means can have real effects (High and Dillard 2012). Protests with real implications for political entities are organized via hashtags and mesh networks (Hu 2014).

FIXED AND FLEXED

The advent of communication technologies has often been heralded as signaling the arrival of greater flexibility in the creation of networked ties (Rainie and Wellman 2012). Indeed this is the very argument on which networked individualism rests. Communication technology introduces flexibility into our networks through the reduced influence of time, geographic location, and local community on our ability to reach out to a vast potentiality of network connections. People can maintain relationships with distant others through social network sites, build communities of practice through micro-blogging, and look for new connections and diverse forms of support through joining online communities. If local networks do not suit for some reason, online communication allows people to create networks of their own choosing.

At the same time, some types of communication technology can actually introduce rigidity into our social relationships and performances. For example, our use of SNS may produce increased fixedness within our networks. For example, prior to the advent of SNS, people had the ability to leave particular networks behind during geographic relocations. High school friends would fade away to be replaced by college pals. Those who might view each other's youthful indiscretions might not be around to disclose these indiscretions to a young professional's new career-based network. Now, SNS users keep their network connections with them as they move from one geographic location to the next. Facebook accounts become a holding place for a variety of ties from different social and temporal spaces. While fixed networks can help build social capital (Ellison et al. 2007), network rigidity may also make the reinvention and growth of self over time more difficult to communicate and perhaps more difficult to experience.

In other evidence of rigidity, identity performances online are more persistent, replicable, and scalable (boyd, 2011). The communication choices that we make to portray our image online must be carefully selected to meet standards of appropriateness in wider and more varied audiences. Although the flexible spaces of the internet offer the possibility of rich identity play and experimentation, when identity performances are for fixed networks we may find ourselves editing, scrubbing, and creating identities that are compressed versions of ourselves in order to meet the simultaneous gazes of friends, acquaintances, family, colleagues, and employers (Child et al. 2011; McEwan and Mease 2012).

The persistence of online identity performance can also bleed into our concerns about offline identity representations (McEwan and Mease 2012). The ubiquity of photography through cell phone cameras means that almost any moment can be captured. Ephemeral moments can then become immortalized through sharing on social sites. Friends may photograph each other at social events and choose to post pictures that are less than flattering. Individuals making a quick run to the store in pajama pants may find that their casual sartorial choice has been sent to a widely viewed cruel humor site (People of Wal-mart, n.d.). People in the background of pictures may appear over and over in others' newsfeeds as pictures are shared, commented on, and discussed.

Both flexible and fixed network spaces have their advantages and disadvantages. In addition, flexibility and fixedness represent two ends of a continuum and online (and offline) spaces can be more or less fixed or flexible). However, these terms allow people to move beyond false dichotomies of online/offline and real/fake in their understanding of how internet technologies work. Doing so can help further understanding of how norms and outcomes in particular online spaces vary.

STRONG TIES, WEAK TIES

There is no question in the literature that people can and do engage in relational communication via CMC. Yet, both scholars and laypeople raise ongoing concerns that online communication lacks the richness of face-to-face communication and might lead to shallower, more brittle social relationships (Kraut, Patterson, Lundmark, Kiesler, Mukophadhyay, and Scherlis 1998; Turkle, 2011). As an example Baym (2010) reviewed several Dear Abby and Dear Ann letters wherein the writers expressed fears that connections on the internet would make people less likely to want to communicate with coworkers and family.

The concern often seems to be that if we use communication channels that are geared toward lightweight communication and the maintenance of weak ties, we run the risk of weakening our close ties. Such a phenomenon would be concerning for several reasons. Weak tie networks may be less able to provide person-centered social support. It may be more difficult to convert perceived social support from weak tie networks into instrumental support. Weak ties may not provide the care and affection that people need to thrive (Floyd 2006). However, just because we use mediated communication for weak ties does not mean that using these forms of communication with strong ties will weaken those ties. Strong ties tend to engage in multiplexity, meaning that they use a variety of media including various communication technologies and face-to-face communication to interact. So while it might be true that most communication on SNS is less intimate (most likely due to the need to perform appropriately for audiences across contexts), this does not mean that communicating with strong ties via SNS will make our relationship with that individual less intimate because it is likely that we are communicating with those ties in a variety of other ways.

Furthermore, although several venues for online communication, including SNS and online communities, currently engender weak tie connections that can be difficult to convert to close tie connections this does not mean that this will be the case forever. Early research on internet communication suggested that the internet would have an overall negative impact on social relationships (Kraut et al. 1998; Nie 2001; McPherson et al. 2006). However, this assumption was based in part on the nature of the early adopters. Early adopters did tend to be individuals who were lonelier and had less strong tie connections in their pre-internet networks. As more people moved into online communication environments, the internet has been shown to facilitate social communication more than it detracts from the phenomenon (Kraut et al. 2002). Humans may yet find better and better ways to harness weak ties as well as create lasting and more meaningful relationships via CMC.

In addition, it should be remembered that strong ties do not spring from the earth fully formed. With the exception of immediate family members, most strong ties become so because the tie has been cultivated from the network of weak ties. Greater access to weak ties increases the possibilities of one's future close tie network. Not all weak ties will become strong ties, but a greater number of weak ties provide greater choice and flexibility regarding which weak tie network connections do become strong ties.

Weak ties also are beneficial components of one's social network. Not every tie can be a strong, close one. Weak ties allow for the diffusion of information and greater access to network resources. Weak ties can provide diversity of information and increase the amount of perceived support a person feels they have access to.

Communication technology can facilitate both weak and strong ties. Different rules and norms for different channels have begun to emerge (Bryant and Marmo 2012; Grelhesl and Punyanunt-Carter 2012; McEwan 2013a; McLaughlin and Vitak 2012; Park et al. 2009; Raacke and Bonds-Raacke 2008). We begin to see that different types of media facilitate different types of ties. In part this may be due to the particular affordances of a medium; in part this may be due to the emergent norms of a medium.

Media that promote openness, visibility of network connections, the simultaneous dissemination of messages to multiple and varied segments of one's network appear to promote weak ties. Social network sites may engender context collapse (Marwick and boyd 2011), but as people learn to use them they learn to curate their messages in order to create messages that are appropriate for a wide swath of contexts (Hogan 2010; McEwan and Mease 2012). On the other hand, the more privacy a medium affords, the more likely that medium is to be used for strong tie communication. This effect can be seen in how people use the most common form of mobile communication, texting. Although it is true that mobile communication can be stored, passed on, and replicated, texting still feels very private to texters. The communication is sent directly from person to person and the message can be read silently. This allows close relational partners to send each other intimate, caring, and affectionate messages throughout the day. In addition, because people are rarely without their mobile phone they can build a sense of presence with each other by sending frequent messages and being perpetually available for contact.

Of course, if people use technology to shift their concentration to strong ties and similar others, they may risk telecocooning (Kobayashi and Boase 2014) and may miss the potential advantages of communicating with more diverse weak tie connections. The strategy that is likely most beneficial for individuals and networks is a blend of weak tie and strong tie communication. Yes, there is a finite amount of time for communication, and yes, online communication can pull people away from co-present others, but people show a remarkable ability to weave online and offline communication through their daily life. A person could quickly send a text to a romantic partner, then like a friend's Facebook comment, while waiting for a different friend to show up at a face-to-face meeting for coffee. If anything, technology appears to assist us in moving through and managing a multiverse of communicative ties rather than restricting us to weak ties or turning our close tie relationships into more shallow connections.

EXPANDING TIME

Another concern was that more online communication with weak ties would necessarily take people away from close relationships because the amount of time available to communicate with others is a finite resource (McPherson et al. 2006). Time, is of course, a finite resource, but although online communication has pulled away from face-to-face interactions in some ways, communicators have been able to use communication technology to expand the amount of time available for communication activities. For one, we can engage in communication in the interstices. Communicators can insert interpersonal communication into spaces that previously might have been lost to communication activities. Time between meetings, riding buses, and waiting for others can now be used to check in with networks and send messages.

Communication can also be quicker as we engage by sending short text-based messages back and forth. No longer do we need to attempt to reach out, contact someone, and set up an appointment for when we will engage in communication. Time is saved from not having to engage in pre-communication communication.

Some venues of communication may replace previous activities but it may be that the activity that they displace is entertainment—not interpersonal communication. For example, the amount of time Americans spend watching television is shrinking while overall media consumption grows (Nielsen 2013, 2014). Social network sites serve co-functions of facilitating interpersonal connection and providing entertainment. When we entertain ourselves through scrolling through our social media feeds, we also may be connecting with others or storing information that can reduce uncertainty and be put to use in future interactions.

A MIRROR TO OURSELVES

Although communicating with weak ties via online communication has the potential to expand our experiences through connections with weak ties, there is also the concern that communicating via the internet may be more like holding up a mirror to ourselves rather than conversing with a fully realized, separate other. The hyperpersonal model points to this concern in recognizing that the people communicating via CMC may experience idealized perceptions of the messages of others. In the reduced cue environment of CMC interactions, receivers interpret the communications of their co-interactants in ways that are favorable to receivers' worldview (Walther 1996). In particular, receivers may interpret senders as being similar others (Walther 1996). Processes such as solipsistic interjection may enhance receivers' perceptions of the similarity of senders in CMC interactions. Solipsistic interjection may allow people to feel closer to co-communicators in reduced cue environments, particularly reduced cue environments that lack audio because they feel closer to others when they read the co-communicator's messages in their own voice. Not only does "hearing" a CMC co-interactant in one's own voice create feelings of closeness, but the way one behaves toward that co-communicator has a strong influence on our impressions of that person. Walther and Tong (2014) found that when people communicated disagreement or agreement through CMC they ended up disliking or liking their CMC partner based on their own rather than their partner's behavior. Computer-mediated communication processes and reduced cue environments may drive communicators to imagine or invent characteristics for their CMC partner that have more to do with themselves than the communication or characteristics of their partner.

Online communication may not meet the promises of expanding our perspectives and world views if we find ourselves engaged primarily in communication with ourselves when engaging with online co-communicators. People may walk away from these interactions feeling intense connections and a sense that others agree with their particular viewpoints because they have connected more strongly with their sense of self than the human being on the other side of the mediated interaction.

WE MOVE FORWARD

Understanding the processes involved in online communication in its entirety is a daunting prospect. Technologies change quickly and the effect of technology on human interaction is varied. However, while communication technologies are sure to adapt, evolve, and change over time—barring some catastrophic event—we will not be returning to the days before the internet. Thus, academics, pundits, and the general public must move away from either/or, good/bad style arguments in order to really delve into how people adapt technology to their interpersonal communication purposes. We must also move from comparing online and offline communication. People do not communicate either only online or only offline (Ellison 2013). Neither is online communication necessarily purely good or purely bad for communication, relationships, society, or individuals. People have developed a multiplex of communication strategies in order to maintain network connections of varying degrees of closeness. The processes underlying message production and relational development mesh with the affordances of various mediated channels to influence our networked society.

This is not to say that a particular medium has no effect. As McLuhan (1964) argued, to say how communicators use media as the only driver of media effects, "is the numb stance of the technological idiot" (18). The structure of media shapes the communication choices that we make and different packages of affordances can facilitate different types of communicative interactions. On the other hand communicative decisions also drive how we engage with communication technology. People develop rules and norms that drive competence using particular types of technology. These processes will drive our communication and our society to new edges and new frontiers. We will not be able to turn back the clock on innovations that have already occurred nor would focusing on preventing new innovation prove anything but futile. Rather, we must focus our attention on better understanding communication technology and how it influences people and society in order to better navigate the challenges that can arise from the use of communication technologies. Despite the daunting nature of the task of studying and understanding the nature of communication technology, continuing to pursue questions related to the recursive influences between technology, communication, and society is a worthy and necessary goal.

Bibliography

Adams, Tim. 2014. "Not tonight, darling: why is Britain having less sex?" The Guardian. September 28. Accessed October 1, 2014. http://www.theguardian.com/lifeandstyle/2014/sep/28/-sp-not-tonight-darling-why-britain-having-less-sex.

Adams, Rebecca G. 1998. "The Demise of Territorial Determinism: Online Friendships." In *Placing Friendship In Context,* edited by Rebecca G. Adams and Graham Allen, 153-182. Cambridge, UK: Cambridge University Press.

Adelman, Mara B., Mac R. Parks, Mac R., and Terrance L. Albrecht. 1987. "Beyond Close Relationships: Support in Weak Ties." In *Communicating Social Support,* edited by Terrance L. Albrecht and Mara B. Adelman, 126 -147. Newbury Park, CA: Sage.

Agneessens, Filip, Hans Waege, and John Lievens. 2006. "Diversity in Social Support by Role Relations: A Typology." *Social Networks* 28: 427-441. doi:10.1016/j.socnet.2005.10.001.

Akbulut, Yavuz, and Selim Günüç. 2012. "Perceived Social Support and Facebook Use Among Adolescents." *International Journal of CyberBehavior, Psychology, and Learning* 2: 30-41. doi: 10.4018/ijcbpl.2012010101.

Albrecht, Terrance, and Mara B. Adelman. 1987. "Communication Networks as Structures of Social Support." In *Communicating Social Support,* edited by Terrance L. Albrecht and Mara B. Adelman, 40 -60. Newbury Park, CA: Sage.

Altheide, David L. 2000. "Identity and the Definition of the Situation in a Mass-Mediated Context. *Symbolic Interaction* 23:1-27. doi: 10.1525/si.2000.23.1.1.

Altman, Irwin, and Dalmus Taylor. 1973. *Social Penetration: The Development of Interpersonal Relationships.* New York: Holt, Rinehart, and Winston.

Anderson, Benedict. 1991. *Imagined Communities: Reflections on the Origin and Spread of Nationalism.* Revised Edition. London and New York: Verso.

Antheunis, Marjolijn L., and Alexander P. Schouten. 2011. "The Effects of Other-generated and System-Generated Cues on Adolescents' Perceived Attractiveness on Social Network Sites." *Journal of Computer-Mediated Communication* 16:391-406. doi: 10.1111/j.1083-6101.2011.01545.x.

Antonnuci, Toni C. 1990. "Social Supports and Social Relationships." In *Handbook of Aging and the Social Sciences* edited by Robert H. Binstock and Linka K. George, 205-226. San Diego, CA: Academic Press.

Applegate, James L. (1980). Person- and position-centered teacher communication in a day care center: A case study triangulating interview and naturalistic methods. *Studies in Symbolic Interaction* 3:59-96.

Appiah, Kwame A. 2006. *Cosmopolitanism: Ethics in a World of Strangers.* New York: Norton.

Arguello, Jamie, Brian S. Butler, Elisabeth Joyce, Robert Kraut, Kimberley S. Ling, and Xiaoqing Wang. 2006. "Talk to Me: Foundation for Successful Individual-Group Interactions in Online Communities." Proceedings of the SIGCHI Conference on Human Factors in Computing Systems, Montreal Quebec, Canada. April 22-28.

Asch Solomon E. 1956. "Studies of Independence and Conformity. A Minority of One Against a Unanimous Majority. *Psychological Monograph, 70.*

Bagozzi, Richard P., and Utpal M. Dholakia. 2002 "Intentional Social Actions in Virtual Communities." *Journal of Interactive Marketing* 16 2:2-21. doi:10.1002/dir.10006.

Bales, Robert F. 1950. *Interaction Process Analysis: A Method for the Study of Small Groups.* Cambridge, MA: Addison-Wesley.

Barak, Azy, Meyran Boniel-Nissim, and John Suler 2008. "Fostering Empowerment in Online Support Groups." *Computers in Human Behavior* 24:1867-1883. doi: 10.1016/j.chb.2008.02.004.

Barak, Azy, and Michel Dolev-Cohen. 2006. "Does Activity Level in Online Support Groups for Distressed Adolescents Determine Emotional Relief." *Counselling and Psychotherapy Research* 6:186–190. doi:10.1080/14733140600848203.

Bargh, John A., Katelyn Y.A. McKenna, and Grainne M. Fitzsimons. 2002. "Can You See the Real Me? Activation and Expression of the 'True Self' on the Internet." *Journal of Social Issues* 58:33-48. doi:10.1111/1540-4560.00247.

Bargh, John A., and Katelyn Y. A. McKenna. 2009. "The Internet and Social Life." *Annual Review of Psychology* 55:573-590. doi: 10.1146/annurev.psych.55.090902.141922.

Bauerlein, Mark. 2009. *The Dumbest Generation: How the Digital Age Stupefies Young Americans and Jeopardizes our Future (or, Don't Trust Anyone Under 30).* New York: Penguin.

Baxter, Leslie A., and Barbara M. Montgomery. 1998. A Guide to Dialectical Approaches to Studying Personal Relationships. In *Dialectical Approaches to Studying Personal Relationships,* edited by Barbara M. Montgomery and Leslie A. Baxter, 1-15. New York: Psychology Press.

Baym, Nancy. 2010. *Personal Connections in the Digital Age.* Cambridge: Polity Press.

Baym, Nancy, Yan Bing Zhang, Adrienne Kunkel, Andrew Ledbetter, and Mei-Chen Lin. 2007. "Relational Quality and Media Use in Interpersonal Relationships." *New Media & Society* 5:735-752. doi:10.1177/1461444807080339.

Beck, Ulrich. 2006. *Cosmopolitan Vision.* Polity.

Beck, Ulrich, and Nathan Sznaider. 2006. "Unpacking Cosmopolitanism for the Social Sciences: A Research Agenda." *The British Journal of Sociology* 57 1:1-23. doi: 10.1111/j.1468-4446.2006.00091.x.

Bell, Robert A., Nancy Buerkel-Rothfuss, and Kevin Gore. 1987. "Did You Bring the Yarmulke for the Cabbage Patch Kid?" The Idiomatic Communication of Young Lovers." *Human Communication Research* 14:47-67. doi:10.1111/j.1468-2958.1987.tb00121.x.

Bell, Robert and Jonathan Healey. 1992. "Idiomatic Communication and Interpersonal Solidarity in Friends' Relational Cultures." *Human Communication Research* 18:307-335. doi: 10.1111/j.1468-2958.1992.tb00555.x.

Berger, Charles R., and Richard J. Calabrese. 1975. "Some Explanations in Initial Interaction and Beyond: Toward a Developmental Theory of Interpersonal Communication." *Human Communication Research* 1:99–112. doi:10.1111/j.1468-2958.1975.tb00258.x.

Bernstein, Michael S., Eytan Bakshy, Moira Burke, and Brian Karrer. 2013. "Quantifying the Invisible Audience on Social Networks." *CHI2013,* Paris, France. doi:10.1145/2470654.2470658.

Bevan, Jennifer L., Pei-Chern Ang, and James B. Fearns. 2014. "Being Unfriended on Facebook: An Application of Expectancy Violation Theory." *Computers in Human Behavior* 33:171-178. doi: 10.1016/j.chb.2014.01.029.

Bimber, Bruce. 2000. "Measuring the Gender Gap on the Internet." *Social Science Quarterly* 81:868-879.

Bindley, Katherine 2011. "When Children Text All Day, What Happens to Their Social Skills?" Accessed December 9. http://www.huffingtonpost.com/2011/12/09/children-texting-technology-social-skills_n_1137570.html.

Bine, Anne-Sophie 2013. "Social Media is Redefining 'Depression.'" October 28. Accessed January 30 2015. http://www.theatlantic.com/health/archive/2013/10/social-media-is-redefining-depression/280818/.

Blanchard, Anita, and Tom Horan. 1998 "Virtual Communities and Social Capital." *Social Science Computer Review* 16:293-297. doi:0.1177/089443939801600306.

Bliezner, Rosemary, and Rebecca G. Adams. 1992. *Adult Friendship.* Sage: Newbury Park, CA.

Bolger, Niall, Adam Zuckerman, and Ronald C. Kessler. 2000. "Invisible Support and Adjustment to Stress." *Journal of Personality and Social Psychology* 79: 953-961. doi:10.1037//0022-3514.79.6.953.

Bond, Rod and Peter B. Smith. 1996. "Culture and Conformity: A Meta-Analysis of Studies Using Asch's (1952b, 1956) Line Judgment Task." *Psychological Bulletin,* 119:111-137.

Boneva, Bonka, and Robert Kraut (2002). "Email, Gender, and Personal Relationships." In *The Internet in Everyday Life,* edited by Barry Wellman and Caroline Haythornthwaite, 372-403. Malden, MA: Blackwell.

Bowman, Jonathan M., and Roger C. Pace. 2014. "Dual-Tasking Effects on Outcomes of Mobile Communication Technologies." *Communication Research Reports* 31:221-231. doi: 10.1080/08824096.2014.907149.

boyd, danah. 2009. "Social Media is Here to Stay. Now What?" Accessed February 20, 2012. http://www.danah.org/papers/talks/MSRTechFest2009.html.

boyd, danah. 2011. "Social Network Sites as Networked Publics: Affordances, Dynamics, and Implications." In *A Networked Self: Identity, Community, and Culture on Social Network Sites,* edited by Zisi Papacharissi, 39-58. New York: Routledge.

boyd, danah. 2014. *It's Complicated: The Social Lives of Networked Teens.* Yale University Press. New Haven, CT.

boyd, danah, and Nicole B. Ellison. 2007. "Social Network Sites: Definition, History, and Scholarship." *Journal of Computer-Mediated Communication* 13: doi: 10.1111/j.1083-6101.2007.00393.x.

Bonetti, Luigi, Marilyn Anne Campbell, and Linda Gilmore. 2010. "The Relationship of Loneliness and Social Anxiety with Children's and Adolescents Online Communication." *Cyberpscyhology, Behavior, and Social Networking* 13:279-285. 2010. doi:10.1089/cyber.2009.0215.

Bourdieu, Pierre. 1986. "The Forms of Capital." In *Handbook of Theory and Research for the Sociology of Education,* edited by J. G. Richardson, 241-248. New York: Greenwood Press.

Braithwaite, Dawn O., Vincent R. Waldron, and Jerry Finn. 1999. "Communication of Social Support in Computer-Mediated Groups for People with Disabilities." *Health Communication* 11: 123-151. doi:10.1207/s15327027hc1102_2.

Brandtweiner, Roman, Elisabeth Donat, and Johann Kerschbaum. "How to Become a Sophisticated User: A Two-Dimensional Approach to E-literacy." *New Media and Society* 12:813-833. doi:10.1177/1461444809349577.

Bratskeir, Kate. 2013. "Unplug from technology: 19 ways to spend time off the grid." February 27. The Huffington Post. http://www.huffingtonpost.com/2013/02/27/unplug-from-technology_n_2762116.html

Brody, Nicholas, Charee M Mooney, Stacy A. Westerman, and Patrick McDonald. 2009. "lts gt 2gthr l8r: Text Messaging as a Relational Maintenance Tool." *Kentucky Journal of Communication* 28:109–127.

Brody, Nicholas and Jorge Pena 2015. "Equity, Relational Maintenance, and Linguistic Features of Text Messaging. *Computers in Human Behavior* 49:499-506. doi: 10.1016/j.chb.2015.03.037

Brodken, Jon 2012. "119 Million Americans Lack Broadband Internet." FCC Reports.

Bryant, Erin M., and Jennifer Marmo. 2010. "Relational Maintenance Strategies on Facebook." *The Kentucky Journal of Communication.* http://kycommunication.com/jenniferpdf/Bryant.pdf

Bryant, Erin M., and Jennifer Marmo. 2012. "The Rules of Facebook Friendship: A Two-Stage Examination of Interaction Rules in Close, Casual, and Acquaintance Friendships." *Journal of Social and Personal Relationships* 29:1013-1035. doi: 10.1177/0265407512443616.

Bryant, Erin M., Jennifer Marmo, and Artemio Ramirez, Jr. 2011. A Functional Approach to Social Networking Sites. In *Computer- Mediated Communication in Personal Relationships,* edited by Kevin B. Wright and Lynne M. Webb, 3-20. New York : Peter Lang.

Brubaker, Jed R., Funda Kivran-Swaine, Lee Taber, and Gillian R. Hayes. 2012. "The Language of Bereavement and Distress in Social Media." Proceedings of the Sixth Annual International Conference on Weblogs and Social Media, Palo Alto, California, June 4-7.

Burke, Moira, Robert Kraut, and Cameron Marlow. 2011. "Social Capital on Facebook: Differentiating Uses and Users." Proceedings of the SIGCHI Conference on Human Factors in Computing Systems, Vancouver, British Columbia, May 7-12. doi: 10.1145/1978942.1979023.

Burke, Moira, Robert Kraut, and Diane Williams. 2010. "Social use of Computer-Mediated Communication by Adults on the Autism Spectrum." Proceedings of the 2010 ACM Conference on Computer Supported Cooperative Work, Savannah, Georgia, February 6-10.

Burleson, Brant, R. 1987. "Cognitive Complexity." In *Personality and Interpersonal Communication* edited by James C. McCroskey and John A. Daly. 305-349. Newbury Park, CA: Sage.

Burleson, Brant R. 2003. "Emotional support skill." In *Handbook of Communication and Social Interaction Skills* edited by John O. Greene and Brant R. Burleson. 551-594. Mahwah, NJ: Lawrence Erlbaum.

Burleson, Brant R. 2008. "What Counts as Effective Emotional Support?: Explorations of Individual and Situational Differences." In *Studies in Applied Interpersonal Communication* edited by Michael T. Motley, 207-228. Thousand Oaks, CA: Sage.

Burleson, Brant. R. 2010. "Explaining Recipient Responses To Supportive Messages: Development and Tests of a Dual-Process Theory. In *New Directions in Interpersonal Communication Research* edited by Sandi W. Smith and Steven R. Wilson, 159-179. Thousand Oaks, CA: Sage.

Burleson, Brant R., and Erina MacGeorge. 2002. "Supportive Communication." In *Handbook of Interpersonal Communication* (3rd Ed.) edited by Mark L. Knapp and John A. Daly, 374-424. Thousand Oaks, CA: Sage.

Burt, Ronald. 1995. *Structural Holes: The Social Structure of Competition.* Cambridge. MA: Harvard University Press.

Calhoun, Craig J. 2002. "The Class Consciousness of Frequent Travelers: Toward a Critique of Actually Existing Cosmopolitanism." *The South Atlantic Quarterly* 101 4: 869-897. doi: 10.1215/00382876-101-4-869.

Canary, Daniel J., and Laura Stafford. 1993. "Preservation of Relational Characteristics: Maintenance Strategies, Equity, and Locus of Control." In *Interpersonal Communication: Evolving Interpersonal Relationships,* edited by Pamela J. Kalbfleisch, 237-259. Hillsdale, NJ: Lawrence Erlbaum.

Canary, Daniel J., and Laura Stafford. 1994. "Maintaining Relationships Through Strategic and Routine Interaction. In *Communication and Relational Maintenance,* edited by Daniel J. Canary and Laura Stafford, 3-21. San Diego, CA: Academic Press.

Canary, Daniel J., Laura Stafford, Kimberley S. Hause, and Lisa A. Wallace. 1993. "An Inductive Analysis of Relational Maintenance Strategies: Comparisons among Lovers, Relatives, Friends, and Others." *Communication Research Reports* 10:5-14. doi: 10.1080/08824099309359913.

Canary, Daniel J., Laura Stafford, Beth A. Semic. 2002. "A Panel Study of the Associations between Maintenance Strategies and Relational Characteristics." *Journal of Marriage and the Family* 64:395-406. doi: 10.1111/j.1741-3737.2002.00395.x.

Campbell, Scott W., and Nojin Kwak. 2010. "Mobile Communication and Social Capital: An Analysis of Geographically Differentiated Usage Patterns." *New Media and Society* 12:435-451. doi: 10.1177/1461444809343307.

Campbell, Scott W., Rich Ling, and Joesph B. Bayer. 2014. "The Structural Transformation of Mobile Communication: Implications for Self and Society." In *Media and Social Life,* edited by Mary Beth Oliver and Arthur A. Raney, 176-196. New York: Routledge.

Campbell, Soctt and Michael R. Neer. 2001. "The Relationship of Communication Apprehension and Interaction Involvement to Perceptions of Computer-Mediated Communication." *Communication Research Reports* 18:391-398. doi: 10.1080/08824090109384820.

Campbell, Scott and Yong Jin Park. 2008. "Social Implications of Mobile Telephony." *Sociological Compass* 2:371-387. doi: 10.1111/j.1751-9020.2007.00080.x.

Caplan, Scott E. 2005. "A Social Skill Account of Problematic Internet Use." *Journal of Communication* 55:721-736. doi:10.1111/j.1460-2466.2005.tb03019.x.

Carey, John. 1980. "Paralanguage in Computer Mediated Communication." Proceedings of the 18th annual meeting of the Association for Computational Linguistics and Parasession on Topics in Interactive Discourse, (pp. 67-69). Philadelphia: University of Pennsylvania.

Carpenter, Christopher J., and Erin L. Spottswood. 2013. "Exploring Romantic Relationships on Social Networking Sites using the Self-Expansion Model." *Computers in Human Behavior* 29:1531-1537. doi: 10.1016/j.chb.2013.01.021.

Carr, Caleb T. and Rebecca A. Hayes. 2015. "Social Media: Defining, Developing, and Divining." *Atlantic Journal of Communication* 23:46-65. doi: 10.1080/15456870.2015.972282

Carr, Nicholas. 2010. "Does the internet make you dumber?" The Wall Street Journal. June 5. Accessed October 1, 2014. http://on.wsj.com/1mO7heT.

Carr, Nicholas. 2008. "Is Google Making Us Stupid." The Atlantic. July 1. Accessed January 30, 2005. http://www.theatlantic.com/magazine/archive/2008/07/is-google-making-us-stupid/306868/

Carroll, Brian and Katie Landry. 2010. "Logging on and Letting out: Using Online Social Networks to Grieve and Mourn." *Bulletin of Science, Technology, & Society* 30:34–349. doi: 10.1177/0270467610380006.

Casey-Campbell, M., and Martin L. Martens. 2009. "Sticking It All Together: A Critical Assessment of the Group Cohesion-Performance Literature." *International Journal of Management Reviews* 11:223-246. doi:10.1111/j.1468-2370.2008.00239.x.

Castells, Manuel. 2001. *The Internet Galaxy: Reflections on the Internet, Business, and Society.* Oxford: Oxford University Press.

Castells, Manuel, Mireia Fernandez-Ardevol, Jack Qiu, and Araba Sey. 2004. "The Mobile Communication Society: A Cross-Cultural Analysis of Available Evidence on the Social uses of Wireless Communication Technology." *International Workshop on Wireless Communication Policies and Prospects: A Global Perspective.* 84 1:119-120. doi: 10.1111/j.1944-8287.2008.tb00398.x.

Chen, Adrian. 2012a. "Unmasking Reddit's Violentacrez, The Biggest Troll on the Web." Accessed June 6, 2014. http://gawker.com/5950981/unmasking-reddits-violentacrez-the-biggest-troll-on-the-web.

Chen, Adrian. 2012b. "Reddit's Biggest Troll Fired from his Real World Job." Accessed June 6, 2014. http://gawker.com/5951987/reddits-biggest-troll-fired-from-his-real-world-job-reddit-continues-to-censor-gawker-articles.

Chen, Yi-Fan, and James E. Katz. 2009. "Extending Family to School Life: College Students' use of the Mobile Phone." *International Journal of Human-Computer Studies* 67:179-191. doi: 10.1016/j.ijhcs.2008.09.002.

Cheney, George and Karen L. Ashcraft Karen L. 2007. "Considering "The Professional" in Communication Studies: Implications for Theory and Research within and beyond the Boundaries of Organizational Communication." *Communication Theory* 17:146-175. doi: 10.1111/j.1468-2885.2007.00290.x.

Chesley, Noelle. 2005. "Blurring Boundaries?" Linking Technology Use, Spilloer, Individual Distress, and Family Satisfaction." *Journal of Marriage and Family* 67:1237-1248. doi:10.1111/j.1741-3737.2005.00213.x.

Child, Jeffrey T., Sandra Petronio, Esther A. Agyeman-Budu, and David A. Westermann. 2011. "Blog Scrubbing: Exploring Triggers that Change Privacy Rules. *Computers in Human Behavior* 27:2017-2027. doi:10.1016/j.chb.2011.05.009.

Christensen, Miyase. 2012. "Online Mediations in Transnational Spaces: Cosmopolitan (re) Formations of Belonging and Identity in the Turkish Diaspora." *Ethnic and Racial Studies* 35 5: 888-905. doi: 10.1080/01419870.2011.628039.

Christensen, Toke H. 2009. "'Connected Presence' in Distributed Family Life." *New Media and Society* 11 3:433--451. doi: 10.1177/1461444808101620.

Clark, Margaret S., and Judson Mills. 1979. "Interpersonal Attraction in Exchange and Communal Relationships." *Journal of Personality and Social Psychology* 37:12-24. doi: 10.1037/0022-3514.37.1.12

Cluley, Graham. 2012. "Poll Reveals Widespread Concern over Facebook Timeline." Accessed March 2, 2013. http://nakedsecurity.sophos.com/2012/01/27/poll-reveals-widespread-concern-over-facebook-timeline.

CNN. 2012. "Interview with Violentacrez. Anderson Cooper 360." Accessed June 6, 2014. https://www.youtube.com/watch?v=s6plIjdaVGA.

Cohen, Sheldon. 2004. "Social Relationships and Health." *American Psychologist* 59: 676-684. doi:10.1037/0003-066x.59.8.676.

Cohen, Sheldon. 1988. "Psychosocial Models of the Role of Support in the Etiology of Physical Disease. *Health Psychology* 7: 269-297.

Cole, Helena, and Mark D. Griffiths. 2007. "Social Interactions in Massively Multiplayer Online Roleplaying Games. *Cyberpsychology and Behavior* 10:575-583. doi: 10.1089/cpb.2007.9988.

Confino, Jo. 2013. "How technology has stopped evolution and is destroying the world." The Guardian. July 11. Accessed October 1, 2014. http://www.theguardian.com/sustainable-business/technology-stopped-evolution-destroying-world.

Cooley, Charles H. 1902. *Human Nature and the Social Order.* New York: Scribner's.

Corman, Steve R., and Craig R. Scott. 1994. "Perceived Networks, Activity, Foci, and Observable Communication in Social Collectives." *Communication Theory* 4:171-190. doi:10.1111/j.1468-2885.1994.tb00089.x

Corn, David. 2012. "Secret Video: Romney Tells Millionaire Donors What he Really Thinks of Obama Voters." Accessed August 31. http://www.motherjones.com/politics/2012/09/secret-video-romney-private-fundraiser.

Coulson, Neil S., Heather Buchanan and Aimee Aubeeluck. 2007. "Social Support in Cyberspace: A Content Analysis of Communication Within a Huntington's Disease Online Support Group." *Patient Education & Counseling* 68:173-178. doi: 10.1016/j.pec.2007.06.002.

Coulson, Neil. S., and Rebecca Knibb. 2007. "Coping with Food Allergy: Exploring the Role of the Online Support Group." *Cyberpsychology and Behavior* 10: 147-150. doi:10.1089/cpb.2006.9978.

Cowden, Kelly R. 2012. "The Relational Maintenance Function of Facebook Status Updates." Paper presented at the annual meeting of the National Communication Association, Orlando, FL.

Craig, Elizabeth, and Kevin B. Wright. 2012. "Computer-Mediated Relational Development and Maintenance on Facebook." *Communication Research Reports* 29:119-129. doi: 10.1080/08824096.2012.667777.

Craven, Paul, and Barry Wellman. 1973. "The Network City." *Sociological Inquiry* 43:57-88. doi:10.1111/j.1475-682X.1973.tb00003.x

Culnan, Mary J., and Myles L. Markus. 1987. "Information Technologies." In *Handbook of Organizational Communication,* edited by, Frederic M. Jablin, Linda L. Putnam, Karlene H. Roberts, and Lyman W. Porter, 420–444. Newbury Park, CA: Sage.

Cummings, Jonathon N., Lee Sproull and Sara B. Kiesler. 2002. "Beyond Hearing: Where Real-World and Online Support Meet." *Group Dynamics: Theory, Research, and Practice* 6: 78-88. doi: 10.1037//1089-2699.6.1.78.

Cunningham, Carolyn. 2013. *Social Networking and Impression Management: Self-presentation in the Digital Age.* Lanham, MD: Lexington.

Cutrona, Carolyn E. 1996. "The Interplay of Negative and Supportive Behaviors in a Marriage. In *Handbook of Social Support and Family* edited by Gregory R. Pierce, Barbara R. Sarason, and Irwin G. Sarason, 173-194. New York: Plenum.

Cutrona, Carolyn E., and Julie Suhr 1992. "Controllability of Stressful Events and Satisfaction with Spouse Support Behaviors." *Communication Research* 19: 154-174. doi: 10.1177/0099365092019002002.

Cutrona, Carolyn. E, and Julie Suhr. 1994. "Social Support Communication in the Context of Marriage: An Analysis of Couples' Supportive Interactions." In *Communication of Social Support: Messages, Interactions, Relationships, and Community* edited by Brant R. Burleson, Terrance L. Albrecht, & Irwin G. Sarason, 113 -135. Thousand Oaks, CA: Sage.

Daft, Richard, and Robert Lengel. 1984. "Information Richness: A New Approach to Managerial Information Processing and Organizational Design." In *Research in Organizational Behavior,* edited by, Barry Staw and Larry Cummings, 191-233. Greenwich, CT: JAI Press.

Daft, Richard, and Robert Lengel. 1986. "Organizational Information Requirements, Media Richness, and Structural Design." *Management Science* 32:554-571. doi:10.1287/mnsc.32.5.554.

Daft, Richard, Robert Lengel, and Linda Klebe Trevino. 1987. "Message Equivocality, Media Selection, and Manager Performance. Implications for Information Systems." *MIS Quarterly* 11:355-366. doi:10.2307/248682.

Dailey, Rene. M., Alexa D. Hampel, and James B. Roberts. 2010. "Relational Maintenance in On-Again/Off-Again Relationships: An Assessment of how Relational Maintenance, Uncertainty, and Commitment Vary by Relationship Type and Status." *Communication Monographs* 77:75-101. doi: 10.1080/03637750903514292.

Dainton, Marianne. 2000. "Maintenance Behaviors, Expectations for Maintenance, and Satisfaction: Linking Comparison Levels to Relational Maintenance Strategies." *Journal of Social and Personal Relationships* 17:827-842. doi: 10.1177/0265407500176007.

Dainton, Marianne. 2013. "Relationship Maintenance on Facebook: Development of a Measure, Relationship to General Maintenance and Relationship Satisfaction." *College Student Journal* 47:113-121.

Dainton, Marianne, and Brooks Aylor. 2002. "Patterns of Communication Channel Use in the Maintenance of Long-Distance Relationships. *Communication Research Reports* 19:118-129. doi:10.1080/08824090209384839.

Daley, Shannon G. 2013. "Social Networking and Other Technologies: Capturing the Attention and Maintaining the Social Significance of an Issue for Young People." *The Philanthropist* 25 2. http://thephilanthropist.ca/index.php/phil/article/view/970/0.

Davis, Becca. 2013. "Has technology ruined communication?" Boston Urban News. November 25. Accessed October 1, 2014. http://www.theguardian.com/lifeandstyle/2014/sep/28/-sp-not-tonight-darling-why-britain-having-less-sex.

Davies, Celia. 1996. "The Sociology of Professions and the Profession of Gender." *Journal of the British Sociological Association* 30:661-678. doi: 10.1177/0038038596030004003.

Davis, Daniel C., Margaeux B. Lippman, Timothy W. Morris, and Jessica A. Tougas. 2013. Face-off: Different ways identity is privileged through Facebook. In *Social Networking and Impression Management in the Digital Age,* edited by Carolyn Cunningham, 61-82. Lanham, MD: Lexington

Davis, Katie. 2011. "Tensions of Identity in a Networked Era: Young People's Perspectives on the Risks and Rewards of Online Self-expression." *New Media & Society* 14:634-651. doi: 10.1177/1461444811422430.

Davison, Kathryn P., James W. Pennebaker, and Sally S. Dickerson. 2000. "Who Talks? The Social Psychology of Illness Support Groups. *American Psychologist, 55,* 205-217. doi:10.1037//0003-066x55.2.205.

Day, S. 2013. "Self-Disclosure on Facebook: How Much Do we Really Reveal?" *Journal of Applied Computing and Information Technology, 17,* http://www.citrenz.ac.nz/JACIT1701/2013Day_Facebook.html.

Dean, Alfred, & Nan Lin. 1977. "The Stress Buffering Role of Social Support: Problems and Prospects for Systematic Investigation." *Journal of Health and Social Behavior* 32: 321-341.

DeAndrea, David C. 2014. "Advancing Warranting Theory." *Communication Theory* 24:186-204. doi:10.1111/comt.12033.

Debatin, Bernhard, Jennette P. Lovejoy, Ann-Kathrin Horn, and Brittany N. Hughes. 2009. "Facebook and Online Privacy. Attitudes Behaviors and Unintended Consequences." *Journal of Computer-Mediated Communication* 15:83-108. doi:10.1111/j.1083-6101.2009.01494.x de Filippi, Primavera. 2014. "It's Time to Take Mesh Networks Seriously (And Not Just for the Reasons You Think." January 2. Accessed February 20, 2015. http://www.wired.com/2014/01/its-time-to-take-mesh-networks-seriously-and-not-just-for-the-reasons-you-think/

DeGroot, Jocelyn M. "Facebook Memorial Walls and CMC's Effect on the Grieving Process." Paper presented at the annual meeting of the National Communication Association, San Diego, California, November 27, 2008.

DeGroot, Jocelyn, M. 2012. "Maintaining Relational Continuity with the Deceased on Facebook." *OMEGA – Death and Dying* 65:195-212. doi:10.2190/OM.65.3.c.

Delanty, Gerard. 2009. *The Cosmopolitan Imagination.* Cambridge: Cambridge University Press.

Derlega, Valerian, J. and Alan L. Chaikin. 1977. "Privacy and Self-Disclosure in Social Relationships." *Journal of Social Issues* 33:102-115. doi:10.1111/j.1540-4560.1977.tb01885.x.

Di Gennero, Corinna, and William H. Dutton. 2007. "Reconfiguring Friendships: Social Relationships and the Internet. *Information, Communication, & Society* 10:591-618. doi:10.1080/13691180701657949.

Dimmick, John, Susan Kline, and Laura Stafford. 2000. The Gratification Niches of Personal Email and the Telephone: Competition, Displacement, and Complementarity, *Communication Research* 27:227-48.

Dimmick, John, John C. Feaster, and Gregory Hoplamazian. 2011. "News in the Interstices: The Niches of Mobile Media in Space and Time." *New Media and Society* 13:23–39. doi: 10.1177/1461444810363452.

Dindia, Kathryn, and Daniel J. Canary. 1993. "Definitions and Theoretical Perspectives on Maintaining Relationships." *Journal of Social and Personal Relationships* 10:163-173. doi: 10.1177/026540759301000201.

DiPrete, Thomas, Andrew Gelman, Tyler McCormack, Julein Teitler, and Tian Zheng. 2011. "Segregation in Social Networks Based on Acquaintanceship and Trust." *American Journal of Sociology* 116:1234-1283. doi:10.1086/659100.

Donath, Judith S. 1999. "Identity and Deception in the Virtual Community." In *Communities in Cyberspace,* edited by P. Kollock and M. Smith London: Routledge.

Donath, Judith and danah boyd. 2004. "Public Displays of Connection." *BT Technology Journal* 22: 71-82. doi:10.1023/B:BTTJ.0000047585.06264.cc.

Domahidi, Emese, Ruth Festl, and Thorsten Quandt. 2014. "To Dwell among Gamers: Investigating the Relationship between Social Online Game use and Gaming-Related Friendship." *Computers in Human Behavior* 35:107-115. doi:10.1016/j.chb.2014.02.023.

Drentea, Patricia., & Moren-Cross, Jennifer L. 2005. "Social Capital and Social Support on the Web: The Case of an Internet Mother Site." *Sociology of Health and Illness* 27: 920-943. doi: 10.1111/j.1467-9566.2005.00464.x

Dubrovsky, Vitaly J., Sara Kiesler, and Beheruz N. Sethna. 1991. "The Equalization Phenomenon: Status Effects in Computer-Mediated and Face-to-Face Decision-Making Groups." *Human Computer Interaction* 6:119-46. doi: 10.1207/s15327051hci0602_2

Duggan, Maeve. 2013. "Photo and Video Sharing Grow Online." *Pew Research Center.* Accessed Month Day. http://www.pewinternet.org/files/old-media/Files/Reports/2013/PIP_Photos%20and%20videos%20online_102813.pdf.

Duggan, Maeve and Aaron Smith. 2013. "Social Media Update 2013." *Pew Research Internet Project.* Accessed August 12, 2014. http://www.pewinternet.org/2013/12/30/social-media-update-2013/.

Duran, Robert L., Lynne Kelly, and Teodora Rotaru (2011). "Mobile Phones in Romantic Relationships and the Dialectic of Autonomy versus Connection." *Communication Quarterly* 59:19-36. doi: 0.1080/01463373.2011.541336

du Pre', Athena. 2010. *Communicating about Health: Current Issues and Perspectives.* Mountain View, CA: Mayfield Publishing Company.

Dunbar, Robin I. M. 1992. "Neocortex Size as a Constraint on Group Size in Primates." *Journal of Human Evolution* 22:469-493. doi:10.1016/0047-2484(92)90081-J.

Dunbar, Robin I. M. 1998. "The Social Brain Hypothesis." *Evolutionary Anthropology* 6:178-190. doi:10.1002/(SICI)1520-6505(1998)6:5[178::AID-EVAN5]3.0.CO;2-8.

Dunleavy, Katie N., and Melanie Booth-Butterfield. 2009. "Idiomatic Communication in the Stages of Coming Together and Falling Apart." *Communication Quarterly* 57:416-432. doi: 10.1080/01463370903320906.

Dutton, William, Ellen Johanna Helsper, and Monica M. Gerber. 2009. The Internet in Britain, 2009. Oxford England. *Oxford Internet Institute.* http://dx.doi.org/10.2139/ssrn.1327033.

Drushel, Bruce E. 2013. "Virtual Closets: Strategic Identity Construction and Social Media." In *Social Networking and Impression Management in the Digital Age,* edited by, Carolyn Cunningham, 149-163. Lanham, MD: Lexington.

Eklund, Lina, and Kristine Ask. 2013. "The Strenuous Task of Maintaining and Making Friends: Tensions between Play and Friendship in MMOs." Proceedings of DiGRA 2013: DeFragging Game Studies, Atlanta, GA

Ellison, Nicole B. 2013. "Social Media and Identity." *Future identities: Changing Identities in the UK – the next 10 years.* UK Government Foresight Project. London.

Ellison, Nicole B., Rebecca Gray, Jessica Vitak, and Andrew T. Fiore. 2013 "Calling All Facebook Friends: Exploring Requests for Help on Facebook. In Proceedings of the 7ᵗʰ Annual International Conference on Weblogs and Social Media. (pp. 155-164). Washington, DC: Association for the Advancement of Artificial Intelligence.

Ellison, Nicole B., Rebecca Heino, and Jennifer Gibbs. 2006. "Managing Impressions Online: Self-presentation Processes in the Online Dating Environment." *Journal of Computer-Mediated Communication* 11:415-441. doi:10.1111/j.1083-6101.2006.00020.x.

Ellison, Nicole B., Charles Steinfield, and Cliff Lampe. 2011. "Connection Strategies: Social Capital Implications of Facebook –Enabled Communication Strategies." *New Media and Society* 13:873-892.

Ellison, Nicole B., Charles Steinfield, and Cliff Lampe. 2007. "The Benefits of Facebook "Friends": Social Capital and College Students' use of Online Social Network Sites." *Journal of Computer Mediated Communication.* 12:1143-1168 doi:10.1111/j.1083-6101.2007.00367.x

Ellison, Nicole, Jessica Vitak, Rebecca Gray, and Cliff Lampe. 2014. "Cultivating Social Resources on Social Network Sites: Facebook Relationship Maintenance Behaviors and Their Role in Social Capital Processes." Journal of Computer-Mediated Communication, 19:855-870. doi:10.1111/jcc4.12078.

Engleberg, Elisabeth and Lennart Soberg, 2004. "Internet use, Social Skills, and Adjustment," *Cyberpsychology and Behavior* 7:41-47. doi: 10.1089/109493104322820101.

Etzioni, Amitai, Oren and Etzioni. 1999. "Face-to-Face and Computer-Mediated a Communities, a Comparative Analysis." *The Information Society.* 15:241-248. doi:10.1080/019722499128402.

Erickson, Christine. September 21 2012. "A Brief History of Text Messaging." Accessed September 10, 2014. http://mashable.com/2012/09/21/text-messaging-history/

Esterling, Brian A., Luciano L'Abate, Edward J. Murray, and James W. Pennebaker. 1999. "Empirical Foundations for Writing in Prevention and Psychotherapy: Mental and Physical Health Outcomes." *Clinical Psychology Review, 19,* 79-96. doi: 10.1016/s0272-7358(98)00026-4.

Facebook.com (n.d). "Statement of Rights and Responsibilities." Accessed February 9, 2012. www.facebook.com/legal/terms.

Farley, Tom. 2005. "Mobile Telephone History." Accessed September 2, 2014. http://www.privateline.com/archive/TelenorPage_022-034.pdf

Feeney, Brooke, C. and Collins Nancy L. (2014). "A New Look at Social Support: A Theoretical Perspective on Thriving Through Relationships. *Personality and Social Psychology Review, OnlineFirst.* doi: 10.1177/1088868314544222

Feld, Scott L. 1981. "The Focused Organization of Social Ties. *American Journal of Sociology* 86:1015-1035. http://www.jstor.org/stable/2778746.

Festinger, Leon. 1950. "Informal Social Communication." *Psychological Review* 57:271-282. doi:10.1037/h0056932.

Finholt, Tom, and Lee. S. Sproull. 1990. "Electronic Groups at Work." *Organization Science* 1:41-64. doi10.1287/orsc.1.1.41.

Flaherty, Lisa M., Kevin J. Pearce, and Rebecca B. Rubin. 1998. "Internet and Face-to-Face Communication: Not Functional Alternatives." *Communication Quarterly* 46:250-268. doi: 10.1080/01463379809370100.

Flanagin, Andrew J. 2005. "IM Online: Instant Messaging Use Among College Students. *Communication Research Reports,* 22:175-187.

Floyd, Kory. 2006. *Communicating affection: Interpersonal behavior and social context.* New York: Cambridge University Press.

Fogel, Joshua, and Elham Nehmad. 2009. "Internet Social Network Communicates: Risk Taking, Trust, and Privacy Concerns." *Computers in Human Behavior* 25:153-160. doi: 10.1016/j.chb.2008.08.006.

Forest, Amanda L., and Joanne Wood. 2012. "When Social Networking is Not Working: Individuals with Low Self-Esteem Recognize but Do Not Reap the Benefits of Self-Disclosure on Facebook." *Psychological Science,* 23: 295-302. doi: 10.1177/0956797611429709.

Fox, Jesse, and Katie M. Warber. 2013. "Romantic Relationship Development in the Age of Facebook: An Exploratory Study of Emerging Adults' Perceptions, Motives, and Behaviors." *Cyberpsychology, Behavior, and Social Networking* 16:3-7. doi:10.1089cyber.2012.0288.

Fox, Susannah. 2011. "In the Moment of Need." *Pew Internet and the American Life Project.* Accessed July 2, 2014. http://www.pewinternet.org/2011/02/28/in-the-moment-of-need/

Fox, Susannah and Maeve Duggan. 2013. "Health Online 2013." *Pew Internet and American Life Project.* Accessed July 2, 2014. http://www.pewinternet.org/files/old-media//Files/Reports/PIP_HealthOnline.pdf

Fulk, Janet, Joseph Schmitz, and Daehee Ryu. 1995. "Cognitive Elements in the Social Construction of Communication Technology." *Management Communication Quarterly* 8:259-288. doi:10.1177/0893318995008003001.

Gaudin, Sharon. 2011. "Google Works to Soothe Users over Real Name Controversy." Accessed November 5, 2013. http://www.computerworld.com/article/2509435/web-apps/google-works-to-soothe-users-over-real-name-controversy.html.

Gajjala, Radhika, 2012. *Cyberculture and the subaltern: Weavings of the virtual and real.* Lanham, MD: Rowman & Littlefield.

Gergen, Kenneth J. 2002. "The Challenge of Absent Presence." In *Perpetual Contact: Mobile Communication, Private Talk, Public Performance,* edited by James E. Katz, and Mark A. Aakhaus, 227-241. Cambridge, UK: Cambridge University Press.

Gibbs, Jennifer L., Nicole B. Ellison, and Rebecca D. Heino. 2006. "Self-presentation in Online Personals: The Role of Anticipated Future Interaction, Delf-disclosure, and Perceived Success in Internet Dating." *Communication Research* 33:152-177. doi:10.1177/0093650205285368.

Gilbert, Eric, and Karrie Karahalios. 2009. "Predicting Tie Strength with Social Media." Proceedings of the SIGCHI Conference on Human Factors in Computing Systems. Boston, Massachusetts, April 6.

Gittell, Ross, and Avis Vidal. 1998. *Community Organizing: Building Social Capital as a Development Strategy.* Thousand Oaks, CA: Sage.

Gladstone Brooke. 2014. "Dissecting the Media After Michael Brown." *On The Media.* August 22. Accessed September 15, 2014. http://www.onthemedia.org/story/on-the-media-2014-08-22/.

Goffman, Erving. 1959. *The Presentation of self in Everyday Life.* New York: Doubleday.

Goffman, Erving. 1967. *Interaction Ritual: Essays on face-to-face Behavior.* Garden City, NJ: Anchor/Doubleday.

Goffman, Erving. 1971. *Relations in Public: Micro Studies of the Public Order.* New York: Harper.

Goldman, Eric. 2013. "Some Concerns about Facebook's "'Graph Search.'" Accessed Month Day. http://www.forbes.com/sites/ericgoldman/2013/01/16/some-concerns-about-facebooks-graph-search/

Good, Chris. 2013. "The Lesson of Mitt Romney's 47-percent Video: Be Nice to the Wait Staff?" Accessed August 31 http://abcnews.go.com/blogs/politics/2013/03/the-lesson-of-mitt-romneys-47-percent-video-be-nice-to-the-wait-staff/.

Goodboy, Alan K. and Scott A. Myers. (2010). "Relational Quality Indicators and Love Styles as Predictors of Negative Relational Maintenance Behaviors in Romantic Relationships. *Communication Reports* 23: 65-78. doi: 10.1080/08934215.2010.511397.

Gouldner, Alvin. 1960. "The Norm of Reciprocity: A Preliminary Statement." *American Sociological Review* 25:161-178.

Granitz, Neil, and James C. Ward. 1996. "Virtual Community: A Socio-Cognitive Analysis." *Association for Consumer Research* 23:161-166.

Granovetter, Mark S. 1973. The Strength of Weak Ties. *The American Journal of Sociology* 78:1360-1380. http://www.jstor.org/stable/2776392.

Granovetter, Mark S. 1983. The Strength of Weak Ties: A Network Theory Revisited. *Sociological Theory* 1:201-233. doi:10.2307/202051

Gray, Emma. 2012. "Relationships and technology: Is texting ruining romance?" *The Huffington Post*, January 20. Accessed October 1, 2014. http://www.huffingtonpost.com/2012/01/20/relationships-technology-texting-romance_n_1219841.html.

Green, Melanie C. 2007. "Trust and Social Interaction on the Internet." In *Oxford Handbook of Internet Psychology*, edited by, A. Joinson, 43-51. Oxford: Oxford University Press.

Greenfield, Rebecca. 2012. "The Internet Has Been Making us Crazy for at Least 16 Years." *The Wire*, July 9. Accessed April 13, 2015. http://www.thewire.com/technology/2012/07/trend-watch-internet-making-us-crazy/54323/

Grellhesl, Melanie, and Narissra M. Punyanunt-Carter. 2012. "Using the Uses and Gratifications Theory to Understand Gratifications Sought through Text Messaging Practices of Male and Female Undergraduate Students. *Computers in Human Behavior* 28:2175-2181. doi: 10.1016/j.chb/2012.06.024.

Griffiths, Mark D., Mark N.O. Davies, and Darren Chappell. 2003. "Breaking the Stereotype: The Case of Online Gaming." *CyberPsychology & Behavior* 6:81-91. doi: 10.1089/109493103321167992.

Griffiths, Mark D., Mark N.O. Davies, and Darren Chappell. 2004. "Demographic Factors and Playing Variables in Online Computer Gaming." *Cyberpsychology and Behavior* 7:479-487. doi: 10.1089/cpb.2004.7.479.

Griggs, Brandon, and Doug Gross. 2013. "5 Things we learned at SXSW 2013." Accessed March 13. http://www.cnn.com/2013/03/13/tech/innovation/5-things-sxsw/?hpt=us_t4.

Guastella, Adam. J. , and Mark R. Dadds. 2006. "Cognitive-Behavioral Models of Emotional Writing: A Validation Study. *Cognitive Therapy and Research* 30: 397-414. doi: 10.1007/s10608-006-9045-6.

Guerrero, Laura K., and, Peter A. Anderson. (1991). The waxing and waning of relational intimacy: Touch as a function of relational stage, gender, and touch avoidance. *Journal of Personal and Social Relationships* 8:147-165. doi:10.1111/j.1475-6811.1995tb00088.x.

Gui, Marco, and Gianluca Argentin. 2011. "Digital Skills of Internet Natives: Different Forms of Digital Literacy in a Random Sample of Northern Italian High School Students." *New Media & Society* 13:963-980. doi:10.1177/1461444810389751.

Gupta, Aditi, Hemank Lamba, Ponnurangam Kumaraguru, and Anupam Joshi. 2013. "Faking Sandy: Characterizing and Identifying Fake Images on Twitter during Hurricane Sandy." Proceedings of the 22nd international conference on World Wide Web Companion, Rio de Janeiro, May 13-17.

Hall, Jeffrey A., and Nancy K. Baym (2011). "Calling and Texting (too much): Mobile Maintenance Expectations, (over)Dependence, Entrapment, and Friendship Satisfaction." *New Media & Society* 14: 316.331, doi:10.1177/1461444811415047.

Hampton, Keith N., Lauren Sessions Goulet, Lee, Rainie, and Kristen Purcell, K. (2011). "Social Networking Sites and Our Lives." *Pew Internet and American Life Project*. Accessed July 8, 2013. http://pewinternet.org/2011/06/16social-networking-sites-and-our-lives/.

Hampton, Keith N., Lauren F. Sessions, Eun Ja Her, and Lee Rainie. 2009. "Social Isolation and New Technology. How the Internet and Mobile Phones Impact American's Social Networks." *Pew Internet and American Life Project*. Accessed November 3, 2013. http://www.pewinternet.org/files/old-media/Files/Reports/2009/PIP_Tech_and_Social_Isolation.pdf.

Hannerz, Ulf. 1990. "Cosmopolitans and Locals in World Culture." *Theory, Culture and Society* 7 2:237-251. doi: 10.1177/026327690007002014.

Hannerz, Ulf. 1996. *Transnational Connections: Culture, People, Places.* Psychology Press.

Hannerz, Ulf. 2006. "Two Faces of Cosmopolitanism: Culture and Politics." *Documentos CIDOB, Dinámicas Interculturales* 7:3-29. doi: 10.1002/9780470693681.ch5.

Hansen, David. 2011. *The Teacher and the World: A Study of Cosmopolitanism as Education.* Florence, Kentucky: Routledge.

Harper, Helen, Thomas W. Bean, and Judith Dunkerly. 2010. "Cosmopolitanism, Globalization and the Field of Adolescent Literacy." *Canadian and International Education/Education* 39 3:1-13. http://ir.lib.uwo.ca/cgi/viewcontent.cgi?article=1056&context=cie-eci

Haythornthwaite, Caroline. 2002. "Strong, Weak, and Latent Ties and the Impact of New Media." *The Information Society* 18:385-401. doi:10.1080/01972240290108195.

Haythornthwaite, Caroline. 2001. "Exploring Multiplexity: Social Network Structures in a Computer-Supported Distance Learning Class." *The Information Society* 17: 211-226. doi: 10.1080/01972240152493065.

Haythornthwaite, Caroline, and Barry Wellman. 1998. "Work, Friendship, and Media use for Information Exchange in a Networked Organization." *Journal of the American Society for Information Science* 49:1101-1114.

Helgeson, Vicki S., Sheldon Cohen, Richard Schulz, and Joyce Yasko. 2000. "Group Support Interventions for Women with Breast Cancer: Who Benefits From Whom? *Health Pscyhology* 19: 107-114. doi: 10.1037//0278-6133.19.2.107.

Henderson, Samantha, and Michael Gilding. 2004. "'I've Never Clicked This Much with Anyone in my Life': Trust and Hyperpersonal Communication in Online Friendships." *New Media and Society* 6:487-506. doi:10.1177/146144804044331.

Hess, Jon A. (2000). "Maintaining Nonvoluntary Relationships with Disliked Partners: An Investigation in the Use of Distancing Behaviors." *Human Communication Research* 26:458-488. doi: 10.1111/j.1468-2958.2000.tb00765.x.

High, Andrew C. and James Price Dillard. (2012). "A Review and Meta-Analysis of Person-Centered Messages and Social Support Outcomes." *Communication Studies* 63: 99-118. doi: 10.1080/10510974.2011.598208.

High, Andrew C., Anne Oeldorf-Hirsch, and Saraswathi Bellur. 2014. "Misery Rarely Gets Company: The Influence of Emotional Bandwidth on Supportive Communication on Facebook." *Computers in Human Behavior* 34:79-88. doi: 10.1016/j.chb.2014.01.037

High, Andrew C., and Denise Solomon. 2011. "Locating Computer-Mediated Social Support within Online Communication Environments." In *Computer-Mediated Communication in Personal Relationships* edited by Kevin B. Wright and Lynne M. Webb, 119-136. New York: Peter Lang.

Hill, Russell A., and Robin I. M. Dunbar. 2003. "Social Network Size in Humans." *Human Nature* 14:53-72. doi:10.1007/s12110-003-1016-y.

Hobfall, Stevan E. 2009. "Social Support: The Movie." *Journal of Social and Personal Relationships*, 26:93-101. doi: 10.1177/0265407509105524.

Hogan, Bernie. 2010. "The Presentation of Self in the age of Social Media: Distinguishing Performances and Exhibitions Online. *Bulletin of Science, Technology and Society* 30 6:377–386 doi: 10.1177/0270467610385893.

Holmstrom, Amanda J. 2012. "What Helps–and What Doesn't–When Self-Esteem is Threatened?: Retrospective Reports of Esteem Support." *Communication Studies* 63: 77-98. doi:10.1080/10510974.2011.586399

Hong, Seoyeon, Edson Tandoc, Eunjin Anna Kim, Bokyung Kim, and Kevin Wise (2012). "The Real You? The Role of Visual Cues and Comment Congruence in Perceptions of Social Attractiveness from Facebook Profiles. *Cyberpsychology, Behavior, and Social Networking* 15:339-344. doi:10.1089/cyber.2011.0511.

Houser, M. L., Fleuriet, C., & Estrada, D. (2012). The cyber factor: An analysis of relational maintenance through the use of computer-mediated communication. *Communication Research Reports, 29,* 34-43. doi: 10.1080/08824096.2011.639911.

Hoybye, Mette. T., Christoffer, Johansen., and Tine Tjornhoj-Thomsen.2005. "Online Interaction: Effects of Storytelling in an Internet Breast Cancer Support Group." *Psycho-Oncology* 14: 211–220. doi:10.1002/pon.837.

Hull, Glynda A., and Amy Stornaiuolo. 2014. "Cosmopolitan Literacies, Social Networks, and "Proper Distance: Striving to Understand in a Global World". *Curriculum Inquiry* 44 1:15-44. doi: 10.1111/curi.12035.

Hu, Elise. 2014. "How Hong Kong Protesters Are Connecting Without Cell or Wi-Fi Networks." *All Tech Considered,* September 29. Accessed October 2, 2014. http://www.npr.org/blogs/alltechconsidered/2014/09/29/352476454/how-hong-kong-protesters-are-connecting-without-cell-or-wi-fi-networks.

Hunt, Daniel, David Atkin, and Archana Krishnan. 2012. "The Influence of Computer-Mediated Communication Apprehension on Motives for Facebook Use." *Journal of Broadcasting and Electronic Media* 56:187-202. doi:10.1080/08838151.2012.678717.

Hur, Jane, and Mayank Gupta. 2013. "Growing Up in the Web of Social Networking: Adolescent Development and Social Media." *Adolescent Psychiatry* 3 3:233-244. doi: 10.2174/2210676611303030004.

Igarashi, Tasuku, Jiro Takai, and Toshikazu Yoshida, T. 2005. "Gender Differences in Social Network Development via Mobile Phone Text Messages: A Longitudinal Study." *Journal of Social and Personal Relationships* 22:691–713. doi: 10.1177/0265407505056492.

Ishii, Kenichi. 2006. "Implications of Mobility: The uses of Personal Communication Media in Everyday Life." *Journal of Communication,56,* 346-365. doi:10.1111/j.1460-2466.2006.00023.x.

Israel, Barbara, A., and Toni C. Antonucci. 1987. "Social Network Characteristics and Psychological Well-Being: A Replication and Extension." *Health Education Quarterly, 14,* 461-481. doi: 10.1177/109019818701400406.

Ito, Mizuko, and D. Okabe. 2005. "Technosocial Situations: Emergent Structuring of Mobile E-mail use." In *Personal, Portable, Pedestrian: Mobile phones in Japanese life,* edited by Mizuko Ito, Daisuke Okabe, and Misa Matsuda, 257-273. Cambridge, MA: MIT Press.

Jacobson, David. 1999. "Impression Formation in Cyberspace: Online Expectations and Offline Experiences in Text-based Virtual Communities." *Journal of Computer-Mediated Communication* 5 doi:10.1111/j.1083-6101.1999.tb00333.x.

James, William. 1890. *The Principles of Psychology.* Mineola, NY: Dover.

Jiang, L. Crystal, Natalie N. Bazarova, and Jeffrey T. Hancock. 2013. "From Perception to Behavior: Disclosure Reciprocity and the Intensification of Intimacy in Computer-Mediated Communication. *Communication Research* 40:125-145. doi: 10.1177/0093650211405312

Jiang, L. Crystal, Natalie N. Bazarova, and Jeffrey T. Hancock. 2011. "The Disclosure-Intimacy Link in Computer-Mediated Communication: An Attributional Extension of the Hyperpersonal Model." *Human Communication Research* 37:58-77. doi: 10.1111/j.1468-2958.2010.01393

Jiang, L. Crystal, and Jeffrey T. Hancock. 2013. "Absence Makes the Communication Grow Fonder: Geographic Separation, Interpersonal Media, and Intimacy in Dating Relationships." *Journal of Communication* 63:556-577. doi:10.1111/jcom.12029.

Jin, Borae , and Namkee Park. 2013 . " Mobile Voice Communication and Loneliness: Cell Phone use and the Social Skills Deficit Hypothesis ." *New Media and Society* 15 :1094 –1111 . doi: 10.1177/1461444812466715.

Jin, Borae, and Jorge F. Pena. 2010. "Mobile Communication in Romantic Relationships: Mobile Phone use, Relational Uncertainty, Love, Commitment, and Attachment Styles." *Communication Reports* 23:39-51. doi: 10.1080/08934211003598742.

Johnson, Amy Janan, and Jennifer A. H. Becker. 2011. "CMC and the Conceptualization of 'Friendship': How Friendships Have Changed with the Advent of New Methods of Interpersonal Communication." In *Computer-Mediated Communication in Personal Relationships,* edited by Kevin B. Wright and Lynne M. Webb, 225-243. New York: Peter Lang.

Johnson, Amy Janan, Michel M. Haigh, Jennifer, A. H. Becker, Elizabeth A. Craig, and Shelley Wigley. 2008. "College Students' use of Relational Management Strategies in Email in

Long-Distance and Geographically Close Relationships." *Journal of Computer-Mediated Communication* 13:381-404. doi: 10.1111/j.1083-6101.2008.00401.x

Johnson, Amy Janan, Michel Haigh, Elizabeth A. Craig, and Jennifer A. H. Becker. 2009. "Defining and Measuring Relational Closeness: The Test Case of Close Long Distance Friendships." *Personal Relationships* 16:631-646.

Joinson, Adam, N. 2008. "Looking At, Looking Up, or Keeping Up With People?" Proceedings of the twenty-sixth annual CHI conference on Human factors in computing systems. doi:10.1145/1357054.1357213.

Joinson, Adam, N. 2001. "Self-Disclosure in Computer-Mediated Communication: The Role of Self-Awareness and Visual Anonymity." *European Journal of Social Psychology* 31:177-192. doi: 10.1002/ejsp.36.

Joyce, Elisabeth, and Robert E. Kraut. 2006. "Predicting Continued Participation in Newsgroups." *Journal of Computer-Mediated Communication* 11:723-747. doi:10.1111/j.1083-6101.2006.00033.x.

Jung,Yumi, Rebecca Gray, Cliff Lampe, and Nicole B. Ellison. 2013. "Favors from Facebook Friends: Unpacking Dimensions of Social Capital." Proceedings of the SIGCHI Conference on Human Factors in Computing Systems, April 27-May2, Paris, France. doi:10.1145/2470654.2470657

Jurgenson, Nathan. 2012. "The IRL fetish." June 28. *The New Inquiry*. Accessed July 17, 2012. http://thenewinquiry.com/essays/the-irl-fetish/.

Jurgenson, Nathan. 2011. "Digital Dualism versus Augmented Reality." February 23. *Cyborgology*. Accessed January 22. http://thesocietypages.org/cyborgology/2011/02/24/digital-dualism-versus-augmented-reality/.

Kasesniemi, Eija-Liisa, and Pirjo Rautiainen. 2002. "Mobile Culture of Children and Teenagers in Finland." In *Perpetual Contact: Mobile communication, private talk, and public performance,* edited by James E. Katz and Mark Aakhaus, 170- 192. Cambridge, UK: Cambridge University Press.

Katz, Elihu, James G. Blumer, and Michael Gurevitch. 1973. "Utilization of Mass Communication by the Individual." In *The Uses of Mass Communications: Current Perspectives of Gratifications Research,* edited by James G. Blumer and Elihu Katz, 19-32. Beverly Hills, CA: Sage.

Katz, James E. 2008. "Mainstreamed Mobiles in Daily Life: Perspectives and Prospects." In *Handbook of Mobile Communication Studies,* edited by James E. Katz, 443-446. Cambridge, MA: MIT.

Keaten, James A. and Lynne Kelly. 2008. "'Re: We Really Need to Talk:' Affect for Communication Channels, Competence, and Fear of Negative Evaluation." *Communication Quarterly* 56:407-426. doi:10.1080/01463370802451646.

Kiesler, Sara, Jane Siegel, and Timothy W. McGuire, 1984. "Social Psychological Aspects of Computer-Mediated Communication." *American Psychologist, 39,* 1123-1134. doi: 10.1037//0003-066x.39.10.1123

Kim, Hyo, Gwang Jae Kim, Han Woo Park, and Ronald E. Rice. 2007. "Configurations of Relationships in Different Media: FtF, Email, Instant Messenger, Mobile Phone, and SMS." *Journal of Computer-Mediated Communication* 12:1183-1207. doi: 10.1111/j.1083-6101.2007.00369.x.

Kleingold, Pauline. 2013. "Cosmopolitanism." *The International Encyclopedia of Ethics* doi: 10.1002/9781444367072.wbiee629.

Klosowski, Thorin. 2014. "The biggest tech industry buzzwords, defined for normal people. Lifehacker. April 18. Accessed October 1, 2014. http://lifehacker.com/the-biggest-tech-industry-buzzwords-defined-for-normal-1564463267.

Knapp, Mark L., Anita Vangelisti, and John P. Caughlin. 2014. *Interpersonal Communication and Human Relationships.* Boston: Pearson.

Kobayashi, Tetsuro, and Jeffrey Boase. (2014). "Tele-Cocooning: Mobile Texting and Social Scope." *Journal of Computer-mediated Communication* 19:681-694. doi: 10.1111/jcc4.12064

Kolo, Castulus, and Timo Bauer. 2004. "Living a Virtual Life: Social Dynamic of Online Gaming." Accessed November 7, 2013. http://realities.id.tue.nl/wp-content/uploads/2010/03/kolo-baur-2004.pdf.

Koltay, Tibor. 2011. "The Media and the Literacies: Media Literacy, Information Literacy, and Digital Literacy." *Media, Culture, and Society.* 33:211-221. doi: 10.1177/0163443710393382.

Kramer, Adam D. I., Jamie E. Guillory, and Jeffrey T. Hancock. 2014. "Experimental Evidence of Massive-scale Emotional Contagion through Social Networks. *Proceedings of the National Academy of Sciences for the United States of America* 111:8788-8790. doi:10.1073/pnas.1230040111.

Krämer, Nicole C., and Stephan Winter. 2008. "Impression Management 2.0. The Relationship of Self-esteem, Extraversion, Self-efficacy, and Self-Presentation within Social Networking Sites." *Journal of Media Psychology* 20:106–116. doi: 10.1027/1864-1105.20.3.106.

Kraut, Robert, Sara Kiesler, Bonka Boneva, Jonathon Cummings, Vicki Helgeson, and Anne Crawford. 2002. "Internet Paradox Revisited." *Journal of Social Issues* 58:49-74. doi: 10.1111/1540-4560.00248.

Kraut, Robert, Michael Patterson, Vicki Lundmark, Sara Kiesler, Tridas, Mukophadhyay, and William Scherlis. 1998. "Internet Paradox: A Social Technology That Reduces Social Involvement and Psychological Well-Being?" *American Psychologist* 53:1017-1031. doi:10.1037/0003-066x.53.9.1017.

Kuznekoff, Jeffrey. 2013. "Comparing Impression Management Strategies Across Social Media Platforms." In *Social Networking and Impression Management in the Digital Age,* edited by Carolyn Cunningham, 15-34. Lanham, MD: Lexington.

Kyriakidou, Maria. 2008. "Mediated Cosmopolitanism: Global Disasters and the Emergence of Cosmopolitan Solidarity." *Global Studies Journal* 1:123-130. doi:10.1515/comm.2008.018

Lakey, Brian, and Edward Orehek. 2011. "Relational Regulation Theory: A New Approach to Explain the Link Between Perceived Social Support and Mental Health." *Psychological Review* 118: 482-495. doi: 10.1037/a0023477

Lampe, Cliff and Erik. Johnston. 2005. "Follow the (Slash) Dot: Effects of Feedback on New Members in an Online Community." Proceedings of the 2005 International ACM SIG-GROUP Conference on Supporting Group Work, New York, New York, November 6-9.

Lampe, Cliff , Nicole Ellison , and Charles Steinfield . 2006 . " A Face(book) in the Crowd: Social Searching vs. Social Browsing ." Proceedings of the 2006 20th Anniversary Conference on Computer Supported Cooperative Work, New York, New York.

La Rocca, James M., James S. House, and John R. P. French. 1980. "Social Support, Occupational Health, and Stress. *Journal of Health and Social Behavior* 21:201-218. doi: 10.2307/2136616.

Lea, Martin, and Russell Spears. 1992. "Paralanguage and Social Perception in Computer-Mediated Communication." *Journal of Organizational Computing* 2:321-341. doi: 10.1080/10919399209540190.

Lea, Martin, O'Shea, Tim, Fung, Pat, and Russell Spears. 1992. "Flaming' in Computer-Mediated Communication: Observations, Explanations, Implications." In *Contexts of Computer-Mediated Communication,* edited by Martin Lea, 89-112. Hertfordshire, UK: Harvester Wheatsheaf.

Leary, Mark R. 1996. *Self-presentation: Impression Management and Interpersonal Behavior.* Madison, WI: Brown and Benchmark.

Leary, Mark R., and Robin M. Kowalski. 1990. "Impression Management: A Literature Review and Two-component Model." *Psychological Bulletin* 107:34-47. doi:10.1037/0033-2909.107.1.34

Ledbetter, Andrew M. 2009a. "Measuring Online Communication Attitude: Instrument Development and Validation." *Communication Monographs* 76:463-486. doi: 10.1080/03637750903300262.

Ledbetter, Andrew M. 2009b. "Patterns of Media use and Multiplexity. Associations with Sex, Geographic Distance, and Friendship Interdependence." *New Media and Society* 11:1187-1208. doi:10.1177/1461444809342057.

Ledbetter, Andrew M. 2010a. "Content- and Medium- Specific Decomposition of Friendship Relational Maintenance: Integrating Equity and Media Multiplexity Approaches." *Journal of Social and Personal Relationships* 27: 938-955. doi:10.1177/0265407510376254.

Ledbetter, Andrew M. 2010b. "Family Communication Patterns and Communication Competence as Predictors of Online Communication Attitude: Evaluating a Dual Pathway Model." *Journal of Family Communication* 10:99-115. doi:10.1080/15267431003595462.

Ledbetter, Andrew M., and Jeffrey H. Kuznekoff. 2012. "More than a Game: Friendship Relational Maintenance and Attitudes toward Xbox LIVE Communication." *Communication Research* 39:269-290. doi: 10.1177/0093650210397042.

Ledbetter, Andrew M., and Joseph P. Mazer. 2014. "Do Online Communication Attitudes Mitigate the Association between Facebook Use and Relational Interdependence? An Extension of Media Multiplexity Theory." *New Media & Society* 16:506-822. doi:10.1177/1461444813495159.

Ledbetter, Andrew M., Joseph P. Mazer, Jocelyn, M. DeGroot, Kevin R. Meyer, Yuping Mao, and Brian Swafford. 2011. Attitudes Toward Online Social Connection and Self-Disclosure as Predictors of Facebook Communication and Relational Closeness. *Communication Research* 38: 27-53. doi: 10.1177/0093650210365537.

Lee, Suk-Jae, Brian M. Quigley, Mitchell S. Nesler, Amy B. Corbett, and James T. Tedeschi. 1999. "Development of a Self-presentation Tactics Scale." *Personality and Individual Differences* 26:701-722. doi: 10.1016/S0191-8869(98)00178-0.

Leung, Louis. 2007. "Stressful Life Events, Motives for Internet Use, and Social Support Among Digital Kids. *Cyberpsychology & Behavior* 10:204-214. doi:10.1089/cpb.2006.9967

Leung, Louis, and Paul S. N. Lee. 2005. "Multiple Determinants of Life Quality: The Roles of Internet Activities, Use of New Media, Social Support, and Leisure Activities. *Telematics and Informatics* 22:161-180. doi:10.1016/j.tele.2004.04.003.

Lenhart, Amanda. 2010. "Is the Age at Which Kids Get Cell Phones Getting Younger?" *Pew Internet and American Life Project.* Accessed September 3, 2014. http://www.pewinternet.org/2010/12/01/is-the-age-at-which-kids-get-cell-phones-getting-younger/.

Lenhart, Amanda, Rich Ling, Scott Campbell, and Kristen Purcell. 2010. "Texts and Mobile Phones." *Pew Internet and American Life Project.* Accessed September 2, 2014. http://pewinternet.org/Reports/2010/Teens-and-Mobile-Phones.aspx.

Lewis, Kevin, Jason Kaufman, Marco Gonzalez, Andreas Wimmer, and Nicholas Christakis. 2008. "Tastes, Ties, and Time: A New Social Network Dataset Using Facebook.com." *Social Networks* 30:330-342. doi:10.1016/j.socnet.2008.07.002.

Lewis, Nathaniel M. 2012. "Remapping Disclosure: Gay Men's Segmented Journeys of Moving Out and Coming Out." *Social and Cultural Geography,* 13:211-231. 10.1080/14649365.2012.677469

Li, Honglei 2004. "Virtual Community Studies: A Literature Review, Synthesis and Research Agenda." Proceedings of the Americas Conference on Information Systems, New York, New York, August 2004.

Licklider, Joseph C. R. 1968. "The Computer as Communication Device." *Science and Technology.* doi: 10.1016/B978-0-08-010970-1.50022-X.

Licoppe, Christian. 2004. "Connected Presence: The Emergence of a new Repertoire for Managing Social Relationships in a Changing Communications Technoscape." *Environment and planning: Society and space* 22:135–156. doi: 10.1068/d323t.

Licoppe Christian, and Jean Phillippe Heurtin. 2001. "Managing one's Availability to Telephone Communication through Mobile Phones: A French Case Study of the Development Dynamics of the use of Mobile Phones." *Personal and Ubiquitous Computing* 5:99-108. doi: 10.1007/s007790170013.

Lifton, Robert Jay. 1992. *The Protean Self: Human Resilience in an Age of Fragmentation.* New York: Basic Books.

Lin, Chieh-Peng, and Anol Bhattacherjee. 2009. "Understanding Online Social Support and Its Antecedents: A Socio-Cognitive Model." *The Social Science Journal* 46:724-737. doi: 10.1016/j.soscij.2009.03.004.

Lin, Kuan-Yu, and Hsi-Peng Lu. 2011. "Why People Use Social Networking Sites: An Empirical Study Integrating Network Externalities and Motivation Theory." *Computers in Human Behavior* 27:1152-1161. doi: 10.1016/j.chb.2010.12.009

Lin, Nan. 1986. "Conceptualizing Social Support." In *Social support, Life Events, and Depression* edited by Nan Lin, Alfred Dean, and Walter M. Ensel, 17-30. Orlando, FL: Academic.

Lin, Nan, Walter M. Ensel, and John C. Vaughn. 1981. "Social Resources and Strength of Ties: Structural Factors in Occupational Status Attainment." *American Sociological Review* 46:393-405. http://www.jstor.org/stable/2095260.

Ling, Richard. 2008. *New Tech, New Ties.* Cambridge, MA: MIT Press

Ling, Richard, and Jonathan Donner. 2014. *Mobile Communication.* Cambridge, UK: Polity.

Ling, Richard, and Birgitte Yttri. 2002. "Hyper-Coordination via Mobile Phones in Norway." In *Perpetual Contact: Mobile communication, private talk, and public performance,* edited by Jack E. Katz and Mark Aakhaus, 139-169. Cambridge, UK: Cambridge University Press.

Litt, Eden, 2013a. "Measuring Users' Internet Skills: A Review of Past Assessments and a Look Towards the Future." *New Media and Society* 15:612-630. doi: 10.1177/1461444813475424.

Litt, Eden. 2013b. "You've Got Mad Skillz: Exploring the Role of Privacy Skills and Knowledge in Social Media Use." *CSCW2013: Networked Privacy Workshop.* doi: 10.1016/j.chb.2013.01.049.

Livingstone, Sonia and Ellen Helsper. 2009. "Balancing Opportunities and Risks in Teenagers' Use of the Internet: The Role of Online Skills and Internet Self-Efficacy." *New Media and Society* 12:309-329. doi:10.1177/1461444809342697.

Lo, Shao-Kang, Chih-Chien Wang, and Wenchang Fang. 2005. "Physical Interpersonal Relationships and Social Anxiety among Online Game Players." *Cyberpsychology & Behavior* 8:15-20. doi:10.1089/cpb.2005.8.15.

Lott, Albert J., and Bernice E. Lott. 1965. "Group Cohesiveness as Interpersonal Attraction: A Review of Relationships with Antecedent and Consequent Variables." *Psychological Bulletin* 64:259-309. doi:10.1037/h0022386.

Ludden, Jennifer. 2010. "Teen Texting Soars; Will Social Skills Suffer?" Accessed October 10, 2013. http://www.npr.org/templates/story/story.php?storyId=126117811.

MacGeorge, Erina L., Bo Feng, and Brant R. Burleson. 2011. "Supportive Communication" In *Handbook of Interpersonal Communication (4th Ed.)* edited by Mark L. Knapp and John A. Daly, 317-354. Thousand Oaks, CA: Sage.

Markus, M. Lynne. 1994. "Electronic Mail as the Medium of Managerial Choice." *Organization Science* 5:502-527. doi:10.1287/orsc.5.4.502.

Marsden, Peter. V. 1987. Core discussion networks of Americans. *American Sociological Review, 51,* 122-131. doi:10.2307/2095397.

Marwick, Alice, and danah boyd. 2011. "I Tweet Honestly, I Tweet Passionately: Twitter Users, Context Collapse, and the Imagined Audience." *New Media & Society* 13:114-133. doi:10.1177/1461444810365313.

Mastre, Brian. 2010. "Has Social Media Killed Social Skills?" Accessed September 2, 2013. http://www.wowt.com/home/headlines/Has_Social_Media_Killed_Social_Skills_106742408.html.

Maguire, Kathy C. and Terry A. Kinney. 2010. When Distance is Problematic: Communication, Coping, and Relational Satisfaction in Female College Students' Long-Distance Dating Relationships. *Journal of Applied Communication Research* 28: 27-46.doi: 10.1080/00909880903483573.

Malinowski, Bronislaw (1923). "The Problem of Meaning in Primitive Languages." In *The Meaning of Meaning,* edited by C. K. Ogden and I. A. Richards, 296-336. London: Routledge and Kegan Paul.

Markus, M. Lynne. (1994). "Electronic Mail as the Medium of Managerial Choice." *Organization Science* 5:502-527. doi:10.1287/orsc.5.4.502.

Martin, Judith N., and Thomas K. Nakayama. 2007. *Intercultural Communication in Contexts.* New York: McGraw-Hill.

Matsuda, Misa 2005. "Mobile Communication and Selective Sociality." In *Personal, Portable, Pedestrian: Mobile phones in Japanese life,* edited by Mizuko Ito, Daisuke Okabe, and Misa Matsuda, 123-142. Cambridge, MA: MIT Press.

Mazer, Joseph P. and Andrew M. Ledbetter. 2012. "Online Communication Attitudes as Predictors of Problematic Internet use and Well-being Outcomes." *Southern Journal of Communication* 11:403-419. doi:10.1080/1041794x.2012.686558.

McCallister, Lynne, and Claude S. Fischer. 1978. "A Procedure for Surveying Personal Networks." *Sociological Methods and Research* 7:131-148. doi:10.1177/004912417800700202.

McCormick Naomi B. and John W. McCormick. 1992. "Computer Friends and Foes: Content of Undergraduates' Electronic Mail." *Computers in Human Behavior.* 8:379-405. doi: 10.1016/0747-5632(92)90031-9

McCroskey, James C. 1977. "Oral Communication Apprehension: A Summary of Recent Theory and Research." *Human Communication Research* 4:78-96. doi:10.1111/j.1468-2958.1977.tb00599.x.

McCroskey, James C. 1970. "Measures of Communication-Bound Anxiety." *Speech Monographs* 37:269-277. doi:10.1080/03637757009375677.

McCroskey, James C. and Virginia Richardson. 1977. "Communication Apprehension as a Predictor of Self-Disclosure." *Communication Quarterly, 25,* 40-43.doi:10.1080/01463377709369271.

McCroskey, James C. and Michael E. Sheahan. 1978. "Communication Apprehension, Social Preference, and Social Behavior in a College Environment." *Communication Quarterly* 26: 41-45. doi:10.1080/01463377809369292.

McEwan, Bree. 2013a. "Choosing Channels: Exploring Multiple Motivations for Exploring Communication Medium Choice." Paper presented at a meeting of the International Association of Relationship Researchers, Louisville, Kentucky, October 4-6.

McEwan, Bree. 2013b. "Sharing, Caring, and Surveilling on Social Network Sites: An Actor-Partner Interdependence Model Investigation of Facebook Relational Maintenance." *Cyberpsychology, Behavior, and Social Networking* 16:863-869. doi:10.1089/cyber.2012.0272

McEwan, Bree. 2013c. "Retention and Resources: How Social Network Resources Relate to Institutional Commitment." *Journal of College Student Retention: Research, Theory, and Practice* 15:113-128. doi:10.2190/CS.15.1.g

McEwan Bree, Jennifer (Marmo) Fletcher, Jennifer Eden, Erin (Bryant) Sumner (2014). "Development and Validation of a Facebook Relational Maintenance Measure." *Communication Methods and Measures* 8:244-263. doi: 10.1080/19312458.2014.967844

McEwan, Bree, and Laura K. Guerrero. 2012. "Maintenance Behavior and Relationship Quality as Predictors of Perceived Availability of Resources in Newly Formed College Friendship Networks." *Communication Studies* 63:421-440. doi:10.1080/10510974.2011.639433.

McEwan, Bree, and Laura K. Guerrero. 2010. "Freshmen Engagement through Communication: Communication Skills as Predictors of Friendship Formation Strategies and Rewarding Social Networks among College Freshmen." *Communication Studies* 61:445-463. doi:10.1080/10510974.2010.493762.

McEwan, Bree, and Dakota Horn. (2015) "ILY & Can U Pick up Some Milk: Effects of Relational Maintenance via Text Messaging on Relational Satisfaction and Closeness in Dating Partners." paper presented at a meeting of the Central States Association Communication, Madison, WI.

McEwan, Bree, and Jennifer Mease. 2013. "Compressed Crystals: A Metaphor for Mediated Identity Expression." In Carolyn Cunningham (Ed.). *Social Networking and Impression Management: Self-presentation in the Digital Age. (*pp. 85-106). Lanham, MD: Lexington.

McEwan, Bree, and Miriam Sobré -Denton. 2011. "Virtual Cosmopolitanism: Constructing Third Cultures and Transmitting Social and Cultural Capital through Social Media." *Journal of International and Intercultural Communication* 4:252-258. doi:10.1080/17513057.2011.598044.

McEwan, Bree, and David Zanolla. 2013. "When Online Meets Offline: A Field Investigation of Modality Switching." *Computers in Human Behavior* 29:1565-1571. doi:10.1016/j.chb.2013.01.020.

McKenna, Katelyn Y. A., Amie S. Green, and Marci E.J. Gleason. 2002. "Relationship Formation on the Internet: What's the Big Attraction?" *Journal of Social Issues* 58:9-31. doi:10.1111/1540-4560.00246.

McKenna, Katelyn Y. A., and John A. Bargh. 1998. "Coming Out in the Age of the Internet: "Demarginalization" Through Virtual Group Participation." *Journal of Personality and Social Psychology* 75:681-694. doi:10.1037/0022-3514.75.3.681.

McKenna, Katelyn Y. A., and John A. Bargh. 1999. "Causes and Consequences of Social Interaction on the Internet: A Conceptual Framework. *Media Psychology* 1:249-269. doi:10.1207/s1532785xmep0103_4.

McLaughlin, Caitlin and Jessica Vitak. 2011. "Norm Evolution and Violation on Facebook." *New Media and Society* 14:299-315. doi: 10.1177/1461444811412712.

McLaughlin, Margaret L., Kerry K. Osborne, and Christine B. Smith. 1995. "Standards of Conduct on Usenet." In *CyberSociety: Computer-Mediated Communication and Community,* edited by Steve Jones, 90-111. London: Sage.

McLuhan, Marshall. 1964. *Understanding media: The extensions of man.* Cambridge, MA: MIT Press.

McPherson, Miller, Lynn Smith-Lovin, and Matthew E. Brashears. 2006. "Social Isolation in America: Changes in Core Discussion Networks over two Decades." *American Sociological Review* 71:353-375. doi: 10.1177/000312240607100301.

Mead, George H. 1934. *Mind, Self, and Society: From the Standpoint of a Social Behaviorist.* Chicago, IL: The University of Chicago Press.

Mehrabian, Albert. 1971. *Silent Messages.* Oxford, UK: Wadsworth.

Melenhorst, Anne-Sophie, Wendy A. Rogers, and Don G. Bouwhuis. 2006. "Older Adults' Motivated Choice for Technological Innovation: Evidence for Benefit-Driven-Selectivity." *Psychology and Aging* 21:190-195. doi:10.1037/0882-7974.21.1.190.

Messman, Susan J., Daniel J. Canary, and Kimberley S. Hause. 2000. "Motives to Remain Platonic Equity, and the Use of Maintenance Strategies in Opposite-Sex Friendships." *Journal of Social and Personal Relationships* 17:67-94. doi:10.1177/0265407500171004.

Metzger, Miriam J., Andrew J. Flanagin, and Ryan Medders. 2010. "Social and Heuristic Approaches to Credibility Evaluation Online." *Journal of Communication* 60:413-439. doi:10.1111/j.1460-2466.2010.01488.x.

Miczo, Nathan, Theresa Mariani, and Crystal Donahue. 2011. "The Strength of Strong Ties: Media Multiplexity, Communication Motives, and the Maintenance of Geographically Close Friendships." *Communication Reports* 24:12-24. doi:10.1080/08934215.2011.555322.

Mignolo, Walter. 2010. "Cosmopolitanism and the De-Colonial Option." *Studies in Philosophy and Education* 2:111-127. doi: 10.1007/s11217-009-9163-1.

Mikal, Jude P., Ronald E. Rice, Audrey Abeyta, and Jenica DeVilbiss. 2013. "Transition, Stress, and Computer-Mediated Social Support." *Computers in Human Behavior* 29:A40-A53. doi:10.1016/j.chb.2012.12.012.

Miller, Danny. 2013. "What is the Relationship between Identities that People Construct, Express, and Consume Online and those Offline?" *Future Identities: Changing Identities in the UK – the next 10 years.* UK Government Foresight Project. London.

Miller, Hugh. 1995. "The Presentation of Self in Electronic Life: Goffman on the Internet." Paper presented at a meeting of the Embodied knowledge and Virtual Space Conference, London, June.

Miller, Kent D., Frances Fabian, and Shu-Jou Lin. 2009. "Strategies for Online Communities." *Strategic Management Journal* 30:305-322. doi:10.1002/smj.735.

Miller-Ott, Aimee E., Lynne Kelly, and Robert L. Duran. 2012. "The Effects of Cell Phone usage Rules on Satisfaction in Romantic Relationships." *Communication Quarterly* 60:17-34. doi: 10.1080/01463373.2012.642263.

Miyata, Kakuko, Jeffrey Boase, Barry Wellman, and Ken'ichi Iked. 2005. "The Mobile-izing Japanese: Connecting to the Internet by PC and Webphone in Yamanashi." In *Personal, Portable, Pedestrian: Mobile phones in Japanese life,* edited by Mizuko Ito, Daisuke Okabe, and Misa Matsuda, 143-164. Cambridge, MA: MIT Press

Mo, Pheonix K. H., and Neil S. Coulson. 2009. "Living with HIV/AIDS and Use of Online Support Groups. *Journal of Health Psychology* 15:339-350. doi: 10.1177/1359105309348808.

Mo, Pheonix K. H., and Neil S. Coulson. 2010. "Empowering Processes in Online Support Groups among People Living with HIV/AIDS: A Comparative Analysis of Lurkers and Posters." *Computers in Human Behavior* 26:1183-1193. doi:10.1080/08870446.2011.592981.

Moore, Eric G., Sanal K. Mazvancheryl and Lopo L. Rego 1996. "The Bolo Game: Exploration of a High-Tech Virtual Community." *Advances in Consumer Research* 23:167-171.

Morris Merrill, and Christien Ogan. 1996. "The Internet as Mass Medium." *Journal of Computer-Mediated Communication* 1. doi:10.1111/j.1083-6101.1996.tb00174.x.

Myers, David. 1987 . "Anonymity is Part of the Magic: Individual Manipulation of Computer-Mediated Communication Contexts ." *Qualitative Sociology* 10 :251 –266 . doi: 10.1007/BF00988989.

Nabi, Robin L., Abby Prestin, and Jiyeon So. 2013. "Facebook Friends with (Health) Benefits? Exploring Social Network Site Use and Perceptions of Social Support, Stress, and Well-Being." *Cyberpsychology, Behavior, and Social Networking* 16:721-727. doi: 10.1089/cyber2012.0521.

Nagourney, Eric. 2005. "Web sites celebrate a deadly thinness." June 7. Accessed January 30, 2015. http://www.nytimes.com/2005/06/07/health/nutrition/07eat.html?pagewanted=all.

Nardi, Bonnie, and Justin Harris. 2006. "Strangers and Friends: Collaborative Play in World of Warcraft." Paper presented at a meeting for *Computer-Supported Cooperative Work,* Banff, Alberta, Canada, November 4-8.

Neighmond, Patti. 2014. "For the children's sake, put down that smartphone." Morning Edition. April 21. Accessed October 1, 2014. http://www.npr.org/blogs/health/2014/04/21/304196338/for-the-childrens-sake-put-down-that-smartphone.

Newman, Mark W., Debra Lauterbach, Sean A. Munson, Paul Resnick, and Margaret E. Morris. 2011. "It's Not That I don't Have Problems, I'm Just Not Putting Them on Facebook: Challenges and Opportunities in Using Online Social Networks for Health." Proceedings of the ACM 2011 Conference on Computer Supported Cooperative Work, Hangzhou, China, March 19-23.

Newman, Stephanie. 2013. "Is Technology Ruining Our Lives." April 5. *Psychology Today.* Accessed April 13, 2015. https://www.psychologytoday.com/blog/apologies-freud/201304/is-technology-ruining-our-lives

New Oxford American Dictionary. 3rd ed. New York: Oxford University Press, 2010. Also available at http://www.oxforddictionaries.com/us/.

Nie, Norman H. 2001. "Sociability, Interpersonal Relations and the Internet: Reconciling Conflicting Findings." *American Behavioral Scientist* 45:420-435. doi: 10.1177/00027640121957277.

Nielson. 2014. "Shifts in viewing: The cross-platform report Q2 2014." Accessed October 1, 2014. http://www.nielsen.com/us/en/insights/reports/2014/shifts-in-viewing-the-cross-platform-report-q2-2014.html

Nielson. 2013a. "A look across media: The cross-platform report, Q3 2013." Accessed October 1, 2014. http://www.nielsen.com/us/en/insights/reports/2013/a-look-across-media-the-cross-platform-report-q3-2013.html

Nielson. 2013b. *The Mobile Consumer: A Global Snapshot.* Accessed August 10, 2014. http://www.nielsen.com/content/dam/corporate/us/en/reports-downloads/2013%20Reports/Mobile-Consumer-Report-2013.pdf.

Nielson. 2011. *The Mobile Media Report.* Accessed August 10, 2014. http://www.nielsen.com/content/dam/corporate/us/en/reports-downloads/2011-Reports/state-of-mobile-Q3-2011.pdfNonnecke, Blair, and Jenny Preece. 2000. "Lurker Demographics: Counting the Silent." Proceedings of the SIGCHI Conference on Human Factors in Computing Systems. Chicago, April, 1-6.

Nonnecke, Blair, and Jenny Preece. 2001. "Why Lurkers Lurk." Americas Conference on Information Systems 2001.

Nonnecek, Blair, and Jenny Preece. 2003. "Silent Participants: Getting to Know Lurkers Better." In *From Usenet to CoWebs: Interacting with Social Information Spaces,* edited by C. Lueg and D. Fisher, 110-132. London: Springer.

Nonnecke, Blair, Jenny Preece, and Andrews, Dorine. 2004 "What Lurkers and Posters Think of Each Other." *System Sciences.* Proceedings of the 37th Annual Hawaii International Conference. doi:10.1109/HICSS.2004.1265462.

Norris, Fran H., and Kaniasty, Krzysztof. 1996. "Received and Perceived Social Support in Times of Stress: A Test of the Social Support Deterioration Deterrence Model." *Journal of Personality and Social Psychology* 71:498-511. doi: 10.1037/0022-3514.71.3.498.

O'Connell, Lenahan. 1984. "An Exploration of Exchange in Three Social Relationships: Kinship, Friendship, and the Marketplace." *Journal of Social and Personal Relationships* 1:333-345. doi: 10.1177/0265407584013006.

Oldenburg, Ray. 1989. *The Great Good Place: Cafés, Coffee Shops, Community Centers, Beauty Parlors, General Stores, Bars, Hangouts, and How They Get You Through the Day.* New York: Marlowe & Company.

Oglosky, Brian G., & Bowers, Jill, R. (2013). "A Meta-Analytic Review of Relationship Maintenance and its Correlates. *Journal of Social and Personal Relationships* 30:343-367. doi: 10.1177/0265407512463338.

Onnela, Jukka-Pekka., Jari Saramäki, Jörkki Hyvönen, Gábor Szabó, David Lazer, Kimmo Kaski, Janos Kértesz, and Albert-László. Barabási. 2007. "Structure and Tie Strengths in Mobile Communication Networks." *Proceedings of the National Academy of Sciences* 104:7332-7336. doi: 10.1073/pnas.0610245104.

Ossola, Alexandra. 2015. A new kind of social anxiety in the classroom. January 14. Accessed January 30, 2015. http://www.theatlantic.com/education/archive/2015/01/the-socially-anxious-generation/384458/.

O'Sullivan, Patrick B. 2005. "Masspersonal Communication: Rethinking the Mass-Interpersonal Divide." Paper presented at a meeting of the International Communication Association, New York, New York.

O'Sullivan, Patrick, B., and Andrew J. Flanagin. 2003. "Reconceptualizing 'Flaming' and Other Problematic Messages." *New Media and Society* 5:69:94. doi: 10.1177/1461444803005001908

Oswald, Debra, L., and Eddie M. Clark. (2006). "How do Friendship Maintenance Behaviors and Problem Solving Styles Function at the Individual and Dyadic Levels?" *Personal Relationships* 16:99-115. doi:10.1111/j.1475-6811.2006.00121.x

Oswald, Debra, L., Eddie M. Clark and Cheryl M. Kelly. (2004). "Friendship Maintenance: An Analysis of Individual and Dyadic Behavior." *Journal of Social and Clinical Psychology* 23:413-441. doi:10.1521/jcsp.23.3.413.35460.

Owen, Jason E., Laura Boxley, Michael Goldstein, Jennifer H. Lee, Nancy Breen, N., and Julia H. Rowland. 2010. Use of Health-Related Online Support Groups: Population Data from the California Health Interview Survey Complementary and Alternative Medicine Study. *Journal of Computer-Mediated Communication* 15:427-446. doi:10.1111/j/1083-6101.2010.01501.x

Palmgreen, Phillip 1984. "Uses and Gratifications: A Theoretical Perspective." *Communication Yearbook* 8:20-55.

Pahnila, Seppo, and Juhani Warsta. 2012. "Assessing the Factors that Have Had an Impact on Stickiness in Online Game Communities." PACIS 2012 Proceedings. Paper 106. http://aisel.aisnet.org/pacis2012/106.

Palen, Leysia, Marilyn Salzman, and Ed Youngs. 2000. "Going Wireless: Behavior and Practice of New Mobile Phone Users." Proceedings of the 2000 ACM conference on Computer Supported Cooperative Work, Phiadelphia, Pennsylvania, December 2-6.

Papacharissi, Zisi. 2013. "A Networked Self: Identity Performance and Sociability on Social Network Sites." In *Frontiers in New Media Research,* edited by F. L. F. Lee, L. Leung, J. L. Qui, and D. S. C. Chu. New York: Routledge.

Park, Namsu, Kerk F. Kee, and Sebastian Valenzuela. 2009. "Being Immersed in Social Networking Environment: Facebook Groups, Uses and Gratifications and Social Outcomes." *Cyberpsychology & Behavior* 12:729-733. doi:10.1089/cpb.2009.0003.

Park, Sora. 2012. "Dimensions of Digital Media Literacy and the Relationship with Social Exclusion." *Media International Australia* 142: 87-100.

Parks, Malcom R., and Kory Floyd.1996." Making Friends in Cyberspace." *Journal of Computer-Mediated Communication* 1 doi: 10.1111/j.1083-6101.1996.tb00176.x.

Parks, Malcom R., and Lynne D. Roberts. 1998. "Making Moosic: The Development of Personal Relationships Online and a Comparison to Their Off-Line Counterparts." *Journal of Social and Personal Relationships* 15:517-537. doi: 10.1177/0265407598154005.

Patterson, Brian and Tarda K. Godycz. 2009. "The Relationship between Computer-Mediated Communication and Communication Related Anxieties." *Communication Research Report* 17:278-287. 2001. doi: 10.1080/08824090009388775.

Pena, Jorge and Jeffrey T. Hancock. 2006. "An Analysis of Socioemotional and Task Communication in Online Multiplayer Video Games." *Communication Research* 33:92-109. doi: 10.1177/0093650205283103.

Pennebaker, James W. 1997. "Writing about Emotional Experiences as a Therapeutic Process." *Psychological Science* 8:162-166. doi: 10.1111/j/1467.9280.1997.tb00403.x.

People of Walmart (n.d.) "People of Wal-mart" Last modified October 1, 2014. http://www.peopleofwalmart.com/

Perlow, Leslie, A. 2012. *Sleeping with your smartphone: How to break the 24/7 habit and change the way you work.* Boston, MA: Harvard Business Press.

Petronio, Sandra. 2002. *Boundaries of Privacy: Dialectics of Disclosure.* New York: State University of New York Press.

Pettigrew, Jonathan. 2009. "Text Messaging and Connectedness within Close Interpersonal Relationships." *Marriage and Family Review* 45:697-716. doi: 10.1080/01494920903224269.

Pew Internet and American Life Project. 2014a. "Cell Phone and Smartphone Ownership Demographics." Accessed September 2, 2014. http://www.pewinternet.org/data-trend/mobile/cell-phone-and-smartphone-ownership-demographics/.

Pew Internet and American Life Project. 2014b. "Internet user Demographics." Accessed March 3, 2014. http://www.pewinternet.org/data-trend/internet-use/latest-stats/

Pew Internet and American Life Project. 2013a. "Cell Phone Activities." Accessed September 3, 2014.. http://www.pewinternet.org/data-trend/mobile/cell-phone-activities/.

Pew Internet and American Life Project. 2013b. "Social Networking Fact Sheet." Accessed March 3 2014. http://www.pewinternet.org/fact-sheets/social-networking-fact-sheet/

Pew Internet and American Life Project. 2012. "Trend data (Adults)." Accessed September 7, 2013. http://www.pewinternet.org/Static-Pages/Trend-Data-(Adults)/Online-Activites-Total.aspx.

Pfister, Damien Smith, and Jordan Soliz. 2011. "(Re) Conceptualizing Intercultural Communication in a Networked Society." *Journal of International and Intercultural Communication* 4:246-251. doi: 10.1080/17513057.2011.598043.

Phillips, Whitney 2011. "Meet the Trolls." *Index on Censorship* 20:68 -7Pierce6. doi: 10.1177.0306422011409641.

Pierce, Tamyra 2009. "Social anxiety and technology: Face-to-face communication versus technological communication among teens." *Computers in Human Behavior, 25,* 1367-1372.

Pinker, Susan. 2015. "Can Students have too much tech?" The New York Times. January 30. Accessed January 30, 2015. www.nytimes.com/2015/01/20/opinion/can-students-have-too-much-tech.html.

Platt, Carrie Anne, Renee Bourdeaux, and Nancy DiTunnariello. 2014. "Should I Text or Should I Call?: How College Students Navigate Mediated Connections with Family." *Emerald Media and Communication Studies.*

Politwoops. 2014. "Deleted Tweets From Politicians." Sunshine Foundation. Accessed October 2 2014. http://politwoops.sunlightfoundation.com/

Poole, Marshall Scott, Michael Holmes, and Gerardine DeSanctis. 1991. "Conflict Management in a Computer-Supported Meeting Environment." *Management Science* 37:926-953. doi:10.1298/mnsc.37.8.926.

Porter, Constance E . 2004 . " A Typology of Virtual Communities: A Multi-Disciplinary Foundation for Future Research ." *Journal of Computer-Mediated Communication* 10 1 . doi: 10.1111/j.1083-6101.2004.tb00228.x.

Preece, Jenny. 2000. *Online Communities: Designing Usability, Supporting Sociability.* New York: Wiley.

Preece, Jenny. 2001. "Sociability and Usability: Determining and Measuring Success." *Behavior and Information Technology Journal* 20 5:347-356. doi:10.1080/01449290110084683.

Putnam, Robert D. 2000. *Bowling Alone: The Collapse and Revival of American Community.* New York: Simon and Schuster.

Qian, Hua and Craig R. Scott. 2007. "Anonymity and Self-Disclosure on Weblogs." *Journal of Computer-Mediated Communication* 12:1428-1451. doi:10.1111/j.1083-6101.2007.00380.x.

Raacke, John, and Jennifer Bonds-Raacke. 2008. "MySpace and Facebook: Applying the Uses and Gratifications Theory to Exploring Friend-Networking Sites." *CyberPsychology & Behavior* 11:169-174. doi:10.1089/cpb.2007.0056.

Rabby, Michael K. and Joseph B. Walther. 2002. "Computer-Mediated Communication Effects on Relationship Formation and Maintenance." In *Maintaining Relationships through Communication: Relational, Contextual, and Cultural Variations,* edited by Daniel J. Canary and Marianne Dainton. Mahwah, 141-162. NJ: Lawrence Erlbaum.

Radovanovic, D., and M Regnedda. (2012). "Small Talk in the Digital Age: Making Sense of Phatic Posts." Proceedings of the #MSM2012 Workshop. Accessed November 1, 2012. http://ceur-ws.org/Vol-838/paper_18.pdf

Rainie, Lee, and Barry Wellman. 2012. *Networked: The New Social Operating System.* Cambridge: MIT Press.

Rains, Stephen A., and Young, Valerie. 2009. "A Meta-Analysis of Research on Formal Computer-Mediated Support Groups: Examining Group Characteristics and Health Outcomes." *Human Communication Research* 35:309-336. doi: 10.1111/j.1468-2958.2009.01353.x.

Ramirez, Artemio, Jr. 2008. "An Examination of the Tripartite Approach to Commitment: An Actor-Partner Interdependence Model Analysis of the Effect of Relational Maintenance Behavior." *Journal of Social and Personal Relationships* 25:943-965. doi: 10.1177/0265407508100309

Ramirez, Artemio, Jr. and Kathy Broneck. 2009. "'IM Me:' Instant Messaging as Relational Maintenance and Everyday Communication. *Journal of Social and Personal Relationships* 26:291-314. doi. 10.117/0265407509106719.

Ramirez, Artemio, Jr., John Dimmick, John Feaster, and Shu-Fang Lin. 2008. "Revisiting Interpersonal Media Competition: The Gratification Niches of Instant Messaging, Email and the Telephone. *Communication Research*, 35: 529-547. doi:10.1177/0093650208345979

Ramirez, Artemio, Jr. and Shuangyue Zhang. 2007. "When Online Meets Offline: The Effect of Modality Switching on Relational Communication." *Communication Monographs* 74:287-310. doi:10.1080/03637750701543493.

Ramirez, Artemio, Jr. and Zuoming Wang. 2008. "When Online Meets Offline: An Expectancy Violations Theory Perspective on Modality Switching." *Journal of Communication* 58:20-39. doi: 10.1111/j.1460-2466.2007.00372.x

Rawlins, W. K. (1994). Being there and growing apart: Sustaining friendships during adulthood: In *Maintaining Relationships Through Communication*, edited by Daniel J. Canary and Laura Stafford, 141-162. Mahwah, NJ; Lawrence Erlbaum.

In *Computer-Mediated Communication in Personal Relationships,* edited by Kevin B. Wright and Lynne M. Webb, 98-118. New York: Peter Lang.

Roberts, Jeff J. July 12. "Facebook Search Warrants a New Tool for U.S. Law Enforcement." Accessed March 2, 2013. http://www.huffingtonpost.com/2011/07/12/facebook-search-warrant_n_896328.html.

Roberts, Sam, Robin I.M. Dunbar, Thomas Pollet, and Toon Kruppens. 2009. "Exploring Variation in Active Network Size." *Social Networks* 31:138-146. doi: 10.1016/j.socnet.2008.12.002.

Roberts, Sam G. B., and Robin I.M. Dunbar. 2011. "The Costs of Family and Friends: An 18-Month Longitudinal Study of Relationship Maintenance and Decay." *Evolution and Human Behavior* 32:186-197. doi:10.1016/j.evolhumbehav.2010.08.005.

Robinson, Laura. 2007. "The Cyberself: The Self-ing Project goes Online, Symbolic Interaction in the Digital Age." *New Media & Society* 9:93-110. doi: 10.1177/1461444807072216.

Rogers, Everett M. 2003. *Diffusion of Innovations (5th Ed.).* New York: Free Press.

Rheingold, Harold. 1998. "The Community of the Future." In *Virtual communities*, edited by Frances Hesselbein, Marshall Goldsmith, Richard Beckhard, and R. F. Schubert. San Francisco, CA. Jossey-Bass.

Rheingold, Harold. 2001. *The Virtual Community: Homesteading on the Electronic Frontier.* (2nd ed). Boston. MIT Press.

Rice, Ronald E., and Gail Love. 1986. "Electronic Emotion: Socioemotional Content in a Computer-Mediated Communication Network." *Communication Research* 14:85-108. doi:10.1177/009365087014001005.

Ridings, Catherine M., David Gefen, and Bay Arinze. 2002. " Some Antecedents and Effects of Trust in Virtual Communities ." *Journal of Strategic Information Systems* 11 3–4 :271 –295 . doi: 10.1016/S0963-8687(02)00021-5.

Ridings, Catherine M., and David Gefen. 2004. "Virtual Community Attraction: Why People Hang out Online." *Journal of Computer-Mediated Communication* 10 doi: 10.1111/j.1083-6101.2004.tb00229.x.

Ridings, Catherine , David Gefen, and Bay Arinze. 2002 . " Some Antecedents and Effects of Trust in Virtual Communities ." *Journal of Strategic Information Systems* 11 3–4 : 271 –295 . doi:10.1016/S0963-8687(02)00021-5.

Riordan, Monica and Roger R. Kreuz. 2010. "Cues in Computer-Mediated Communication: A Corpus Analysis." *Computers in Human Behavior* 26(6):1806-1817. doi:10.1016/j.chb.2010.07.008.

Rosenbaum, James, Benjamin K. Johnson, Peter A. Stepman, and Koos C. M. Nuijten. 2013. "Looking the Part, and Staying True: Balancing Impression Management on Facebook." In *Social Networking and Impression Management in the Digital Age,* edited by, Carolyn Cunningham, 35-59. Lanham, MD: Lexington.

Rui, Jian Raymond, and Michael A. Stefanone. 2013. "Strategic Image Management Online. *Information, Communication, and Society* 16 8:1286-1305. doi:10.1080/1369118x.2013.763834.

Ruppel, Erin, K., and Tricia Burke. 2014. "Complementary Channel Use and the Role of Social Competence. *Journal of Computer-Mediated Communication* 20: 37-51. doi: 10.1111/jcc4.12091

Sacks, Harvey, Emanuel A. Schegloff, and Gail Jefferson. 1978. "A Simplest Systematics for the Organization of Turn-Taking for Conversation." In *Studies in the Organization of Conversational Interaction,* edited by J. N. Schenkein, 7–55. New York: Academic Press.

Sarason, Barbara R., Irwin G. Sarason, T. Anthony Hacker, and Robert B. Basham. 1985. "Concomitants of Social Support: Social Skills, Physical Attractiveness, and Gender. *Journal of Personality and Social Psychology* 49:469-480. doi:10.1037//0022-3514.49.2.469.

Schiffrin, Holly, Anna Edelman, Melissa Falkenstern, and Cassandra Stewart. 2010. The Associations among Computer-Mediated Communication, Relationships, and Well-Being. *Cyberpsychology, Behavior, and Social Networking* 13:299-306. doi:10.1089/cyber.2009.0173.

Scott, Craig R., and Erik C. Timmerman. 2005. "Relating Computer Communications and Computer-Mediated Communication, Apprehensions to new Communication Technology use in the Workplace. *Communication Research* 32:683-725. doi: 10.1177/0093650205281054.

Seligman, Molly. 2012. "Facebook: Friend or Faux?" *Journal of Infant, Child, and Adolescent Psychotherapy* 4:415-421. doi: 10.1080/15289168.2011.618424.

Shachaf, Prina, and Noriko Hara. 2010. "Beyond Vandalism: Wikipedia Trolls." *Journal of Information Science,* 36: 357–370. doi: 10.11771016555150365390.

Sharkey, William F., and Laura Stafford. 1990. "Responses to Embarrassment." *Human Communication Research* 17:315-342. doi:10.1111/j.1468-2958.1990tb00235.x.

Shaw, Lindsay. H., and Larry M. Gant. 2002. "In Defense of the Internet: The Relationship between Internet Communication and Depression, Loneliness, Self-esteem, and Perceived Social Support." *Cyberpsychology and Behavior* 5:157-171. doi: 10.1089/109493102753770552.

Shirky, Clay. 2008. *Here Comes Everybody: The Power of Organizing without Organizations.* New York: Penguin.

Short, John A., Ederyn Williams, and Bruce Christie. 1976. *The Social Psychology of Telecommunications.* New York: John Wiley & Sons.

Sherblom, John C., Lesley A. Withers, and Lynette G. Leonard. 2013. "The Influence of Computer-Mediated Communication (CMC) Competence on Computer-supported Collaborative Learning (CSCL) in Online Classroom Discussions." *Human Communication* 16:31-39. doi: 10.4018/978-1-61520-827-2.ch001.

Siegel, Jane, Vitaly Dubrovsky, Sara Kielser, and Timothy McGuire. 1986. "Group Processes in Computer-Mediated Communication." *Organizational Behavior and Human Decision Processes* 37:157-187. doi:10.1016/0749-5978(86)90050-6.

Spitzberg, Brian. 2006. "Preliminary Development of a Model and Measure of Computer-Mediated Communication (CMC) Competence." *Journal of Computer-Mediated Communication* 11: 629-666. doi:10.1111/j.1083-6101.2006.00030.x.

Spitzberg, Brian H., and William R. Cupach. 1989. *Handbook of Interpersonal Competence Research.* New York: Springer-Verlag.

Smith, Aaron. 2015. "U.S. Smartphone Use in 2015." *Pew Internet and American Life Project.* April 1. Accessed April 13, 2015. http://www.pewinternet.org/2015/04/01/us-smartphone-use-in-2015/

Smith, Aaron. 2014. "5 facts about online dating." *Pew Research Center.* February 13. Accessed October 1, 2014. http://www.pewresearch.org/fact-tank/2014/02/13/5-facts-about-online-dating/.

Smith, Aaron. 2013. "Smartphone Ownership 2013". *Pew Internet and American Life Project.* Accessed January 10, 2014. http://www.pewinternet.org/2013/06/05/smartphone-ownership-2013/

Smyth, Joshua M. 2007. "Beyond Self-Selection in Video Game Play: An Experimental Examination of the Consequences of Massively Multiplayer Online Role-Playing Game Play." *Cyberpsychology & Behavior* 10:717-721. doi:10.1089/cpb.2007.9963.

Sobré-Denton, Miriam. 2011. "The Emergence of Cosmopolitan Group Cultures and its Implications for Cultural Transition: A Case Study of an International Student Support Group." *International Journal of Intercultural Relations* 35 1:79-91. doi: 10.1016/j.ijintrel.2010.09.007.

Sobré-Denton, Miriam, and Nilanjana Bardhan. 2013. *Cultivating Cosmopolitanism for Intercultural Communication: Communicating as a Global Citizen.* Kentucky: Routledge.

Sobré-Denton, Miriam, Robert Carlsen and Veronica Greuel. 2014. "Opening Doors, Opening Minds: A Cosmopolitan Pedagogical Framework to Assess Learning for Global Competency in Chicago's Underserved Communities." *International Journal of Intercultural Relations* 40 1:141-153. doi: 10.1016/j.ijintrel.2013.12.001.

Sobré-Denton, Miriam. In press. "Virtual Intercultural Bridgework and Intercultural New Media Studies: Social Media, Virtual Cosmopolitanism, and Community Building." *New Media and Society.*

Sorrells, Kathryn. 2012. *Intercultural Communication: Globalization and Social Justice.* Thousand Oaks, CA: Sage.

Sprecher, Susan, Pepper Schwartz, John Harvey, and Elaine Hatfield. 2008. "TheBusinessofLove.com: Relationship Initiation at Internet Matchmaking Services." In *The handbook of Relationship Initiation,* edited by, Susan Sprecher, Amy Wenzel, and John Harvey, 249 – 265.

Sproull, Lee, and Sara Kiesler. 1986. "Reducing Social Context Cues: Electronic Mail in Organizational Communication." *Management Science* 32:1492-1512. http://dx.doi.org/10.1287/mnsc.32.11.1492.

Srivastava, Lara. 2005. "The Mobile Makes its Mark." In *Handbook of Mobile Communication Studies,* edited by James Katz, 15-28. Cambridge, MA: MIT.

Stafford, Laura, and Daniel J. Canary. (1991). Maintenance strategies and romantic relationship type, gender, and relational characteristics. *Journal of Social and Personal Relationships,* 8: 217-242.

Stafford, Laura, John Dimmick, and Susan Kline. 2000. "The Gratification Niches of Personal E-mail and the Telephone: Competition, Displacement, and Complementarity." *Communication Research* 27:227-248. doi:10.1177/009365000027002005.

Stafford, Laura, Susan L. Kline, and John Dimmick. 1999. "Home E-mail: Relational Maintenance and Gratification Opportunities. *Journal of Broadcasting and Electronic Media* 43:659-669. doi:10.1080/08838159909364515

Stafford, Laura, and Andrew J. Merolla. 2007. "Idealization, Reunions, and Stability in Long-Distance Dating Relationships." *Journal of Social and Personal Relationships* 34:37-54. doi:10.1177/0265407507072578.

Steinkuehler, Constance A., and Dmitri Williams. 2006. "Where Everybody Knows Your (Screen) Name: Online Games as "Third Places." *Journal of Computer-Mediated Communication* 11:885-909 doi:10.1111/j.1083-6101.2006.00300.x.

Stern, Gary, M. 2012. "Put the smartphone down: It'll be okay." Fortune. June 21. Accessed October 1, 2014. http://fortune.com/2012/06/21/put-the-smartphone-down-itll-be-okay/.

Stevens, Chandler Harrison. 1981. "Many-to-Many Communication." Sloan White Paper No. 1225-81. Sloan School of Management, MIT. Accessed September 18, 2014. http://dspace.mit.edu/bitstream/handle/1721.1/48404/manytomanycommun00stev.pdf.

Stroebe, Wolfgang and Margaret Stroebe. 1996. "The Social Psychology of Social Support." In *Social Psychology Handbook of Basic Principles,* edited by E. Tory Higgins and Arie W. Kruglanski, 597-621. New York: Guileford.

Suler, John 2005. "The Online Disinhibition Effect." *International Journal of Applied Psychoanalytic Studies* 2:184–188. doi:10.1002/aps.42.

Stutzman, Fred, and Jacob Kramer-Duffield. 2010. "Friends Only: Examining a Privacy Enhancing Behavior in Facebook." Proceedings of the 28th International Conference on Human Factors in Computing Systems, Atlanta, Georgia, April 10-15.

Stutzman, Fred, Ralph Gross, and Alessandro Acquisti. 2012. "Silent Listeners: The Evolution of Privacy and Disclosure on Facebook." *Journal of Privacy and Confidentiality* 4:7-41. doi: 10.1007/11957454_3.

Sudman, Seymour. 1985. "Experiments in the Measurements of the Size of Social Networks." *Social Networks* 7:127-151. doi:10.1016/0378-8733(85)90002-4.

Tang, Lijun. 2010. "Development of Online Friendship in Different Social Spaces." *Information, Communication, & Society* 13:615-633. doi:10.1080/13691180902998639.

Tam, Donna. 2012. "Facebook Resurrects Old Posts on Timeline, Panic Ensues." Accessed Febrary 20, 2013. http://news.cnet.com/8301-1023_3-57519228-93/facebook-resurrects-old-posts-on-timeline-panic-ensues/.

Tate, Ryan. 2013. "Creepy Side of Search Emerges on Facebook." Accessed February 23, 2013. http://www.wired.com/business/2013/02/creepy-graph-searchers/.

Taylor, Alex S., and Richard Harper. 2003. "The Gift of *Gab*?: A Design Oriented Sociology of Young People's Use of Mobiles." *Computer Supported Cooperative Work* 12:267-296. doi: 10.1023/A:1025091532662.

Teng, Ching-I., Ming-Yi Chen, Yun-Jung Chen, and Yi-Jhen Li. 2012. "Loyalty Due to Others: The Relationships among Challenge, Interdependence, and Online Gamer Loyalty." *Journal of   Computer-Mediated   Communication   17*:489-500.   doi:10.1111/j.1083-6101.2012.01586.x.

The Telegraph. (2009). "Twitter and Facebook could harm moral values, scientists warn." April 13. Accessed October 1, 2014. http://www.telegraph.co.uk/science/science-news/5149195/Twitter-and-Facebook-could-harm-moral-values-scientists-warn.html

Thurlow, Crispin, Lara M. Lengel, and Alice Tomic. 2009. *Computer Mediated Communication: Social Interaction and the Internet.* Thousand Oaks, CA: Sage.

Tidwell, Lisa C. and Joseph B. Walther. 2002. "Computer-Mediated Communication Effects on Disclosure, Impressions, and Interpersonal Evaluations: Getting to Know one Another a Bit at a Time." *Human Communication Research* 28:317-348. doi:10.1111/j.1468-2958.2002.tb00811.x.

Titcomb, James. 2012. "Texting, Tweeting, and Social Networking are Behind 'Rough Behavior' of Teens." Accessed September 3, 2013. http://www.dailymail.co.uk/news/article-2138791/Texting-tweeting-social-networking-damaging-childrens-ability-communicate-says-Pratchett.html.

Tong Stephanie, T., and Joseph B. Walther. 2011. "Relational Maintenance and CMC." In *Computer-Mediated Communication in Personal Relationships,* edited by Kevin B. Wright and Lynne M. Webb, 98-118. New York: Peter Lang.

Toma, Catalina L. 2013. "Psychological Benefits and Costs: A Self-Affirmation Framework for Understanding the Effects of Facebook Self-Presentation." In *Social networking and impression management in the digital age*, edited by Carolyn Cunningham, 227-245. Lanham, MD: Lexington.

Tracy, Sarah J., and Angela Trethewey. 2005. "Fracturing the Real-Self Fake-Self Dichotomy: Moving Toward "Crystallized" Organizational Discourses and Identities." *Communication Theory* 15:168-195. doi:10.1111/j.1468-2885.2005.tb00331.x.

Tufekci, Zeynep. 2012. "Social Media's Small, Positive Role in Human Relationships." Accessed January 15, 2013. www.theatlantic.com.

Turkle, Sherry. 2012. "The Flight From Conversation." Accessed January 30, 2015. http://www.nytimes.com/2012/04/22/opinion/sunday/the-flight-from-conversation.html?pagewanted=all&_r=0.

Turkle, Sherry. 2011. *Alone Together: Why we Expect More from Technology and Less From Each Other.* New York: Basic Books.

Turkle, Sherry. 2008. "Always-on/always-on-you: The Tethered Self." In *Handbook of Mobile Communication Studies,* edited by James Katz, 121-137. Cambridge, MA: MIT Press.

Turkle, Sherry. 1995. *Life on the Screen: Identity in the Age of the Internet*. New York: Touchstone.

Turner, Jeanine W., Jean A. Grube, and Jennifer Meyers. 2001. "Developing an Optimal Match within Online Communities: An Exploration of CMC Support Communities and Traditional Support." *Journal of Communication* 5:231-251. doi:10.1111/j.1460-2466.2001.tb02879.x

University of Michigan. 2006. "On the Move: The Role of Cellular Communication in American Life." Department of Communication Studies, Ann Arbor.

Utz, Sonja. 2010. "Show Me Your Friends and I Will Tell you What Type of Person you Are: How One's Profile, Number of Friends, and Type of Friends Influence Impression Formation on Social Network Sites." *Journal of Computer-Mediated Communication* 15:314-335. doi: 10.1111/j.1083-6101.2010.01522.x.

Weston, Kath. 1995. Get Thee to a Big City: Sexual Imaginary and the Great Gay Migration. *GLQ: A Journal of Lesbian and Gay Studies,* 2: 253-277.

Valkenburg, Patti M., Alexander P. Schouten, and Jochen Peter. 2005. "Adolescents' Identity Experiments on the Internet." *New Media and Society* 7:383 -402. doi: 10..1177/1461444805052282.

Valkenberg, Peter M. and Jochen Peter. 2008. "Adolescents' Identity Experiments on the Internet: Consequences for Social Competence and Self-concept Unity. *Communication Research* 35:208-231. doi: 10.1177/0093650207313164.

Valkenburg, Peter, M., and Jochen Peter. 2007. "Preadolescents' and Adolescents' Online Communication and Their Closeness to Friends. *Developmental Psychology,* 43: 267-277.

van den Berg, Pauline. E. W., Theo A. Arentze, Harry J.P. Timmermans. 2012. "New ICTs and Social Interaction: Modelling Communication Frequency and Communication Mode Choice." *New Media and Society* 14:987-1003. doi:10.1177/1461444812437518.

Van Dijk, Jan A. 2005. "The Deepening Divide Inequality in the Information Society." London: Sage.

Vayreda, Agnes, and Charles Antaki. 2009. "Social Support and Unsolicited Advice in a Bipolar Disorder Online Forum." *Qualitative Health Research,* 19:931-942. doi: 10.1177/1049732309338952.

Vitak, Jessica. 2012. "The Impact of Context Collapse and Privacy on Social Network Site Disclosures." *Journal of Broadcasting and Electronic Media* 56:451-470. doi:10.1080/08838151.2012.732140.

Wright, Kevin B. 2012a. "Emotional Support and Perceived Stress among College Students using Facebook.com: An Exploration of the Relationship Between Source Perceptions and Emotional Support." *Communication Research Reports* 29:175-184. doi:10.1080/08824096.2012.695957.

Wright, Kevin. 2012b. Similarity, Network Convergence, and Availability of Emotional Support as Predictors of Strong-Tie/Weak-Tie Support Network Preference on Facebook." *Southern Communication Journal* 77:389-402. doi: 10.1080/1041794X.2012.681003.

Wright, Kevin B., and Sally B. Bell. 2003. "Health-Related Support Groups on the Internet: Linking Empirical Findings to Social Support and Computer-Mediated Communication Theory." *Journal of Health Psychology* 8:39-54. doi:10.1177/1359105303008001429.

Wright, Kevin, Steven Rains, and John Banas. 2012. Weak-Tie Support Network Preference and Perceived Life Stress among Participants in Health-Related, Computer-Mediated Support Groups." *Journal of Computer-Mediated Communication 15:*606-624. doi:10.1111/j.1083-6101.2009.01505.x

Yee, Nick. 2006a. "Motivations for Play in Online Games." *Cyberpsychology & Behavior* 9:772-775. doi:10.1089/cpb.2006.9.772.

Yee, Nick. 2006b. "The Demographics, Motivations and Derived Experiences of Users of Massively-Multiuser Online Graphical Environments." *PRESENCE: Teleoperators and Virtual Environments* 15:309–329. doi:10.1162/pres.15.3.309.

Yeow, Adrian, Samer Johnson, and Samer Faraj. 2006. "Lurking: Legitimate or Illegitimate Peripheral Participation?" Twenty-Seventh International Conference on Information Systems, Milwaukee, Wisconsin, December, 10-13.

Young, Susan. 2012. "4 Ways Texting is Killing our Communication Skills." Accessed July 7. http://www.prdaily.com/Main/Articles/4_ways_texting_is_killing_our_communication_skills_13330.aspx.

Zhao, Shanyang. 2006. "A Call for Differentiated Analyses of Internet Use." *Journal of Computer-Mediated Communication* 11:844-862. doi:10.1111/j.1083-6101.2006.00038.x

Zhao, Shanyang, Sherri Grasmuck, and Jason Martin. 2008. "Identity Construction on Facebook: Digital Empowerment in Anchored Relationships." *Computers in Human Behavior* 24:1816-1836. doi:10.1016/j.chb.2008.02.012.

Index